Critical Theory from the Margins

Critical Theory from the Margins

Horizons of Possibility in the Age of Extremism

SALADDIN AHMED

SUNY PRESS

Published by State University of New York Press, Albany

Printed in the United States of America

For information, contact State University of New York Press, Albany, NY
www.sunypress.edu

Library of Congress Cataloging-in-Publication Data

Name: Ahmed, Saladdin, 1972– author.
Title: Critical theory from the margins : horizons of possibility in the
    age of extremism / Saladdin Ahmed.
Description: Albany, NY : State University of New York Press, [2023] |
    Includes bibliographical references and index.
Identifiers: LCCN 2022053665 | ISBN 9781438494326 (hardcover : alk. paper) |
    ISBN 9781438494333 (ebook) | ISBN 9781438494319 (pbk. : alk. paper)
Subjects: LCSH: Critical theory.
Classification: LCC HM480 .A426 2023 | DDC 303.4—dc23/eng/20230120
LC record available at https://lccn.loc.gov/2022053665

10 9 8 7 6 5 4 3 2 1

To those who never get used to
the violence of the norms
and the norms of subjugation

Contents

Acknowledgments

I owe thanks to everyone in the SUNY Press staff who helped in the creation of this book. I am sincerely grateful to Dr. Michael Rinella, senior acquisition editor at SUNY Press, for all his meticulous and punctual work overseeing the processes from the proposal and manuscript reviews all the way through until the production stage. This is the second time I have the pleasure of working with Dr. Rinella. I am also grateful to the two anonymous reviewers for their constructive comments and insights. Their feedback was extremely helpful, and I am deeply appreciative of both reviews. My deep gratitude also goes to Diane Ganeles for the wonderful job she did overseeing a swift and flawless production process and Carly Miller for her tremendous copyediting assistance and invaluable suggestions.

In 2021, I presented parts of chapter 4 at Wesleyan University in an invited talk hosted by the Department of Philosophy. I would like to thank the faculty and students who enriched the debate through their comments and questions. Also, in November 2021, I had the pleasure of presenting parts of chapters 5 and 6 in the Department of Political Science at Union College. I would like to thank my colleagues there. I would also like to thank my students at Union College, whose courage to unlearn thoughtless norms and question common paradigms (such as "culture") has been a source of further motivation for me during the long writing process.

The appendix to chapter 4 is a discussion of Judith Friedlander's book *Being Indian in Hueyapan*. Friedlander and I discussed my take on her book several times. She read earlier versions closely and provided edits. On short notice, she read the last version as well. I appreciate her help and express gratitude for her outstanding collegiality. Of course, my intention was to use her findings as an anthropologist to reinforce my argument against culturalism. Nonetheless, it was important to make sure that in doing so I did not misrepresent her work.

Parts of chapter 2 have been published by the journal *Critical Sociology* in an article titled "Fascism as an Ideological Form: A Critical Theory," which appeared in the OnlineFirst section of the journal's website on July 15, 2022. Many thanks to the journal's editor David Fasenfest for his impressive work facilitating a timely review process, to the two reviewers for their insightful feedback, and to Taylor & Francis for granting the republication permission.

I have also published parts of chapters 5 and 6 in an article titled "The Marginalized and Critical Theory: Dialectics of Universalism" in *International Critical Thought*, on June 19, 2022. Many thanks to Dr. Wang Zhen and the rest of the editorial staff for all their help with the publication process and the two anonymous reviewers for their useful feedback.

I would like to thank Fred Fuentes for publishing several of my commentaries and thought pieces in *International Journal for Socialist Renewal LINKS* and for the permission to republish two of those pieces in this book. The first one, "Universal Discrimination and the Democratic Camouflaging of Culturalism," published on March 27, 2021, appears, with some editorial changes, in this book as "Universal Discrimination and the Democratic Camouflaging of Culturalism" in the epilogue. "Global Tribalism in the Name of Universality" in the epilogue is a lightly edited version of "Why 'Islamo-leftism' is Just Another Conspiracy Theory," published on March 5, 2021, also in *International Journal of Socialist Renewal LINKS*.

Meridith Murray came to my aid at a critical stage as she worked hard to write the index on short notice, so I am extremely grateful to her. Last but not least, Doug and Michele rented me a beautiful old farmhouse in upstate New York, where this book and other works were written. I am grateful to them and their family for their hospitality. The aura of the house made the lonely process of writing, almost every day for two years, not too tiring.

Introduction

It is extremely disturbing that in liberal democracies, where at least most people are not deprived of the means of education, issues that enjoy overwhelming scientific consensus are still widely denied. It is alarming that seventy-four million American voters[1] cast ballots for a man who shamelessly and repeatedly mocked scientific authorities, including most of those who work within the state apparatuses. It should be shocking that we need to argue for the usefulness of vaccines, as opposed to prayers. Merely thinking about the fact that a sizable portion of the population in the richest and most powerful liberal democracy believe that the world is about ten thousand years old, missing the actual number by nearly five hundred thousand times, is a symptom of something catastrophic in terms of the prospects of enlightenment. Given all this, strong criticism of anti-enlightenment institutions, ideologies, and movements is urgently needed.

Critical Theory's prime significance can be clearly placed against this particular backdrop. There have been various orientations and schools of thought within what has been known as Critical Theory. My main focus is the spectrum that is associated with the Frankfurt School's first generation because the other variations, whether in the institutions that claim the legacy or other, less commercial associations within the academy, often philosophically do not retain the dialectical, or Marxist-materialist, framework, which, I think, is indispensable for a theory whose production of concepts is sensitive to marginalization and is capable of reflecting the epistemology of the marginalized.

Rather than reproducing and perpetually normalizing the dominant mode of perception, which is the perception of the dominant groups, Critical Theory problematizes the violence inherent in the prevalent order. It is inclined to uncover the embedded violence in what the dominant mode of perception perceives as order. To quote Theodor Adorno's *Negative Dialectics*, "If negative dialectics calls for the self-reflection of thinking, the tangible implication is that if thinking is to be true—if it is to be true today, in any case—it must also be a thinking against itself. If thought is not measured by the extremity that eludes the concept, it is from the outset in the nature of the musical accompaniment with which the SS liked to drown out the screams of its victims" (1973, 365). This critical negativity, however, does not and cannot stem from a moral decision, including the moral choice of taking the side of the marginalized because making such a choice does not necessarily entail epistemological emancipation from the dominant mode of perception. One would still perceive the world positively and within the parameters of positivism or another (less or more disguised) form of metaphysics. The point is to produce knowledge despite the oppressive order and through perceiving the world under those very existing conditions of oppression. This does not mean living under conditions of oppression in their immediacy is sufficient or even necessary; in this sense (i.e., in terms of the framework of negativity) what matters the most is not the material but the materialist experience, not the empirical but the political interpretation of the empirical within the critical philosophy of history.[2] That is also to say, it is the materialist philosophy's frame of reference that negatively shapes and historically contextualizes critique as a revolutionary praxis. As chapters 2, 5, and 6 show, such a critique has an immediate emancipatory influence precisely because it is a praxis that aims to reclaim the subject's place as an active creator of and in both history and the social space. It is through this critical negativity that alienation, as the experience of unfreedom, becomes raw material in the production of a collective space of freedom.

There cannot be a possibility of a progressive spatial production without a systematic spatial deconstruction of the regimes of signification that, through their normal function, reproduce marginalization and perpetually naturalize it. Therefore, perceiving the prevalent order from the standpoints of the marginalized bodies and conceiving history from the viewpoint of the excluded are imperative for Critical Theory's power of negation and, thus, emancipatory capacity. Critique can be the locus where creative resistance partakes in the composition of theory, and the latter, through amplifying the emancipatory voices of the marginalized, defies the imposed regime of truth that has been silencing the victims while exploiting their suffering however possible to fortify the prevalent order of social hierarchicalization and spatial segregation, thereby perpetuating a totalitarian system that dictates material and knowledge production. The materialist philosophy and the dialectical method are essential for a critical theory that aims to (1) challenge the epistemological totalitarianism that fictionally includes all only to disguise its actual exclusion of the vast majority who are objects rather than subjects of knowledge production and (2) problematize the moral hegemony that has metaphysicalized various forms of social privilege primarily at the expense of the subclasses within the subaltern, or those Walter Benjamin called "the hopeless ones" (2004, 356).

One of the main merits of Critical Theory, as this book tries to show, concerns epistemic politics of emancipation. Critical epistemic politics, in this sense, is an essential condition of the principle of negativity. This is compatible with Benjamin's theses "On the Concept of History" (2006c), whereby he emphasizes the state of being oppressed and thus experiencing history as a constant state of emergency while at the same time denoting the revolutionary subject as a historical materialist who is motivated by a fidelity to the sufferers of the past and present, not by the promised land of communism in the future.

Adorno too maintained a position of negative epistemology in every aspect of his philosophical, political, and pedagogical projects. Expressing this, he states, "We may not know what absolute good is or the absolute norm, we may not even know what man is or the human or humanity— but what the inhuman is we know very well indeed. I would say that the place of moral philosophy today lies more in the concrete denunciation of the inhuman, than in vague and abstract attempts to situate man in his existence" (Adorno 2000a, 175). There is a continual line of this dialectical negativity that connects Marx's materialism to Critical Theory as advanced by the Frankfurt School's émigrés. At every turn, from the letters of young Marx (1967, 212) to the surviving notes of Benjamin (2004, 356), the negative imperative comes across clearly. Both the urge for taking uncompromising political stances and the motive for philosophizing the world amid overwhelming crises are rooted in a negative genealogy. This is also what makes this tradition potentially cosmopolitan and capable of housing experiences and works of dissent from Asia, Africa, and Latin America as vital concretizing forces for the project's emancipatory objective.

The truth is that European fascism had long been at work in Asia, Africa, and the Americas before the multiple heads of the same beast, of European fascism, brought destruction and death to Europe. For instance, Aimé Césaire (2001), Frantz Fanon (1994), Walter Rodney (1972), Chinua Achebe (2009), and Abdulrazak Gurnah (2020), through various genres of writing, provide clear insights into (what should be called) European fascism in Africa during times long before the emergence of the term "fascism" at the end of World War I. What the British, French, Spanish, Portuguese, Dutch, Belgian, and German governments had been committing outside Europe was not qualitatively different from the Nazi crimes in Europe. Hence, expanding the historical and spatial scope of Critical Theory makes it more Benjaminian, more Adornonian, and even more Marxian than the version that was formed from the moment of Marx and Engels to the moment of Benjamin and Adorno. It should be revived and further revolutionized by making it more faithful to the epistemic politics of the margins. This book is an attempt in that direction.

Granted Critical Theory does not concern itself with articulating particular solutions for most of the social and political issues it problematizes, but in terms of the central question of why the enlightenment has lapsed back into irrationality and violence, Critical Theory's answer is quite tangible, albeit without violating the negativity principle central to its dialectical approaches. The answer is that the enlightenment could not and will not fulfill its emancipatory objectives as long as it, the enlightenment project itself, is manipulated by the privileged, as long as rationality is rendered a mere instrument for fortifying domination. Each historical setback is only more barbaric, irrational, and catastrophic than the prior one especially for the powerless, silenced, and marginalized. Of course, the privileged sustain their own ideologies of nativism, hierarchy, and antagonism, such as nationalism, and their own institutions, such as the nation-state. Therefore, the very defenders of the enlightenment, in societies that are shaped by domination, are the spokespersons of its perverted myths and mystified perversions. By claiming the universalist doctrine of the enlightenment, often unknowingly, they universalize tribalism; by denouncing the marginalized Other in the name of the enlightenment, they push the enlightenment further into the abyss of primordial phobias, including xenophobia. Of course, the principles of the American and French enlightenment are universal, but then that universality was fought for in St. Domingue more eagerly and unanimously than in France or the United States, both of which, in fact, soon after their respective revolutions became a haven for imperialist, colonial, and bourgeois agenda shamelessly expanding the spheres of enslavement of the oppressed in the name of freedom of the few. Just as the human individual as a right holder and a free subject was about to be born, in that very birthplace, humanity was systematically reduced into an entitlement based on race and class. Today, the same remains to be true: universal emancipation is fought for more desperately and more unanimously in the margins of the margins while the centers of class monopoly, tribalization, culturalization, and racialization continue to claim it. Of course, there has also been a continual monopoly of patriarchy on subjecthood, to which women were denied any real claim even in the cases of those who had the privileges of class and/or race because like the rest they were defined in homogenizing collective terms. The persistence of patriarchal hegemony in knowledge production renders feminist epistemology (Harding 1986; Flax 1987) equally essential for reviving the revolutionary foundations of Critical Theory. Indeed, feminists are at the center of the reconstruction of the revolutionary subject in several contemporary movements such as the Naxalite (Roy 2011), the Rojava movement (Bengio 2016; Tax 2016; Hosseini 2016; Knapp, Flach, and Ayboga 2016), the Zapatistas (Mentinis 2006; Klein 2019), Idle No More (Morris 2014; Nicolescu 2018), and Pussy Riot (Gessen 2014; Tolokonnikova and Žižek 2014).

〜

This book is motivated by a sense of urgency as extremism has been on the rise from the Indian subcontinent to the Middle East and from Eastern Europe to Brazil. It draws attention to the ongoing emancipatory struggles in the margins and induces international lessons from them in hope of building a broader, stronger, and more inclusive democratic front in political, intellectual, and educational arenas. The book helps students, intellectuals, scholars, educators, and opinion makers to unlearn false assumptions that are rooted in our epistemic blind spots of privilege. Putting my maxim of learning via *unlearning* at work, this project presents in-depth discursive analyses exposing prejudices embedded in everyday discourses and practices. At the same time, it concretizes lessons we need to learn from the margins for both consistently expanding the scope of emancipation and effectively critiquing exclusionary systems and movements. Thus, this interdisciplinary project will help its reader to (1) problematize totalitarian modes of perception and (2) use marginalized philosophies of resistance to negate totalitarianism.

Chapter 1 tries to problematize the totalitarian nature of the dominant modes of knowledge production and spatial experiences under capitalism. The chapter uses the concept of "spatial aura," as I have theorized it previously (2019d), and critically analyzes examples of spatial production in cafés, museums, and university campuses to expose mechanisms of exclusion through inclusion. This idea is further developed in chapter 4, which is a critique of culturalism and the ways in which the culturalized Other, the marginalized, is denied personhood under the new regime of what I call cultural absolutism or absolute relativism. Absolute relativism is a totalitarian regime of manipulation that fictionally represents all via its spectacles and exhibitions but practically alienates all via totalizing the principle of exchange. It technically mediates unrestricted communication but technologically depoliticizes even what used to be (per Habermas [2015]) bourgeois public sphere. It discursively claims democratic recognition of diversity but spatially demolishes all differences, denying the marginalized a place as soon as s/he dares to claim personhood.[3] As Žižek put it, "The Other is just fine, but only insofar as his presence is not intrusive, insofar as this Other is not really other" (2008b, 41).

The Other is welcome and even encouraged to celebrate the mass-produced identity imposed on them. The Other is alienated through an identity that is meant to define them negatively in relation to the identity of the dominant. At the same time, that mass-produced identity is meant to de-subject the Other because it is molded according to an essentialized and generalized image that has nothing to do with any person or group of people. The very celebrations of diversity in this setting of commercialism, mass production, and mass consumption are founded according to a perception that reduces the individual Other to a unit representative of a collective that is, in turn, assumed to be a homogeneous entity composed of identical units. Ultimately, in everyday social spaces, the Other is compelled to feel out of place simply because the essentialization had already exiled them prior to their actual presence. The very spatial production denies the subject personhood, and this is often intensified through the visual (mis) representation (e.g., flags, imagery that is supposed to symbolize diversity, etc.). The body becomes a subject of its own sharp awareness, perceiving its own movement as a spatial intrusion and stillness as a spatial wound. In fact, the body as a space is also invaded by the alienating imposed identity. The categorical essentialization, spatial alienation, and colonization of the body have been committed through material relations of domination but always with the aid of ideological methods of indoctrination, such as culturalization and the culture industry.

Under the new absolutism, differences are conceived according to the dominant modes of perception, and then each conceived difference is mass-produced according to the dominant modes of knowledge production. Describing the culture industry, Horkheimer and Adorno state, "Something is provided for everyone so that no one can escape; differences are hammered home and propagated. The hierarchy of serial qualities purveyed to the public serves only to quantify it more completely" (2002, 97). The moment the marginalized Other decides to perform any subjectivity, contradicting the identity that had been racially conceived, culturally perceived, and commercially mass-produced, they are swiftly and democratically deported from the public space. If the person somehow manages to retain their individual voice from drowning and demands some sort of justice, groups of public opinion makers might, without any sense of irony, accuse the person of promoting "cancel culture." Again, without any sense of irony, those whose very political activities are in direct opposition to freedom, such as neo-Nazi groups or certain authoritarian state-controlled media, express grievances about the right to free speech. Similarly, denialists who often deny anything from basic logical propositions to well-established scientific facts constantly make up conspiracy theories and absurd narratives while shamelessly accusing their liberal opponents of making up "fake news" and "alternative facts."[4] However, these absurdities are symptoms of a much deeper crisis, some of which critical theorists from Marx and Engels to Horkheimer and Adorno anticipated.

Chapter 2 addresses the question of fascism in today's world while arguing for a critical theory of fascism. The Eurocentric approaches to fascism studies are inseparable from the culturalist mode of perception. However, for the sake of critically analyzing normalized discourses and other forms of racist practices, it was essential to divide the work in terms of problematizing blind spots and omissions in several fields of study as well as various examples of articles, books, and official documents. Arguably, the most challenging aspect of Critical Theory is the task of transforming language as an ideological institution of power while, as a matter of course, critical theorists have nothing but language itself at their disposal for achieving that task. To put this paradoxical challenge in a question form, how can critical theorists ensure that they do not reproduce the dominant mode of perception through their use of linguistic formulas that are inherently bound to reproduce the relations of domination? In other words, if certain discourses and linguistic practices have been advanced as apparatuses of ideological domination in the interest of the privileged, how can those who are adamant to take the side of the marginalized establish a form of theory that is negative as a discourse and negating as praxis?

As of the time of writing this book, the best method I could come up with is one that starts with problematizing the totalitarian space that encapsulates our everydayness, including leisure, consumption, work, production, daydreams, and so on. This is reflected in the structure of this book, with chapter 1 aiming to problematize a space in which we are not only unfree but also unaware of our unfreedom. Referring to other critical theorists and my previous work, I argue that this is precisely what makes neoliberal capitalism by far the most advanced form of hegemony. It seems in a population that lives under a despotic regime, most people have no illusion about the fact that they are politically unfree. This very awareness has resulted in inventing new spaces, albeit in the margins, for resistance and for exercising some form of political, social, intellectual, and aesthetical freedom. It should be clear that I, undoubtedly, prefer the worst liberal democracy over the best despotic regime, but the difference, or the contrast to which I am pointing, has nothing to do with my personal preferences; nor am I trying to equate between a regime that executes people for their political views and a system that respects its citizens' human rights and freedoms. Obviously, there is a world of difference between the two, and those differences must not be ignored under any pretext. What I am alluding to is two different forms (and tools) of the exercise of power in despotic regimes versus liberal democracies. The comparison has to do with two forms of technologies of power: an older and underdeveloped form of totalitarianism that aims to impose unlimited control via coercion if not sheer horror versus a more advanced one that utilizes means of hegemony. Examining the spatial implications of this difference is a main focus in my work.

Inspired by the Frankfurt School's interdisciplinary investigations of fascism, I argue for a critical theory of fascism for conceptualizing the term to make it useful for critical analyses in various spatiotemporal contexts. The debate about the validity and invalidity of various generic and historical definitions of fascism has been dominating much of the scholarship. There is still a sense of scholastic obligation to return to the first historical models of fascism at least in terms of developing definitions, whether historical or generic ones. The orthodox scholarship has constrained the conceptual capacity of the term by relying on Mussolini's Fascism and Hitler's Nazism as the main, if not only, standards for determining what should or should not be considered "fascist." The chapter serves as both a revisit of Critical Theory's approaches to the problem of fascism and the conceptualization of fascism as what I call "ideology form." This critical conceptualization avoids the common oversight that amounts to attributing a philosophical worldview to fascist movements. It also avoids a fallback into Eurocentrism and other forms of reductionism and essentialism, which seems to be a serious problem in fascism studies. In short, I argue that fascism, except when it is capitalized, does not designate a particular ideology or philosophy. Rather, it should be used in reference to a form of ideologies, each with different specific content depending on the historical and spatial contexts in which it emerges.

In chapter 3, the critical analysis of aspects of fascism as an ideology form is continued while refuting the common elitist accounts that blame "the masses" for the rise of fascism. The chapter proposes and argues for a different concept, namely, "mobomass," both to avoid the misleading implications of defining fascism as a "mass" movement and to advance a more effective theory for diagnosing and analyzing fascist phenomena wherever and whenever they may occur. There is a long tradition of bourgeois mobilization of the masses and then blaming the masses for what goes wrong. However, the chapter also makes the correlation between anti-proletarian politics and fascism clearer, and in doing so, the chapter refers to Hannah Arendt and the Frankfurt School.

Chapter 4 is a continuation of the same line of problematization but with a focus on the culturalist mentality and culturalist practices because today's dominant form of racism is culturalism. "Culture" is a pseudo-concept even though it has become a dominant paradigm in the humanities and social sciences. Where it exists, it is inherently political, ideological, and unstable, reflecting the existing social conflicts, yet when it appears discursively in reference to any non-White Other, it is used in order to depoliticize and mystify their affairs and racialize them. In this and other works, I revisit the problem of culturalism as one of today's most common means of ideological hegemony that perpetuate social inequality on various sociopsychological and geographical levels.

By this point the book will have addressed several aspects, mechanisms, examples, and frames of Othering, all of which are characteristic of new forms of racism and absolutism. Concrete reappropriations and applications of Critical Theory from the viewpoint of the marginalized are the focus of the final two chapters. Chapter 5 is a critique of positivism as a pseudo-antipode of superstition, arguing that, if anything, there is a historical and strategical unity between the two. Here too the critique is concrete, as opposed to abstract; the chapter begins with an overview of the similarities between religious and positivist claims of "enlightenment" in their respective identification with the dominant, thus furthering the normalization, legitimization, and eternalization of the processes of the totalitarian exercise of power. Chapter 6 is a more direct but at the same time broader critique of the dominant modes of knowledge production and the dominant modes of perception. In conclusion, the chapter reaffirms that when Critical Theory is reappropriated from the perspective of the marginalized, it becomes even more Benjaminian and more Adornoian in terms of its fidelity to the struggles of the marginalized.

~

By way of concluding this introduction, let us consider an objection that, among other possible objections, could be posed against this project. It is understandable for a reader of this book to indicate that most of the thinkers to whom I refer are European. If it is the marginalized who have the potential epistemic power for emancipation, how come this book invests mainly in a group of European thinkers, from Marx and Engels to Horkheimer and Adorno? One of the most ambitious philosophical objectives of this book is precisely the falsification of today's normalized identitarianism, including the nationalist frame of reference. Without even having to engage in biographical accounts of thinkers such as those mentioned above, this book tries to help its readers to unlearn those dominant, and false, modes of perception, signification, and classification. For the sake of brevity, here it suffices to state the following. Every critical thinker I have relied on, from Marx and Engels to the Frankfurters, was extremely marginalized, in many cases made stateless, and in Benjamin's case even denied not just a place in European universities but also a place to exist. What interests me in this book is their works. It is those very works that are adamantly negative and unapologetically in solidarity with the victims of racism, actual and potential forms of fascism, and capitalism as a global system of marginalization. On that note, the mentality that attributes the enlightenment to Europeans unwittingly renders the enlightenment devoid of its emancipatory cosmopolitan essence. In fact, it is precisely the adoption of such racist lenses, which falsely reduce inclusive projects that were the product of multitudes, that is responsible for turning the project into a nightmare over and over again starting from the immediate aftermath of the French Revolution through the twentieth century and continuing to our day. Attributing the enlightenment project exclusively to Europeans is not different than attributing writing and laws exclusively to Mesopotamians. In fact, going by the dominant racializing/culturalizing mentality, the enlightenment itself would be impossible when the Chinese, Indian, Central Asian, and African earlier inventions in various fields of knowledge are excluded. It is ironic that the same professed right holders of the human civilization, examples of whom are mentioned in the epilogues of this book, are in the first row of the reproducers of exclusionary discourses, ideologies, and regimes of political economy. Somehow, the heirs of the same nationalism that denied every critical thinker from Marx to Benjamin the right of citizenship want us to believe that those thinkers are part of the (racially defined) European legacy.

Politically, in late 2021, none other than the head of one of the notorious surviving totalitarian regimes of the twentieth century, Alexander Lukashenko, put the European Union into a basic test, in which the European political leadership failed badly. Simply by turning the tables, Lukashenko proved that his regime's suppression of protesters, journalists, and opposition figures fades in comparison to the European Union's treatment of refugees, not only in the Mediterranean Sea but also on the Polish border. That treatment amounted to a collective death sentence to refugees whose only fault, one could argue, was that they had indeed believed in the European legacy and claims regarding the Universal Declaration of Human Rights. In fact, many of the victims who were left to die in the cold, including an unknown number of Yezidis who had already been brutalized because of both the construction of states invented by Western colonialism in twentieth century (e.g., Iraq and Syria) and then the partial or near-complete destruction of the same states by Western (neo)liberalization in the twenty-first century.

The system of power relations and the regime of knowledge production, as we learn from Foucault, are inseparable. In the American news industry, often when protests of Black Lives Matter (BLM) and Antifa are mentioned, almost habitually some sort of looting and destruction takes up part of the report—so much so that even the self-proclaimed sympathizers of BLM got into the habit of including a renouncement of violence and looting whenever they mention their supposed support for the movement (as in, "I support BLM, but I am against violence"). These implicit apologies further assert the false accusations against BLM.

How do these kinds of false accusations and assumptions become a normal part of the truth in the first place? For the answer, we should learn to critically examine the prevalent modes of perception, which, as we will discover, are structurally tilted and thus functionally discriminatory from the very first step of the process, that is, at the stage of collecting sensory data. This means the distortion takes place from the very first moment of forming what will be constituting "information." The objective placement of the sensors is tilted. Objectivity itself is unconsciously predetermined, so it will inevitably generate data that are against the interests of the marginalized. This institutionalized slope is not a matter of bad intentions from the side of, say, reporters, journalists, or teachers. In fact, the slope is undetectable, impossible to realize, within the natural capacity of our perception (but "natural" must be read as *sociohistorically naturalized*). Objectivity is measured according to the standards of the dominant, which means all the recognized standards. We may not know what the standards of the silenced would be like simply because they are silenced. Given this and the fact that we do not experience their experiences, phenomenologically the experiences of the marginalized are ruled out in the depiction of the reality. And we should keep in mind that what we call "reality" is necessarily a *depiction* of the world out there, as opposed to *the world out there*. "The reality" as a discursive entity is, therefore, always already a distortion of truth. By virtue of being constructed on the basis of a selective system of fact-collection, it cannot represent the full truth. The missing parts of truth are missing because the objective sensors are simply incapable of recognizing them. The unrecognizable slope in the placement of objectivity, therefore, inevitably results in an unrecognizable distortion of truth. The truth regime serves falsehood, not truth. What we call truth here and now would certainly be false in a world without marginalization. What we call society is only a false image of what is out there. The same is true in the case of what we call nature, history, culture, and so on.

A broken bank machine wins more media time than the injured bodies of the protesters. Yet, when the Proud Boys, Boogaloo militias, and other similar right-wing groups attacked the US Capitol building in Washington, DC, one of the most typical statements by reporters was something along the lines of "I am shocked," or "I would've never imagined something like this." What makes so many genuinely liberal, diversity-loving, and well-educated opinion makers associate the marginalized with violence even if the movement in question is incredibly peaceful, as BLM has been? What kept these same opinion makers from anticipating an attack such as the one on January 6, 2021, despite repeated and multiple violent assaults on people and public institutions by White supremacists? Have we not repeatedly seen that those who claim to represent a higher civilization, those who want to *make it great again* from the Nazis to today's extreme right in the United States, are the same ones who never fail to *destroy it again*? As I will show in chapter 3, fascists might be a minority in today's West, but fascist enablers cannot be assumed to be a negligible minority in terms of numbers. What I term "liquid sentimentalism" seems to have made entire sectors of the academy more concerned about the use of the term "fascism" than the possibility of the rise of fascism. Liquid sentimentalism is at least partly to be blamed for today's state of affairs whereby liberal democracies in the West have come under serious threat, not to mention the endless destructive wars by the United States that left entire societies from Afghanistan to Libya at the mercy of Islamists and the various regional gangs from human traffickers to smugglers of crude oil.

To sum up, this book questions the premises implied in the normalized racist language that is perpetuated in institutions of the nation-state and the elites that are behind the fetish of cultural commodities. It is an attempt to revive and revolutionize Critical Theory by reconceptualizing its fidelity to the epistemic politics of the margins and thereby draw more attention to the emancipatory movements of the marginalized. Considering the essential contributions of the German émigrés of the 1930s who have become known as the first generation of the Frankfurt School, Critical Theory was advanced in the margins at the hands of outcast thinkers who were nonetheless unapologetically critical of the relations of domination. Their simultaneous critique of positivism, instrumental rationalism, and superstitions places them among the most unwavering philosophers of universal emancipation. In the works of Benjamin, Pollock, Kracauer, Horkheimer, Adorno, Löwenthal, Marcuse, and Fromm, the target of critique is one and the same: the totalitarian essence of instrumental reason and the discriminatory regimes of truth that render modernity an extension of the Dark Ages.

To Critical Theory, the enlightenment is both the ultimate problem and the only hope going forward; both the soil on which fascism continues to grow and the philosophical sphere within which anti-fascism must take shape; both the curse of historical marginalization imposed on the colonized and the liberation enterprise the marginalized must own. Using the language of Critical Theory and aiming to reclaim the cosmopolitan project of emancipation to the revolutions of the margins, this book speaks from the viewpoint of the marginalized. It shows that most of the actual defenders of the emancipatory aspects of the enlightenment project have always been in the margins while the elites of the dominant groups not only invented the pseudo-concept of "race" but also engineered, rationalized, and justified countless acts of mass enslavement and genocide on every continent. Incorporating critique of political economy and historiographic research conducted by other critical scholars such as Walter Rodney (2018) and Fernando Grüner (2020), this project draws attention to the fact that the first authentic revolution of universal emancipation took place in the margins while the American Republic and the French Republic continued to practice extreme and violent discrimination across classes and geographies.

Chapter 1

Captives of a Totalitarian Space

Spatial transparency should be understood in two senses simultaneously: first, in the common sense of surveillance objectives, and second, as a characteristic of the capitalist production of space that entails sameness, flatness, and mass reproducibility. We are placed in spaces that are predesigned by the apparatuses of the dual power of capital and the state. Because it is engineered and produced by the ruling groups for the purpose of control and profit, mass manufactured space does not allow its users to lead lives with spatial depths or textures. The common building materials, such as glass, cement, and asphalt, do not hold our traces. The dominant space under capitalism is a space shaped by machines and policed by the state, but, most importantly, its use imposes mechanized modes of being whose activities are inevitably directed toward accumulation, which in turn perpetuates total quantification. Our inability to leave spatial traces of our individual lives and situate ourselves within a spatial continuity renders our experiences auraless. This auralessness is not mere collateral damage. It is, rather, an essential condition of the totalitarian order of the endless accumulation of capital. In that sense, we are captives of a totalitarian space, and our unfreedom is no longer contingent on our individual choices or social position. I base the central argument on an analogy between the social transparency to which we are subjected and the experience of zoo animals.

Only caging can deprive an animal of the interactive spatiality that is at the heart of the unity of her being. Caging creates an existential catastrophe for the animal often reflected in the animal's anomalous behavior, such as walking back and forth endlessly. Constantly living in a transparent space, we have become more like zoo animals who are permanently stripped of their spatiality. Like zoo animals, we are made aware of our existence as displaced bodies violently separated from the world around us. Flattened spaces disorient our animality, without which we could turn into manipulated beings that can only generate and respond to force. Subjugated by the omnipresent gaze, the exhibited bodily existence becomes an unforgettable source of pain, the pain of being eternally separated and individuated. Under the omnipresent gaze, our state of being is that of inmates for whom neither time nor thoughts flow effortlessly as they should. Our being in the world as part of the flow of a larger natural process of becoming is disrupted by the stress of fitting oneself geometrically into a world that is engineered for mass individuals whose movements must be predictable, measurable, and calculable. In the dominant space of total transparency, the ecstasy of mindfulness is shattered by a glassy mode of existence, the edges of which wound the flesh and bone without leaving a trace on the skin. It is a surface that imposes a one-dimensional mode of existence rendering the subject immediately visible and fully governable. In such a mode of existence, melancholy is replaced with depression, the tragic element of art with emotional prostitution, and the potential auratic life of the body with the constant consumption of the commodities of the culture industry. The transformation is almost complete, and the body is almost entirely caged, exiled outside its own spatiality. We have reached a point where all public, social, and private spaces have become secondary to the digital sphere. The digitalization of our desires and our bodiless interactions with the world is just one phenomenon among other phenomena that are symptomatic of ontological deformation. In short, I argue that the totalitarian deprivation of our autonomy to appropriate space and leave auratic traces will result in a permanent (i.e., devolutionary) spatial disability and thus deform us ontologically.

The Totalitarian End Point of Capitalism or Neoliberal Totalitarianism

The spatial crisis we are facing can no longer be diagnosed by the Arendtian theory of public space (Arendt 1998), the Habermasian theory of public sphere (Habermas 2015), or even the Foucauldian anti-panopticism because what is at stake goes far beyond the ultimate failure of bourgeois democracy. The frontier of the spatial struggle has receded from the realm of rights to the most essential ontological boundaries of the concrete human in her social formation and humanity insofar as it assumed to be a species' essence.

Before going further in depicting the ontological dimension, it is crucial to underline the fact that even by the standards of bourgeois liberalism the spatial crisis has reached a catastrophic point because the most public of all spaces (the natural environment) is privatized while, simultaneously, the most private of all spaces (the body) is collectivized. Privatization has imposed a physical end to the public space just as commercialization of the social has abolished all that was once considered the sacred space of intimacy.

The body of the minoritized subject is subjected to totalitarian control. Let us take an example of this. The issue of collectivizing or politicizing reproductive rights (abortion) even in democracies is nothing but a totalitarian process for subjugating every woman's body because the very democratic process of voting on platforms that take particular positions with regard to reproductive rights entails that the body, as the most autonomous individual space, has already been turned into an object of political deliberation, a space on which the collective exercises power. To make things even worse, this democratic collective that is about to exhibit the dictating *general will* includes the citizens who are from the opposite sex. Ultimately, regardless of the outcomes of the voting process, what takes place can be described as a democratic persecution of the individual body, which amounts to *totalitarianism* in the fullest possible sense of the concept. The subject has already been condemned; she is deprived of the right to self-determination even before the political deliberation reaches the stage when people are invited to cast their votes in a public performance usually called an election or a referendum. The tragedy peaks when the condemned is also compelled to freely take part in the collective ceremony, the voting process that has been organized precisely for the purpose of executing the condemned body, the ultimate corner beyond which there is nowhere to withdraw to, the most essential space for subjecthood. When the body becomes an object of political administration and a territory for legislations, personhood had been persecuted and potentially, depending on individual situations, already executed. Depriving a subject from bodily autonomy amounts to captivating them in preparation for slaughtering their personhood analogues to the state of unfreedom imposed on a captive or domestic animal.

The same platforms that concretize the politicization of the most individual spaces of the minoritized in the interest of the dominant groups also concretize the privatization of the most collective of spaces on every possible macro and micro level in order to enlarge the bourgeoisie's ultimate source of power and privilege: private accumulation of capital. A case to point is the legitimization, and eventually legalization, of the exploitation of the bio-space. Since every destruction of the bio-space is by definition of a partial destruction of the conditions of life, often with indefinite consequences extending far beyond the temporality and spatiality of our experiences, there is nothing more deserving of political deliberation and collective defense than the environment. By the same token, the ecological space is inherently inclusive as the broadest but also most essential social space rendering *communistic* political mobilization around universalism and ecologism rationally imperative. Yet today the question of ecology is shamelessly, openly, and democratically subdued to the nationalist, capitalist, and corporative agenda. Just as the exploitation of the so-called natural resources constitutes direct forms of meddling with life as a possibility, the state-backed bourgeois domination and the unlimited commodification of everything is a totalized norm in today's world.

Thus, neoliberalism brought about a totalitarian transformation of the world by virtue of its politicization of all that is private and depoliticization of all that is public. To fully understand the production of this totalitarian space, we need to take a look at the evolvement of the political scene in the birthplace of neoliberalism, in the United States, especially after the fall of the Soviet Union. Up until then, the bogeyman of communism served as the monstrous enemy, which helped shaping the entire political topography from the right to the (relative) left. Despite all the totalizing effects of the propaganda, the American public sphere used to retain a number of political ingredients true to the philosophy of liberalism. For instance, questions of human rights, freedom of expression, anti-authoritarianism, and a sense of solidarity with refugees and exiles were more or less the common ground or at least normal subjects for public debate. That is not to say the climate of opinion in the civil society had a significant impact on American foreign policies that openly supported countless anti-socialist and fascist regimes and movements such as Augusto Pinochet's regime in Chile and the Islamist movement in Afghanistan.[1]

After the fall of the Soviet Union, the political topography underwent a universal erosion, exposing the social nature of what appeared to be political antagonisms formed around ideals. The new ideology is idealism without ideals, falsehood without even superficial ethical claims, which would be a nightmare not only to Marx but to the liberals of the nineteenth century as well. The American society remains geographically scattered with many rural settlements that are as conservative as a group can be. Historically, even in the cities, public space has been rather hazy mainly because since its colonial foundation, capital and labor have been the brute interlocked forces that formed social landscapes. In Europe, Asia, and Africa, capitalism reshaped social spaces that already had long histories, but in the United States (as well as Canada, Australia, New Zealand, and to a lesser degree Latin America), the new space was produced from the beginning of the European colonization on the basis of the capitalist modes of production leading to unprecedented domination of the duality of spaces of production and consumption. Most early non–Native Americans came to the continent either escaping poverty elsewhere or driven by the prospects of wealth making. Of course, there were also those who were brought to America, mainly from the continent of Africa, as enslaved populations.[2] As a result, the formation of the public space has always been profoundly lacking even by European bourgeois standards. For instance, the café as a space for chatting about politics, discussing literature, exchanging news, and most importantly doing nothing other than being an available member of the public was never fully born in the United States. Neither cafés nor their socially nomad but publicly observant occupants have become influential actors in the United States. In fact, even going to a coffeeshop to grab a cup of coffee is seen as too much of a waste of time, and hence the American popular embracement of the drive-thru (invented in the 1930s).

A café has become a space of intensive labor and consumption, on both sides of the counter. On one side there are the workers whose labor force is fully utilized while they are kept isolated from the social space. Thanks to the touch screens, headphones, and meticulous division of the mechanized tasks, every moment of the worker's working time is fully employed toward the maximization of production. On the other side of the counter, we have the rest of the population whose need for stimuli is just as crucial to keep other spaces of production and consumption, from social engineering to banking and marketing, running as flawlessly as possible. It should also be noted that wherever and whenever workers do socialize, which is more regular in the case of bartenders in bars and public dance clubs, their sociability is part and parcel of the so-called customer service. In fact, it is not uncommon, especially in some of the former socialist countries, for bartenders to receive no or very small hourly wages and instead be entirely dependent on tips, which is a neutralized term for the charity given to the bartender as a sociable entity at service.

The Habermasian hero of rational democratic communication is nowhere to be found in the frenzy of caffeinated bodies whose senses are wirelessly occupied and intoxicated bodies whose socialization is even more taxing both societally and rationally. The protagonist of the bourgeois public sphere is already a martyr, like Che, but without enthusiastic followers because unlike communists, liberals are not revolutionaries. We do not hear about Assangists or Snowdenists because liberals fanatically stick to the center of indifference when it comes to any political action that could jeopardize their privileges, jobs, pensions, credit scores, and, of course, absolute obedience to the rule of (bourgeois) state. Therefore, the Arendtian hero of public action is either put in solitary confinement, like Julian Assange, or, like Edward Snowden, forced into hiding under the wings of the authoritarian rival of liberalism, somewhere in the Siberia of the world, in Putin's Russia.

The fall of the Soviet Union brought about more depoliticization of the public space. This deeper erosion of the political coating of the public space rendered private-personal affairs a raw material for political partisans of the mainstream to continue their discursive industry. Quickly, abortion and same-sex marriage became among the most divisive political subjects and hotly debated points of electoral platforms.[3] For instance, the conservatives' opposition to same-sex marriage was among the significant issues in the 2004 elections that led to George W. Bush's second term presidency (Lewis 2005).

When the ruling elites habitually frame capitalism's materialistic vulgarity within religious morality, there is a good chance for fascism to grow gradually not despite of but through democratic practices, procedures, and institutions. Of course, the prevailing order would not call itself fascist, and this is among its least complicated discursive strategies to camouflage. Whether we call the nihilist ideological form in question fascism or not, it is idealism without any ideals, embodied in a system that commits genocide with one hand and donates money to humanitarian organizations with the other. The fear of genetic modification dehumanizing the coming generations is profoundly misplaced. The real threat on humanity is precisely the humanist who is a dull empiricist and self-assuring moralist, a successful pragmatist and faithful philanthropist, a standardized law-abiding citizen and positive hedonist at the same time. These are the traits of the today's bourgeois personality responsible for obliterating even the Habermasian bourgeois public sphere and replacing it with a private sphere without privacy. This protagonist has politicized everything that is not political and depoliticized everything that is political.

The Death of the Last European and the Philosopher of Aura

The concept of aura can aid us in theorizing space without getting lost in either old-fashioned tyranny of metaphysics or the endless secessions of phenomenology. Specifically, it is spatial aura that I have conceptualized as the key to theorizing lived space (2019d). However, before taking another step in that direction, visiting Benjamin's place in-between borders and histories is due.

Benjamin was both a universalist by virtue of being a Marxist and a solitary being by virtue of holding a unique poetic mode of perception. He was a living example of what I call the dialectics of hope and hopelessness.[4] In spite of his communism, he was too sensitive to become a partisan, and in spite of his fascination with the Baudelaireian flâneur (1999, 21; 2005), the allegorical hero endowed with the ability to sense loss, he was too revolutionary to pursue the path of bourgeois narcissism. As his free will would have it, he would not write an autobiography like so many narcissistic bourgeois writers, and as the barbarian turn of events would have it, he would be stuck at a European border denied a corner for existence. Caught up between fascist forces, he was forced to take his own life as quietly as the angel of history turned its back on the oppressed and those who tried to write history from the viewpoint of the silenced.[5] Benjamin's last place and "absent grave" happened to be Portbou, Catalonia (Traverso 2016b, 206)—the same Catalonia only two years earlier had been the world's locus of an anti-fascist, egalitarian, and internationalist struggle, and Portbou had been an essential lifeline for the blockaded revolutionaries.

This dialectics of hope and despair, of the truth of utopia and the reality of hopelessness, was embodied even in his map of friendships on which both Brecht and Adorno had their intimate places. In his own life, Benjamin was madly in love with the great cities of Europe from its eastern ends, Moscow, to its western ends, Paris, including its center, Berlin, which was at a crossroad between "socialism and barbarism" (per Rosa Luxemburg). In fact, Benjamin was standing in the middle of his short forty-eight-year life as "the last European"[6] when Luxemburg, another internationalist, Marxist, Jewish, Berliner (from Poland) at the very end of her own short forty-eight-year life warned about the imminent rise of barbarism.[7] Brushing "history against the grain," Benjamin too at age forty-eight wrote, "There is no document of culture which is not at the same time a document of barbarism" (2006b, 392).

The Benjaminian is torn between the desperate revolution of/by/for those who are denied a space for existence and the ultimate hopelessness that envelopes an auratic being that has been placed in the dehumanizing spaces of capitalism. The Benjaminian body is a space that is stuck between fidelity to the revolution of the "hopeless ones"[8] and the allure of auratic experiences of radical tenderness. The Benjaminian character is a character shaped around the dream of a wall-less world of communism and a stonewalled space of the sweet sorrows of solitude. Therefore, Benjamin was almost messianically situated to secularize "aura" and as a concrete concept independent of the capitalist commodification and everything that renders auratic activity impossible. Benjamin discovered aura, and he stood somewhere in the middle of the polarized positions of his two close friends, Brecht and Adorno, in terms of the former's call for a communist open space in art and society and the latter's fidelity to auratic art as the locus of revolutionary negativity. In his most famous piece of writing, "The Reproducibility of Works of Art" (2006b), Benjamin is torn between the two opposites. He simultaneously mourns and celebrates the destruction of aura. As if trying to free himself from the contradiction generated by his embracing of the messianic role and fidelity to the secularization project, he gives up aura to the cultic value even though he himself had freed aura from the cultic through a long, albeit fragmented and unfinished, struggle that stretched across most of his life as an author.[9]

In Benjamin's project—in the gap that separates the Brechtian and Adornoian Marxisms as well—this contradiction remained unsolved. By this contradiction I mean the problem of critically theorizing communism without the vulgarization implied in the destruction of aura and preserving the aura of works of art without the conservatism of adhering to the ruling class as the legitimate owner of the means of auratic aesthetics. The destruction of aura, Benjamin thought, is inevitable for the democratization of art, but such a destruction, as Adorno rightly argued, would run the risk of ending all that is negative and revolutionary in art and thereby preparing the world for the capitalist totalitarianism embodied in the culture industry. The question remained whether the anti-fascist enterprise of radical critique should be expedited or resisting the destruction of aura should be given the priority.

Spatiality and Conceptualizing Aura

There is, however, a problem in the conceptualization of aura itself that needs to be addressed as a prerequisite for solving the contradiction represented by the Brechtian versus Adornoian polarization. The problem is that neither Benjamin nor Benjamin scholars went beyond the aesthetic boundaries of aura, that is, they focused for the most part on the aura of works of art. There is a much broader and more crucial realm to be looked at, and that is space and spatiality as such.

As I have argued (2019d), the missing concept was *spatial aura*, or aura as an aspect of space. Spatial aura is neither purely subjective nor vaguely phenomenological. Rather, it is a qualitative variable of spatiality. Spatiality to space is what history is to time. At least since Marx's dialectical theorization of history, we do not equate history with the leaner notion of the passage of time. In fact, even traditional historians did everything to distribute value unevenly on the leaner line of the past time in order to problematize, analyze, (re)signify, departmentalize, and rationalize what is then called history. From Marx to Foucault, an anti-metaphysical concept of history is formulated, a concept that does not pass over silenced margins as nonexistent or lesser truths. To the contrary, Marxist materialism and Foucauldian genealogy theorize history by carefully uncovering the official ideologies and discourses, by questioning the accepted modes of knowledge production. They uncover the actuality of social relations that shape the state of affairs in the otherwise absolutized reality and scandalize meta-physics' idealist inductions, which in turn eternalize/naturalize "the truth." In short, both the Marxian and Foucauldian projects aim to expose the historical subversions committed by metaphysicians and their allies against the margins of silence in knowledge production and the silenced margins in social relations.

Spatiality too needs to be theorized within a critical project that is capable of creating a pole-to-pole disturbance in the order of spatial reality and the dominant mode of spatial production. We have learned from Henri Lefebvre that space is both a production and a product (1991), but what became known as the spatial turn was deeply betrayed by institutionalized philosophy, leaving the turn incomplete. Without a corresponding aware-ness of spatiality and revolutionary will for spatial emancipation, we will continue to be passive objects of spatiality. The ruling groups dominate not only the means of material and knowledge production, capital and ideology, but also the means of spatial production, spatiality. These are not different forms of hegemony; rather they should be recognized as the various dimensions of social domination. Outside textbooks that force the world into neatly cut and easily digestible pieces of information, domination in the real world of real human beings is never one-dimensional. Every class oppression, when considered in its existing complexity and predetermining net of circumstances, is also racist. The same is true with regard to the historical racism of capitalist class domination. Put briefly, power is always inevitably formed through actual social relations, which are reflections of the multitude inherent in each human individual, group, and the countless interactions and clashes of interests. If there is one thing to be learned from dialectics it is that no being in the world has a static and one-sided identity—every "being" in its very singularity entails multitudes of identities, which are continually changing within evolving and intermingled frames of reference and relations of power. Therefore, identitarian thought is inevitably anti-thought, a sort of belief-forming activity, which distorts understanding, at best, and prevents it, at worst. It is a falseness that can only regenerate more falsehood. Reductionist notions of power and oppression, whether these notions are counted on communism, anti- or postcolonialism, or any other form of egalitarianism, fall into the broader falsehood oppressive power itself continually produces and reproduces.

The spatial illiteracy at large and the lack of critical spatial awareness more specifically place us at a truly primitive point in the broader project of emancipation. Power, including the power of myths, illusions and superstitions, or capital, is always spatially formed and spatially effective. By the same token, every conception of freedom, in terms of both emancipation and equality, will remain inadequate if it is not premised on the essentiality of spatiality. That is to say, a critical awareness of spatiality is essential for the very philosophical process according to which freedom is conceptualized.

This theorization of spatial aura tries to refute both dull empiricist accounts of space and mystifications of spatial experiences. Aura is simultaneously grounded in the materiality of space and spatiality of consciousness, so it is neither purely physical in the sense of vulgar materialism nor a mere conceptual abstraction produced by a Cartesian consciousness. Spatiality is always inevitably in a state of and immanent transformation, and at the center of its fluctuations and transformations is the concrete human individual as a social entity relatively active while entirely situated in a plane of countless clashing, merging, and re-diverging social forces. Spatiality is overwhelmingly determining of the lives of the human individuals who happened to be in it, but to be in spatiality is also to be a component of it, as its object and subject. The human agent therefore can be the most determining spatial force precisely because her spatiality is existential and all-encompassing.

Conceptualizing aura as a spatial quality allows for solving the forementioned contradiction in Benjamin's aura, and an emancipatory theory of space can be formulated. More specifically, the real problem does not lie in the mechanical reproducibility of works of art or even the capitalist and fascist recontextualization of works of art; rather, the broader mode of spatial production is the problem. The capitalist mode of spatial production is inherently anti-auratic. For the same reason, the produced space under capitalism is inevitably auraless. In such a space, culture in all its forms is employed to produce a single, plain, transparent, space that is stripped of its aura. It is in this sense that auraless space is totalitarian and specific to the capitalist modes of production. Capitalism as a mode of production has never recognized any limits to its manipulation, mobilization, and expansion. All that can be hegemonized is hegemonized in order to more easily exploit all that can be exploited. That is what the endless accumulation of capital requires, and that is the ultimate aspect of the capitalist mode of production.

Totalitarian Space: The Capitalist Graveyard of Aura

This limitless exploitation of both the material and ideological, objective and subjective, political and social, produces one space: the space of total inclusion. Precisely through its total inclusion it excludes all differences, for every object and subject must be subjected to the capitalist modes of production in order to be given a quantifying value without which its existence is not recognized and with which its existence is quantified, voided of difference and the possibility of difference. The power of capital is first and foremost in its quantifying influence that exceeds all objective and subjective boundaries, geographically and politically. Under capitalism, power itself gains a new meaning: power is the power to quantify. However, quantification is inherently totalizing and effectively absolute. That which has been quantified can no longer be a holder of any differentiating quality. That is to say, nothing that is quantified can be unique in any sense because uniqueness is by definition an unrepresentable quality. If the value of an entity is determined by the number that is assigned to that entity, then that entity is something that can be immediately exchanged with an actual or virtual entity that carries the same value. In fact, the moment it was quantified, it was made exchangeable. Thus, the only possible change is a change in the value itself.

In short, by virtue of being admitted into the capitalist space, the entity is quantified, but to be quantified is to be essentially abolished. What remains of the entity, after the inclusion, is all that is not particularly a quality of the entity. It is not something with an exchange value because it *becomes* the exchange value. By becoming an exchange value, however, it simply ceases to be. As an exchangeable quantity, the included "it" does not designate a being (within the space).

Of course, the quantification and value determination are not arbitrary. To the contrary, there is precision in the distribution of value—quantity is itself nothing but utter precision. Moreover, it should be admitted that the process of the value distribution/determination is highly democratic under capitalism. It is a process that is conducted in the market, the crown of liberal democracy. The market, we are told, should enjoy complete freedom in determining the value of everything, from labor force to health and education and from units of time to units of space. Neoliberals go further in their democratic fidelity to demand the absolute freedom of the market. The only problem is that the rule of the market is the most totalitarian form of absolutism that has ever existed. The market is both a quantifying institution and a space of quantification. When the value of everything is determined by or in the market, then everything is quantified whether or not it is actually traded, sold, and bought. It is the totalized rationality of value that actualizes totalitarianism.

Capitalism's promised democracy turns out to be the complete abolishment of all that is not quantifiable. It is a democracy without any democrats. In fact, it is a subjectless democracy, or the de-subjectifying rule of commodities. This is ruling in its purest utilitarian form. It is a system whose operation is almost fully automatized, rendering a government unnecessary, attesting to the wisdom of American libertarianism. American libertarianism, however, very much like religious fundamentalism, has confused perfect totalitarianism for perfect liberty and complete conformity for complete emancipation.

This process of de-subjectification through inclusion is not separate from the process of the capitalist spatial production; rather, they are one and the same. Just as the exclusion of all is accomplished through the de-subjectifying inclusion of all, actual de-diversification is accomplished through the double process of visualizing diversity and totalizing vision. There is no possibility of subjectivity without a subjective realm, which is of course a realm that is not dictated by visibility and transparency. This is why panopticism, not as a design but as a rationality for spatial technologies of power, has been the most significant discovery for totalitarianism.

As we learn from Foucault,[10] the Benthamian discovery is the idea of utilizing light, instrumentalizing transparency, or the dictatorship of vision.

This discovery was bound to finally find the right techniques to actual limitless exercise of power over all the subjugated. It was bound to succeed in occupying the last fortified spaces of the subject. To better pinpoint the dynamics of the production of totalitarian space, we need to consider the process as it happens, in the interaction between the subjective and the objective. As we will see later, the objectified is not only the gazed at but also the gazer. To begin, we need to start from particular cases of subjugations, gazes, and spaces.

Light as a Trap: Death by Exhibition

Democracy under the dictatorship of the market amounts to the rule of commodified humans by humanized commodities. Inclusion and diversity take special meanings in this totalitarian space. Difference is not only welcome but also sought after, albeit in limited quantities and for quantifying purposes. In the world of exchangeability where privilege is determined by the amount of quantifying power, to be included is to be quantified. Since privilege is by definition exclusionary, selective, and discriminatory, its rational claim to inclusivity too is designed to increase the aggregate of the dominant's power. Therefore, capitalist totalitarianism, in its advanced stages, rids itself from hateful compulsiveness that compels the marginalized to seek innovative ways for creating spaces of resistance. Instead, it adopts inclusivity and diversity. The inclusivity and diversity, however, are contingent on the utilitarian principle of complete quantification, which is essential in the production of totalitarian space. Once representatives of difference are selected, their total transparency is proven, and their visual identities are authorized, they will be spatially distributed according to their utilitarian role and worth. Ultimately, whether they end up in the equivalent of a window shop, the police force, somewhere in the pyramid of the culture industry, or the highest political office in the state, their homogenizing effect in the totalitarian space of capitalist democracy is guaranteed. The included (visually different) entity has a utilitarian worth in addition to its immediate value; a utilitarian calculus determines its spatial role (to maximize the aggregate value). Thus, the critical, that is *the negative*, terms of anti-racism and anti-fascism, which already imply the existence of racism and fascism, are substituted with positive terms such as diversity and multiculturalism, which capitalize on every virtual presence of the perceived Other, transforming their bodies to commodities with exhibition values and marketing functions. This is the reason that images of a Black body, whether on university campuses, on managerial teams of corporations, in the leadership circles of mainstream political parties, or in police institutions, are endlessly advertised. The catch is that the spectators will be unconsciously conditioned to perceive the sheer existence of the Other in the institutional or corporate space as a morally praiseworthy democratic accomplishment achieved by the institution or corporation in question. The focus is shifted from existing problems such as institutionalized inequality, spatial discrimination, and perpetuation of racism to an alleged diversifying agenda advanced by the decision makers. Another desired outcome is to turn the marginalized and silenced Other from a potential critic, protestor, or revolutionary, to a grateful subject, and her body from a genealogical record of a history of injustices to an item of advertisement for further promoting the institutional or corporate space in question in the market or the political sphere where rival parties compete for scoring higher moral points that are exchangeable quantifiably (the number of "people of color" is what is counted to collect the symbolic capital) and may be profitable financially.

This kind of inclusivity utilizes the selected individuals as effective means for further totalizing sameness. At the end, similar to a popstar's songs, images of Che Guevara are perfectly accommodatable and liberally commodifiable, just as Martin Luther King Jr., Paulo Freire, Mahatma Gandhi, Nelson Mandela, Frantz Fanon, Emma Goldman, and today's Rojava women fighters are perfectly safe articles of celebration within the liberal engineering of authorized diversity. What can be better than turning revolution from a potential grave of capitalism to a song or a movie that speaks to the democratic inclusivity of the existing order and, at the same time, transforms avant-garde energy into effective entertainment products that in turn help in societal conformity and labor recruitment?

A similar technique of inclusion as a method for concretizing exclusion is displaying the typical photos of smiling faces of Black and Brown recruits on a college website or brochure, alluding to a supposed harmonious space of diversity. More broadly, in the United States, the effective agents of capitalist totalitarianism are not fanatic conservative evangelicals. To the contrary, they are the liberal politicians and billionaires who do allow and even encourage the inclusion of representatives of the marginalized groups. The idiot is not the White billionaire who donates money to the Black Lives Matter movement—which calls for boycotting "White capitalism"—but the White conservative who is surprised by such a move. Inclusivity is the path to true capitalist totalitarianism. The liberal who speaks of diversity and social justice is far ahead of the typical conservative in terms of securing the totalitarian triumph of capitalism.

Old-fashioned fascist models and politicians have always been the worst makers of totalitarianism—their models are too obviously and rigidly exclusionary to have a chance of survival. Among Arendt's thorough observations is her statement that "nothing is more characteristic of the totalitarian movements in general and of the quality of fame of their leaders in particular than the startling swiftness with which they are forgotten and the startling ease with which they can be replaced" (1979, 305). However, what Arendt described is old-fashioned totalitarianism, which is a failed model. Neoliberal capitalism has invented a form of totalitarianism that is not at the mercy of a ruler's compulsive interventions; rather, its endurability is guaranteed through its mechanization of spatial production. The produced space is a space of capitalist social relations, and as such its diversity entails oneness and its inclusivity entails sameness. Instead of antagonizing and thus further politicizing the marginalized, it institutionalizes their political language and commodifies their perceived difference.

After all, there are two obvious signs of living under totalitarianism: (1) not being allowed to call the system totalitarian and (2) not being able to dream of an auratic world. The first is characteristic of the twentieth-century model, under which silencing and forced isolation are the norm, yet it is possible to find and create auratic corners. Losing the ability to sense auratic absence is characteristic of life under the twenty-first-century model of totalitarianism, under which we have lost the ability to be shocked. The auralessness of space under the twenty-first-century totalitarianism is complete not only because it has reached all social and subjective spaces but also because it amounts to murdering the human project of freedom, the potentiality of being a human, without leaving a trace similar to "the perfect crime" Baudrillard pointed to when he wrote about the murder of reality by hyperreality (Baudrillard 2002). Under old-fashioned totalitarianism, aura survives in the traces of the violent crime committed against space, in the ruins of places (e.g., a forgotten house that has become a shelter for stray cats and a home for unwanted plants growing unnoticedly from the cracks of standing and fallen walls). Aura survives in the distances created by the presence of the absent revolutionary and the distance created by the unstoppable interventions of exiles whose bodily existence and even graves continue to serve as a reference to some other place that remains poetic, some other possible world that remains realizable, and some other time that is neither a dead past nor a doomed future but a spatially sculptured rapture erected at the moving border between the possible and the impossible.

The security of totalitarianism is dependent on the destruction of spatial aura. The destruction of spatial aura is, in turn, unattainable without the hegemony of capitalism, the domination of the capitalist mode of production. In a totalitarian space, everything is permitted because nothing fails to meet the condition of auralessness and everything contributes to the normalization of auralessness of the lived space. Under true totalitarianism, imagining another world is impossible, which is precisely why old-fashioned fascists should be considered the stupidest of all totalitarians because if nothing else their very policies of violent exclusion make imagining another world not only possible but also imperative. This also explains why under old-fashioned fascism, so many great works of art are created despite the oppression. Under neoliberal totalitarianism, on the other hand, the very museums and art galleries exemplify the total destruction of aura, including the aura of works of art. For instance, the museumization of Native Americans is the ultimate death sentence on all that was once native American. Such museums are open graves for frozen histories mummified and exhibited to please prostituting gazes of bored consumers. Artifacts from long lost worlds are placed in geometrized and glassified spaces to serve as objects of visual perversion. Yet, the viewer, being a zoofied human thanks to ultimate triumph of exhibition value and the principle of exchange, cannot even realize the perversion implied in enjoying someone's broken skull or framed agony.

A museum site is first and foremost a bureaucratically and commercially maintained spatial graveyard designed for fragmented, abstracted, and deformed articles, including outdated artifacts and remnants of whatever else that had once been part of the body's spatial worlding of the Earth but were later extracted from destroyed worlds. The museum ensures that even the traces of those who had been wiped out will be wiped out. Traces are loci of aura, and as such they make the absence of the victims present. A trace's power is in its resistance to both transparency and disappearance. It is sensible only insofar as it refers to the absent, but it does not surrender itself to a decodifying identity or a clear meaning because that would mean its assimilation. A trace's power is in its fragility, and its fragility is in its intangibility. To be intangible is to resist objectification, to resist becoming an object of vision. Thus, traces are erased by exhibition. When exhibited, what used to be a locus of aura becomes an object of the prostituting gaze.

Hunters are obsessed with keeping a part of the hunted animal as a souvenir (perhaps as a primordial act to brush off any doubts about the ultimate defeat of the dead animal, to ensure that the dead animal will not be back as totem to haunt them). Likewise, victims of genocide are often stripped before they are driven to their death as if by objecting them to unlimited visibility, their death would be more complete. Often the graves of the victimized are vandalized as if the grave is a sign of endurance by other means. The grave as a dark, secluded space is a trace, the dead's final claim to some form of spatiality, the absent presenting its absence to spatially defy time. Thus, the oppressor goes after the grave. A museum could represent a mass grave denied the status of graveness. After claiming their lives, the oppressor now wants to own their traces, crafts, dreamcatchers, and masks to hang them on the wall if possible or place them in glass boxes for every passerby to take a look at them. The final act of elimination is committed by illumination. Light abolishes distance. The victims must be stripped of their clothes, skins, bones, and finally, traces. Every corner for hiding becomes a target until there is nowhere outside the plane of visibility, until there is no distance. In the last account, totalitarianism is a genocidal war against aura, and its most fatal weapon is light.

The absoluteness of the exhibit value renders both the museum articles and the space of the museum auraless. The isolation and visibility of each article are maximized (e.g., in glass boxes, on closely guarded walls, behind fenced spots, etc.). A museum object is the object of endless gazes, just like the remainders of hunted animals. A museum cannot possibly create memory. To the contrary, it replaces memory. If the dead have the privilege of reminiscence (of being in our memory, of being remembered), it is precisely because of their absence. The significance of the trace is that it emphasizes that absence. When the objects that carry the traces of the victims are exhibited, the victims are stripped even from that last spatial claim, the claim of not being here. Their "not being here" is finally transformed into utter and complete nonexistence. The tragedy of the victims is transformed into sheer objects of pure window-shopping. Admittedly, no gods or spirits will revenge for the ultimate elimination of the victims, but the spatial technology inevitably hunts down everyone. The window-shopper falls into the same trap of light. The same light aimed at one side of the glass will illuminate the other side as well. The window-shopper, like the hunter, is doomed by a self-fulfilling prophecy. Radiation is the kind of force that acts as if it is immaterial, that is, supernatural, but when it invades a place, it contaminates the space as such, as opposed to just selected objects or spots.

The visitor of a museum is objectified because they find themselves placed in a space that is ruled by the dictatorship of vision. They immediately become a captive of the same absolutism that rules the plane where endless gazes pass through each other, unable to return each other. Each gaze, therefore, has an objectifying power, and each body, including the gazing one, is objectified. As if everyone is both a strip dancer and a police officer policing only herself to make sure that her presence, appearance, and movements do not violate the order of visual absolutism while partaking in the visual fetish (watching and being watched). Like the exhibited objects, everyone is removed from social and historical contexts, expelled from the subjective space of solitude and forced to comply to the absolute transparency. The absolute transparency is itself also the absolute separation from one's own animality. Subjectivity is the luxury of having a secluded space qua a thinking, sensing, and feeling body. When one is situated on a plane of exhibition, every medium is also a means of visual domination, so the ontological dissolvement is immediate. Glass, lenses, light, and the geometrical distribution of space together create what can be called an ontological guillotine.

The problem is of course more profound. It is not just in the museum that the subject becomes a zoo animal by virtue of being subjected to self-inspection and gazes that endlessly detect it only to pass through it. Social, public, and personal spaces have been sliced open, flattened, illuminated, and set up to maximize visual consumption. The subject has become a zoo animal whose helpless existence is determined by its exhibition value. The moment it loses access to the virtual theater or is no longer being watched, it becomes a victim to its own monstruous inner vacuum. Inexperienced in handling subjectivity and foreign to the space of subjectivity, the subject is faced with an existential crisis as soon as the gaze from without ceases to objectify it. That existential crisis quickly leads to depression, violence, or some other form of malfunction.[11]

To purely exist for the gaze of the other is to be a visual prostitute. The brutality of consumerism and the society of commodity fetishism becomes most apparent in the case of prostitution, but all forms of labor under capitalism are prostitution, as Marx argues (2012, 99–100). Labor, under capitalism, amounts to a spatiotemporal loss of the autonomy of the body because the body has been purchased to be used as a means of production within a process that can only further disempower the laborer. The moment the task is fulfilled (e.g., the service is delivered) and the prostituted body is thrown back into the state of worthlessness, a consumed commodity, an object that has lost its magic. The prostitute loses both the use and exchange values. On another temporal level, the prostitute loses value, continually aging and eventually reaching the point of no value. In the meantime, the youth are continually trained and recruited, ensuring the uninterrupted perpetuation of a world in which the subject is trapped in complete transparency, endless exhibition, and unlimited domination of capital. After losing the autonomy of the body, or the last corner, the subject is forced into realms of disembodiment in a hopeless and nihilistic search for salvation. Thus, online existence and religious fanaticism, or political passivity and extremist nativism, could be two sides of the same coin: fascism.

Chapter 2

Toward a Critical Theory of Fascism

Fascism as an Ideology Form

We have been witnessing a global rise of ultra-nationalism and fanaticism, rendering public awareness and critical analysis of fascism ever more relevant. Fascism, I argue, is an ideological form rather than an ideological system. An ideology form can best be understood as a set of overall characteristics that distinguish a class of ideologies from other classes of ideologies. This theory enhances our capacity for recognizing, problematizing, and critically analyzing both existing and potential variations of fascism. Fascist movements in different sociohistorical and geopolitical circumstances vary in terms of their belief systems, strategies, and politics, so conventional comparative methods and approaches that deduce their criteria from a particular model have restricted the area of fascism studies. I argue for a trans-spatial and transhistorical concept with flexible theoretical applications. My central claim is that fascism denotes a class of ideologies that have a similar form, just as a concept such as egalitarianism, socialism, sexism, or sectarianism makes sense as a form of ideology rather than a particular ideology or philosophy.

Fascism as a Concept

Usually, political concepts such as democracy, socialism, sovereignty, and so forth are not, nor should be, defined on basis of their historical origins. To take the first example in the list, we do not define "democracy" exclusively on the basis of the model invented by ancient Athenians. Yet somehow "fascism" is commonly defined merely by the specifications of the first occurrences of fascism. For the most part, this has crippled critical debates and analytic applications of the concept. Again, if we measured democracy by the earliest historical models in Ancient Greece, we would not be able to justifiably designate any contemporary system of governance as a democracy. In fact, "representative democracy" would be an oxymoron. Just as we continue to reappropriate other political concepts, we should be able to enhance the conceptual boundaries of the term "fascism" without having to always justify its use in terms of the Italian and German models that emerged during the first half of the twentieth century. There is good reason to recover the term as an analytical concept rather than treating it as something from the past. That said, the main objective of this chapter is to argue for a critical theory of fascism as an *ideology form*. There are fascist ideologies and philosophies as opposed to a standard fascist ideology or philosophy. If we use "fascism" as a concept to refer to a class of anti-egalitarian ideological systems that have in common a general framing regarding exclusionism, then we will be better equipped to diagnose fascist politics and movements wherever and whenever they emerge without having to deploy a conventional definition as a measuring device every time.

Ascribing a specific ideological content to fascism in order to define it as a term will inevitably amount to reductionism. To make the point clearer, it might help to consider the nature of the fallacy when committed in terms of other notions. Let us take "sexism" as an example. Sexism may be used to describe a general characteristic of certain ideologies, but it does not denote a particular ideology. We can speak of sexist ideologies, as opposed to *the* ideology of sexism. To assume that sexism is an ideology is to confuse the subject and the predicate. It would also be false to impose a birthdate or a birthplace on sexism simply because it is a *feature* shared by many ideologies and worldviews. Of course, fascism could refer to more than a mere ideological feature, and it could be claimed as an ideology (e.g., Italian Fascism). In this case, we could speak of both the ideological form (of fascism) and a specific ideological content determined in terms of historical and spatial particularities as well as political and societal objectives. In every other case (i.e., when fascism is not claimed as the name of a particular ideology), "fascism" does not denote a particular ideology or philosophy. Even in Italy, it is misleading to analyze today's fascist movements as reoccurrences, duplications, and resurrections of Mussolini's Fascism. We capitalize the "f" when we use the word as a proper noun in reference to the brand Mussolini invented and named. In all other cases (i.e., when the signified is not the ideology of the movement Mussolini founded), fascism is used as a term, and it can be conceptualized and reconceptualized like other terms. The monotheistic (idea of) god happened to also be called God, which is why we capitalize the first letter when the word is used as a proper noun. Otherwise, "god" is an indefinite noun that means "deity" but not any particular deity unless we use other words to qualify the word "god." To insist that there is only one deity, God, is to totalize the monotheistic (idea of) god, which is exactly what monotheists do, situating monotheism in a direct contradiction with philosophical logic.

Without necessarily adopting Plato's entire system of metaphysics and epistemology, it might be helpful to keep in mind the Platonic notion of "form" in order to make sense of the general noun that denotes a class of entities as opposed to a particular one. In this sense, "fascism" should be used as a categorical "form." Only when we specify the form (e.g., Japanese fascism, Aryan fascism, Iranian fascism, Christian fascism, or Islamic fascism) would we be speaking of a particular fascist ideology, of course, without implying that an identity, Japanese, Aryan, Iranian, Christian, or Islamic, is inherently fascist. Indeed, fascism is not unique to any particular region, nationalism, religion, or patriotism; rather, it (and, of course, resistance against it) could appear anywhere and among any particular population just as sexism or racism is not unique to certain ethnic, national, or religious groups. As Enzo Traverso asserts, "Fascism has not only been transnational or transatlantic, but also transhistorical" (Traverso 2019, 20). The realization itself is crucial but not enough; we need a theoretical conceptualization of fascism that reflects its transhistoricality and transgeographicality simultaneously. A definition that is not formulated around, and does not lend itself to, such a theoretical conception will necessarily fail to account for all cases of fascism even if it appears to accurately describe multiple variations.

As early as 1921 Gramsci (1978) emphasized that it is futile to try to explain fascism as a concrete ideological platform. For instance, he wrote, "Fascism has presented itself as the anti-party; has opened its gates to all applicants; has with its promise of impunity enabled a formless multitude to cover over the savage outpouring of passions, hatreds and desires with a varnish of vague and nebulous political ideals" (Gramsci 1978). Ironically, even though Gramsci deduced his conclusions from Mussolini's movement on the eve of the National Fascist Party's reign in Italy, and he did mean Fascism with a capital letter, his account captures what conceptually characterizes fascism better than most of the accounts that followed for decades, especially after World War II. Many of the later accounts insist on formulating their definitions in light of the Fascist and Nazi programs and policies and Mussolini's and Hitler's personalities. In the same article, Gramsci warns against reductionist accounts as he also emphasizes the need for an approach that can best be described as a critical theory, broadly defined as a Marxian, materialist, multidisciplinary theory of society and social movements. Gramsci's work in general anticipates the Frankfurt School's Critical Theory that started to take shape in the 1930s at the hand of a group of Marxists who were widely denounced politically and academically, at home and abroad.

Because fascist movements are discriminatory, chauvinistic, and exclusionary, we should not expect vast similarities between the contents of the ideologies of two fascist movements unless they have in common, say, the same racist agenda. Because "fascism" does not designate any universal set of philosophical principles, even what is universally agreed upon as a textbook case of fascism should be considered as a particular variation of fascism specific to particular sociohistorical circumstances and geopolitical context, keeping in mind that in a drastically different set of circumstances and context, the equivalent ideology would be drastically different. In other words, every fascism, including Mussolini's Fascism, is just a variation of fascism. Using one movement's ideology as a standard model does not help in conceptualizing fascism. Even within the same geography (e.g., Italy or Europe), just as racism has evolved its discursive means and strategies since World War II, we should not expect much resemblance between today's varied iterations of fascism and those from the twentieth century. Most fascist movements are extremely pragmatic and adaptive, so focusing exclusively on historical definitions and origins does little to help in detecting fascism as a remerging or enduring phenomenon.

In fact, even the Nazis never identified themselves as fascists, and admittedly there were significant differences between Italian Fascism and German Nazism. Furthermore, if we were to apply the criteria of the definition provided by the inventors of the term, whereby totalitarianism is at the heart of fascism,[1] Mussolini's Italy itself should not be called fascist, for it was not a totalitarian one-party state for about three-quarters of the duration of the Fascist party's rule, which is something Hannah Arendt noted early in the debates surrounding totalitarianism and fascism (Arendt 1979, 257). Therefore, molding our definition on the Italian and/or German models would render the term useless as a concept. Theoretical flexibility and, thus, potential plural instrumental uses are essential for conceptuality. If the definition of fascism is restricted by a few historical references, it can only function as an ordinary word insofar as a word has a specific meaning and sense.

Because fascism is more of a modern tribalist impulse that manifests itself according to specificities of circumstances as opposed to a set of principles induced from a universal philosophical worldview, it can best be understood as a form of modern exclusionary fanaticism, which can be secular or religious, and racist in the sense of biological or cultural racism. In fact, none other than Giovanni Gentile, the first self-identified philosophizer of "Fascism," makes the point that it does not denote a particular philosophy, thereby easily lending itself to non-Italian, non-European, and non-interwar contexts:

> The doctrine of Fascism is not a philosophy, in the ordinary sense of the term, and still less is it a religion. It is also not an explicated and definitive political doctrine, articulated in a series of formulae. The truth is that the significance of Fascism *is not to be measured in the special theoretical or practical theses that it takes up at one or another time.* As has been said at its very commencement, it did not arise with a precise and determinate program. (2002, 21. Italics added)

Gentile goes on to describe the opportunistic and pragmatic nature of Fascism. As a matter of fact, it is the lack, not the presence, of principles that should be considered as one of the features that characterize fascist movements. However, in their attempts to define fascism as an ideology, scholars have continued to emphasize different criteria in various orders and combinations. The field of fascism studies has been gravely limited by conventional methods that have led to the domination of reductionist accounts intermingled in repetitive scholastic cycles. Even though the conventional approaches may appear diverse, they adopt similar methods for defining fascism and diagnosing fascist movements. These methods amount to searching for and then deploying a particular set of criteria as a test kit or what can be called a *fascismo-meter*. When these fascismo-meters are designed retroactively and Eurocentrically, often they prove to be dysfunctional in terms of their capacity to recognize vast variations of fascist movements. Therefore, I argue for moving toward critical conceptualization and away from traditional definitions. Normal definitions are for normal terms, and as such they could be relatively rigid, lacking theoretical grounding, dialectical viability, and critical potentiality. Concepts, on the other hand, are dialectically flexible because they are constructed through continual theorization. This flexibility also becomes evident and proves to be indispensable in the process of applying the concept in critical analyses of ideologies, discourses, events, and social and political phenomena.

The orthodox rigidity and historical reductionism have implications that reach arenas far beyond academia. What is at stake is not just elusive theoretical methods. The more serious problem is the political implications in terms of comprehending the threat of fascism in contemporary societies. Today, in multiple countries around the world, despite the variations in their influence and nature of democratic institutions, democratic principles are increasingly abolished through systematic violations of everything from laws to basic norms of the public sphere. Yet, we are less and less capable of being shocked by what happens. It is absurd that many of us are alarmed only when someone somewhere carries the swastika flag. It is not that a large number of people are indifferent about the rise of fascism; rather, the majority of people are falsely assured by public opinion makers, including some liberal politicians and educators, until it is too late for civil society to stop the fascist forces. Underestimating the threat of the rise of fascism is not merely the result of theoretical fallacies. Also, it is a fallacy to assume that theoretical fallacies are themselves not socially and politically produced. What we are facing is unconscious denialism within a broader ideological hegemony, which is in turn rooted in material interests and social relations of domination. Even without all the sound arguments that refute reductionist accounts of fascism, we should be able to recognize fascist movements and detect the rise of fascism. Of course, there are also anti-fascist movements, protests, and platforms in every society, but, with more critical education, anti-fascism could be more popular and more effective. The general public should be able to recognize the signs of fascism even in cases that carry little or no resemblance to previous models or current models elsewhere.

Stations in Fascism Studies

The purpose of the following discussion is to contextualize my proposition that fascism should be considered an *ideological form*, as opposed to an ideological system. It should be noted that most of the literature in fascism studies inevitably suffers from various forms of reductionism. For instance, rarely have Spanish, British, Portuguese, Italian, Dutch, German, and Belgian colonial practices outside Europe been considered in the literature about fascism even though those practices both historically and thematically predate what is normally considered the emergence of fascism. Both Aimé Césaire and Frantz Fanon argue that the crimes the Nazis committed in Europe are not dissimilar to the crimes European colonialism had been committing outside Europe for a long time (Césaire 2001, 3; Fanon 1994, 166).

Even studies that trace fascism back to the nineteenth century do so from the perspective of the history of ideas. To be fair, the Marxian accounts tend to stand out for their consideration of the imperialist and colonialist dimensions of fascism. Despite the anti-Marxist testimonies that became fashionable especially in the late 1980s and throughout the 1990s, the Marxist theory seems to offer more robust accounts even today. For example, Karl Polanyi's *The Great Transformation* investigates the political economy of fascism and its connection with capitalism and capitalist crises (Polanyi 2001, originally published in 1944). To Polanyi, "It was a case of symbiosis between movements of independent origin" (250). Polanyi asserts, "The part played by fascism was determined by one factor: the condition of the market system" (250). He shows that fascist movements did not become strong enough to represent a serious international threat until the major crisis of the market economy took place. While I maintain that for investigating the rise of a fascist movement the critique of political economy is indispensable, my objective here is limited, and it concerns a critical conception of the ideological aspects of fascism. That is to say, my attempt here is focused on fascism in the ideological realm, but by no means do I intend to imply that its causes are simply located in the realm of ideology. On the contrary, every fascist ideology, like any other ideological species, is a product of sociohistorical circumstances. By the same token, resisting fascism requires a holistic project to negate the material conditions of domination and dehumanization in addition to political, intellectual, and educational anti-fascist struggles.

Horkheimer conducted a great deal of ideology critique in relation to fascist phenomena, but he also stated that "whoever is not willing to talk about capitalism should also keep quiet about fascism" (Horkheimer 2005, 226). The Frankfurt critical theorists were faithful to Marxist materialism throughout. In their coauthored book, Horkheimer and Adorno point to the systematic generalization of patterns of sameness as something directly related to the mind-numbing standardization within the capitalist modes of material production. They argue that "the more superfluous physical labor is made by the development of technology, the more enthusiastically it is set up as a model for mental work" (2002, 167). Then, they add: "If, even within the field of logic, the concept stands opposed to the particular as something merely external, anything which stands for difference within society itself must indeed tremble. Everyone is labeled friend or foe. The disregard for the subject makes things easy for the administration. Ethnic groups are transported to different latitudes; Individuals labeled 'Jew' are dispatched to the gas chambers" (2002, 167). In 1976, Terry Eagleton published an article titled "What is Fascism?" and it opens by stating, "Only a few years ago, an article with a title such as this would have seemed of merely historical interest" (1976, 100). Fascism, Eagleton maintains, "signifies a massive offensive by the bourgeoisie at a time when the working class is disorganised and defensive, betrayed by a reformist leadership, lacking a revolutionary alternative. The ingredients of fascism, then, are multiple: economic and political crisis, proletarian defeat, failure of social democracy, absence or impotence of revolutionary leadership" (1976, 102). Most importantly, Eagleton realizes that "what is common to all fascist formations, however, is the markedly high degree of relative autonomy which the formation grants to the ideological region" (106). He concludes his paper by stating, "If the notoriously loose and emotive use of the term 'fascist' common to some sectors of the left is a dangerous political imprecision, it can at least serve to remind us that fascism is never far beneath the surface of bourgeois democracy" (108). Eagleton's own statement can also serve to remind us that things have worsened so much that his own paper would most likely not find a home in today's world of peer-reviewed research thanks to the gentrification, if not outright rejection, of Marxist phraseology.

In the 1970s, the totalitarianism theory that had been widely adopted in the West for two decades started to become less and less defendable. Henry Ashby Turner (1972) proposed that fascism should be defined as a reaction to modernization. In terms of his wording, Turner was careful not to sound too confident about what his thesis could accomplish; nonetheless, that thesis soon became the new theory of choice, especially for scholars who were not prepared to entertain the idea of reconsidering their stance on the Marxist theory. Turner's definition also became the subject of criticism even within the anti-Marxist camp. For instance, through reference to some of the primary sources of the Italian fascists, James Gregor argues that the modernization theory would not be applicable to Italian Fascism (1974). Gilbert Allardyce, who along with Henry Ashby Turner, James Gregor, and Ernst Nolte comes from the anti-Marxist camp, argues that the Nazis would not be considered fascist according to the modernization theory because they were very enthusiastic about industrialization (1979, 373). However, Turner himself shows that a generic definition could not hold up to this kind of analysis because even the two supposedly fundamental models of fascism could not be grouped under the term fascism (1972).

One of Gilbert Allardyce's main grievances is that fascism had not been taken seriously and that researchers have not listened to fascists themselves (1979, 368). To Allardyce, there is nothing close to a set of common criteria to determine how or why cases other than the Italian and German models should be considered versions of fascism (1979, 371). However, his observations could be used to arrive at the exact opposite of the conclusion he puts forward. Namely, precisely because "fascism" cannot be soundly defined as a universal ideology or international movement, fascism should not be attributed exclusively to the interwar period in Europe. Because the position that argues for a historical definition has never lost its appeal in the field, those who argue for a generic definition sound unorthodox in comparison. As I will argue, however, we need to go a step further and leave behind this binary of historical versus generic definitions, which should be considered an orthodox binary despite the critical significance of some of the projects. Instead of the search for a shared ideology called "fascism," as I will conclude, we should think of fascism as a set of characteristics of ideologies that otherwise might have very little in common. Such an approach would provide a way out of what seems to be a deadlock created by the endless, and to a great deal repetitive, debate around historical versus generic definitions of fascism.

Most of the problems from the 1960s and 1970s have persisted in fascism studies, and somehow the criticisms of the earlier approaches did not lead to an end to the traditional search for a definition. For the last three decades, Roger Griffin's (1991) work has been widely quoted especially in works that avoid Marxist analysis. Griffin claims to offer a solution for the problem of definitions, and he situates himself in a supposedly unorthodox position, admitting that fascism could take new shapes (2018, 1). He offers what he calls a "palingenetic" account of fascism based on a "definitional minimum" (1991, 13, 50), but his work does not leave behind the reductionist/idealist approaches. Ultimately, Griffin offers yet another typical definition, and if anything, it is a narrow one. In his supposedly minimalist definition of fascism, revolutionism is included. Here is precisely where the anti-communist strategy surfaces in Griffin's work as well. Namely, it is the strategy of pairing communism and fascism as belonging to the "revolutionary" species. This strategy continues to provide scholars who tend to sound critical of conservatism but are nonetheless deeply revisionist and anti-Marxist with a convenient discursive avenue to come across, albeit falsely, as unorthodox or at times even as critical theorists.

Outside the scholarship that got into the propagandist and revisionist habit of pairing fascism with communism, Robert Paxton's work has been among the influential ones. To Paxton, fascism is a "function," a recognizable and traceable political practice. Rejecting the common convention that assumes the existence of particular texts behind every (Western) political movement or phenomenon (Paxton 1998, 4–5), he maintains that "feelings propel fascism more than thought does" (6). Fascist movements adamantly impede prospects of both justice and freedom, which speaks to the anti-revolutionary feature at the heart of fascism. Also, a grievance of fascists is that the bourgeoisie is not exploitive enough (7). Despite the indisputability of these two points, that is, the anti-revolutionary and anti-egalitarian features of fascism, not to mention the continual historical antagonism between fascists and communists across regions and countries, there have been overwhelming attempts to group fascism and communism together. It should go without saying that pairing fascism and communism has been one of the widely adopted strategies of the cold war era, so the pairing itself does not say anything about fascism, but rather it uses fascism to target communism.

There is a somewhat widely adopted comparative method that aims to proof similarities between a contemporary movement with one or both of the historical examples of fascism.[2] It might be helpful to associate the rise of the new far right with Italian Fascism and German Nazism to draw the general public's attention to the ensuing threat, but the method is inherently reductionist and largely ineffective. Moreover, this kind of method makes it easy for others to form counterarguments simply by pointing to dissimilarities between today's far-right movements and the interwar fascist movements in Europe. In other words, the approach renders refuting the conclusion (that fascism is on the rise) by using the same comparative method extremely easy for denialists and apologists who are today's enablers of fascism. In short, despite the good intentions behind employing it, the comparative method could result in the exact opposite of the desired outcome, that is, furthering the false sense of security in the public sphere.

What may be recognizable in fascist doctrines is their relationships with the world. For instance, whether religious or secular, Pan-European or Pan-Slavic, Islamist or Hindutva, they are exclusionary, anti-egalitarian, retroactive, and semi-tribalist in terms of a sharp division between the perceived in-group and the out-group. There were substantial differences even between Italian Fascism and German Nazism in terms of their ideological worldviews, as has been explained repeatedly by historians. The rise of movements that have empowered Modi in India, Erdogan in Turkey, Orbán in Hungary, Trump in the United States, and Bolsonaro in Brazil points to the presence of global conditions that have to do with the current phase of capitalism. Therefore, approaches that tend to ignore the political economy of fascism on both regional and global levels will only continue to distort the real threats of fascism and the fascist dimensions of the existing reality.

Fascism as Ideology Form

A critical theory of fascism necessitates a philosophical conceptualization of analysis. As a sociopolitical phenomenon with vague but potentially detectable features, fascism cannot be comprehended as a specific set of philosophical claims. A philosophy may be fascist, but there is not a universal philosophy of fascism. Like "totalitarianism," "fascism" does not denote a particular ideology or philosophy. Also, like "totalitarianism," "fascism" has commonly been reduced to something less than a useful theoretical concept precisely because most of the political theoreticians failed to break free from the discursive authority of state politicians (Ahmed 2019d, 5). The definitional frame of totalitarianism was drawn mainly to mirror the USSR policies, thanks to Carl Friedrich and Zbigniew Brzezinski's book published in 1956, and to a lesser degree Hannah Arendt's classic published in 1951. Thus, totalitarianism was born dead. From the beginning, the referential rigidity was built into the definition, rendering it conceptually and analytically useless even though it has been serving effectively as an anti-communist propaganda tool. The similarity in the lives of these two terms is that they were deprived of conceptual flexibility from the outset.

Fascism is an orientation characteristic of ideologies that might have nothing in common other than their *form*. This is exactly why two fascist movements could be fatally opposing each other in their politics. As a matter of fact, it is more likely for fascist ideologies from different geographical contexts to contradict each other and fascist movements from different societies to be aggressively antagonistic toward each other simply because each side desperately needs an enemy and qualifies to serve as an enemy simultaneously, for instance Neo-Nazis versus fundamentalist Islamists or Aryanism versus Baathism. What makes the two opposing sides fascist is what they have in common in terms of the nature of their fanaticism, compulsivity, irrationality, intolerance, essentialism, and power-cultism, all of which are ideological characteristics as opposed to ideological specifications.

Therefore, critically examining the form of an ideology is sufficient to determine whether the ideology is fascist or not, regardless of the content of the ideology in terms of its particular similarities or dissimilarities and agreement or disagreement with the doctrines of any other fascist ideology, including Italian Fascism and German Nazism. Of course, examining the ways in which the content operates can also be useful, but it should not be considered decisive in the diagnosis. For instance, whether the ideology demonizes the Other on the basis of perceived "race," faith, culture, nationality, or gender should be considered as specific qualifications of a particular ideology rather than determining whether the ideology is fascist or not. By the same token, whether the essentialized Other in the ideology is Jewish, Arab, Muslim, Black, Catholic, Asian, White, Chinese—or some combination such as a Native American woman, Somali man, or Latin American immigrant—matters only insofar as we study the particularity of a specific case of fascism.

A typological discussion focused on the logic of classification and conceptualization is essential to make my distinction between an ideological form and an ideological system clear. I use "form" in the sense of the compositional frame of a category, that is, the general configuration of entries (with corresponding entities). Each entry that is classified under a particular category/form should be more distinct as a subcategory, and moving down, the divisions continue from the general to the specific. As the number of specifications increases, the ideological systems become more tangible.

A group of ideologies might be classified in terms of nationalism, but ultimately each nationalist ideology aims for a definitive content in terms of, say, the perceived identity of the "national self" or its other. Also, historically, each nationalist ideology could break into multiple, and conflicting, nationalist ideologies diverging from the original ideology in several ways and to various degrees. At the base level of the categorical divisions, the entries are necessarily different and distinct from each other. If A and B are identical, they should be signified through one signifier/entry. However, what makes a number of entries members of the same group of ideologies is what they have in common. Moving upward in the classification system should structurally correspond to a decrease in *content* commonalities and an increase in *form* commonalities.

The higher we look in the vertical classification system, the broader each "ism" is and thus the lower its rate of specifications. That is to say the more we zoom out, the better our perception of the general frames at the expense of the detailed particularities. By the same token, the more we zoom in, the more tangible the identities, the signifiers, become. If we keep zooming in, we will enter a microlevel of resolution, discovering that there are endless units within each entity's unit and so on. Therefore, classification is meant to be a logical process of composition. The plausibility of any particular system of classification depends on its grasp of the actual compositions of the classified.

This proposition is conceptually straightforward and logically clear but essential to avoid orbiting in endless cycles of debates that are often doomed to endlessly bounce back and forth between semantics and observations, with the former often restricting the latter, thereby prolonging the lifespan of the dominant frame of reference. Often our political debates orbit within this kind of sphere, so awareness of the ways in which concepts are created philosophically is indispensable for both critical analysis and theoretical problematization. A term such as democracy, egalitarianism, or fascism should not be used as if it necessarily denotes one ideology. That would substantially restrict our theoretical abilities and analytic capacities and fatally limit progress in the relevant fields of inquiry. When we describe a system or an ideology as being democratic, we make a specific claim within a relatively general proposition. The system or ideology in question could, for instance, be a liberal democracy, a nationalist democracy, a socialist democracy, a direct democracy, and so on.

The same goes for egalitarian/ism. Vastly different ideologies can be classified under egalitarianism, and it would be false to deduce that those ideologies are identical in terms of their content. Their similarity is on the class level; it is a similarity of the general form. They all give substantial weight to "equality," each in a different way and to a different degree. A number of egalitarian ideologies could, at the same time, be classified under democratic ideologies and vice versa. It is possible to designate or soundly argue for recognizing certain socialist ideologies also as democratic ideologies. There have been ideologies and systems described, whether rightly or wrongly, as socialist, but we cannot construct a universal scale of socialism based on socialist ideologies exclusively from a particular geography and history. Socialism continues to be conceptualized and reconceptualized within a large number of worldviews. No historical example of socialism can be seen as an authentic and definitive model.

Similarly, fascism can and should be conceived as a class name, a form of ideology, as opposed to a particular ideology or even a relatively small group of ideologies. Of course, the conceptualization concerns the size of the class. As in any other area of political philosophy, the concept-creation and theorization are strongly intertwined. There are many fascist ideologies, and there is an infinite number of other potential fascist ideologies, movements, forces, and systems that could emerge under other circumstances. Therefore, my theorization of fascism will include describing some specific ideological features, but they should be understood in terms of a description of the general ideological frame that contains fascist ideologies. That is to say, in addition to my arguments for ideology form, I will start advancing an account for what might distinguish fascism as an ideological form. The point then is not what fascist ideologies contain (that would be an impossible task), but what general features they have in common. What I aim to do here is to address the ideological manifestation of "fascism," not its origins or circumstances of growth, which would require adequate investigations in multiple fields. Methods that are based on the assumption that the origins of fascism and the reasons of its growth could be found in the so-called history of ideas could not be more misleading because they commit the typical idealist fallacy. Here, I do not mean to address *why* fascism emerges; instead, I am concerned with the ideological guises of fascism.

Diagnosing Fascism

FASCISM SIGNIFIES A CLASS OF IDEOLOGIES

To argue that fascism is an *ideology form*, as I suggest, should not be read as denying the existence of fascist philosophies, ideologies, and worldviews. To the contrary, a fascist movement has fanatic ideologues and dogmatic followers of a specific set of ideological beliefs and ideals. What my theoretical intervention refutes is the common perception of fascism as one specific ideology. I suggest reconsidering fascism within a system of classification and with a clearer comprehension of the kind of logic classification of ideologies requires.

The concept of "fascism" should be placed in the first layer, that is the broadest level, of the classification system, on the same level as, for instance, cosmopolitanism and democracy. That is to say, initially, what distinguishes fascism is that it is necessarily non-cosmopolitan, anti-egalitarian, and exclusionary. Fascist ideologies are exclusionary but on different nationalist, racist, culturalist, and/or religious bases, which necessitates further breakdown of the main category of fascism into smaller and smaller subgroups. Insisting that an ideology is not fascist if it does not contain the same elements as those contained in Italian Fascism and German Nazism is at best analogous to a position that would recognize schist and gneiss as the standard metamorphic stones for deciding what stones could or could not be considered metamorphic. Some of the scholars who prefer a generic concept implicitly recognize fascism as a category, but more often than not, their conception of the category is too rigidly determined. The equivalent of that in the geological classification of stones would be something along the following lines. Even though marble and quartzite share certain characteristics with both schist and gneiss, they would not be considered metamorphic stones because of their other features. More to the point, what geologists have classified as metamorphosed limestones and metamorphosed sandstones would falsely be excluded from the class of metamorphosed stones.

In any society and at any point in time, a new fascist movement could come up with an entirely new essentialist category to draw the line between the in-groups and out-groups. If fascism studies cannot be useful in aiding us with analytic tools of diagnosis to enable us to recognize new fascist movements, something must be missing in fascism studies. It is time for the field to dispose of the *fascismo-meters* for good and instead allow for more critical theoretical analysis and conceptual creativity. This is especially crucial given the dangerous nature of fascist movements. Using Italian Fascism or German Nazism as the ultimate fascismo-meter or some sort of authenticity test kit will continue to undermine the usefulness of fascism studies. In addition to the theoretical deficiency, the social and political consequences are inestimable, especially at the current historical moment when exclusionary movements are on the rise in various parts of the world and we are in a desperate need to build international anti-fascist awareness.

The Fascist Double Bifurcation

The fascist depiction of the collective self and its Other could not be more contradictory. The collective self, the nation or the racial or religious community, is imagined as an extremely fragile being on the verge of the ultimate destruction at the hands of outside enemies and their collaborators, or those among "us" who betray the nation or community of faith, the unpatriotic, the unfaithful, the immoral, and so forth. At the same time, however, there is always another depiction of the nation or community as an indestructible leviathan with some sort of divine mission and endowed with a superhistorical or a supernatural power to surpass all challenges. The nation, therefore, is assumed to be so great even God put all his trust in it to carry out the divine mission on earth, but somehow it is also so pure and fragile that it could be ruined irreversibly by a few miserable immigrants, leftist educators, or decadent writers and artists. Parallel to this bifurcation of the self-identity, there is another bifurcation pertaining to the fascist self's Other who is also assumed to be both powerful enough to represent an existential threat to "us" and so powerless that it could be no match for "us" in an open conflict of forces. In their study of the anti-Semite discourse in the 1940s United States, Löwenthal and Guterman note this "fantastic fusion of ruthlessness and helplessness" (2021, 69). This contradiction, however, is not arbitrary; rather, it is precisely the "powerlessness" of the marginalized that proves to be an irresistible object of hatred and enmity, as Horkheimer and Adorno also noted (2002, 138).

The fascist obsession with the cult of power can be embodied as the striving for the extensive exercise of power against the Othered, such as Jews. In fact, anti-Semitism is one of the most common aspects of fascist movements, but even this denotes the form of the ideologies in question more than it indicates a similarity of definitive ideological content. Anti-Semitism is common among fascist movements from different parts of the world because historically Jews have been a minority in so many different parts of the world. It is hard to think of any other demarcation of a group of people who, as a result, have been subjected to discrimination so universally and for so long. It is only expected that most fascist movements, given that they are exclusionary, would be obsessed with anti-Semitism. The presupposed otherness of Jews has rendered perceived Jews a convenient candidate as the imagined enemy. Historically, anti-Semitic demonizing myths have accumulated, leading to the creation of a terrific ready-at-hand candidate for the role of the Other. Another way to put it is that because fascist movements are desperate for the image of an enemy, anti-Semitism only intensifies in the age of fascism.

For the fascist, as Löwenthal and Guterman write, "the Jew is not the abstract 'other,' he is the other who dwells in themselves. Into him they can conveniently project everything within themselves to which they deny recognition, everything they must repress" (2021, 89). Precisely because of this, the perceived Jew is accused of being whatever the fascist in-group claims not to be. For many fascists, Marxism is nothing but a creation of world Jewry to destroy capitalism. To isolationist fascists, Jews are the secret manipulators of both capital and global capitalism. If the fascist group is theistic, Jews may be depicted as the ultimate enemies of God. No wonder that Islamist fundamentalists and White supremacist groups, despite their enmity, could come together when it comes to anti-Semitism. A clear case of such an alliance can be seen in the *Journal of Historical Revisionism*, which published hundreds of anti-Semitic articles throughout its twenty-two years of life, 1980–2002. That said, it has become increasingly more common for White supremacist groups to distance themselves from anti-Semitism and instead draw their metaphysical dividing line between Judo-Christianity and Islam in order to essentialize perceived Muslims. In a similar manner, Islamists assume absolute political despotism on the basis of metaphysical absolutism merged with racist and nationalist exclusionism.

While anti-Semitism is one of the most common symptoms of fascism, an ideology could be fascist without necessarily professing anti-Semitism. To reiterate, because Jews have been discriminated against across many regions and ages, it is not surprising that fascist groups reproduce and intensify the existing prejudices against perceived Jews systematically. The same is true in terms of patriarchism and fascism. Almost all societies have been patriarchal and sexist in the last five thousand years, so exclusionary movements tend to push their patriarchalism and sexism even further. Thus, while both anti-Semitism and sexism remain common among many old and new fascist groups, it is possible for fascist groups to condemn anti-Semitism and/or gender inequality, albeit superficially. In fact, there are White supremacist fascist groups who seem to have realized that toning down their anti-Semitism might serve the group well in terms of popularity and mass mobilization against the post-9/11 (imagined) enemy Muslim. While the intensity and criminality of anti-Semitism in Europe cannot be compared with anti-Muslim tendencies in today's Europe or the United States, the irrationality of the exclusionary mentality that has surfaced lately does carry some resemblance with the anti-Semitic discursive strategies (Ahmed 2021a; 2021b).

The Great Little Leader

To the fascist, there is nothing more appealing than sheer power. Whether mystified or vulgarly exhibited, power is the ultimate magical ingredient in every fascist recipe anywhere. The appeal of the father figure is rooted in this, and by politically empowering him, fascist followers fulfill their desire to exercise absolute power, to eliminate all that is powerless, including the marginalized groups whose presence provokes the suppressed, unconscious, individual self-image as hopelessly weak. The fascist is, therefore, exemplary of the narcissist-masochist character whose self-love and self-hate form a bipolar personality pathologically addicted to denialist and suppressive patterns of behavior. The follower finds unique enjoyment is unconditional submission to the leader who provides a sense of moral certainty through the promise of absolute power. The leader intuitively understands the follower's painful narcissistic-masochistic chasm, so he symbolizes both the protective father toward his (the nation's) children and the unforgiving force against the intruding Other. The leader is a "great little man" (Löwenthal and Guterman 2021, 134, 149; Adorno 2001, 142; 2004, 226), someone who is perceived as one of the "people," a true son of the nation, and a father figure endowed with unique abilities to stand for the nation with utmost honesty and selflessness against both inside and outside threats. Whenever "the nation" gains more discursive significance than the state and the leader acts as if he has a national or divine mandate to claim authority over the state institutions, there is reason to search for other signs of fascism.

The "great little man" character is a role, and whoever plays it will also have to fulfill the psychological needs of the followers. In this sense, the movement creates its own leader, even though each leader would of course have their own style of, say, bullying, vulgar exhibition of power, and staged authenticity. We could come up with lists of characteristics and behaviors of fascists leaders by analyzing the personalities of past fascist leaders, but ultimately it is essential to keep in mind that the Führer principle has a particular function in the fascist dynamics. Drastic differences with past examples of the Duce or the Führer should not deceive us in terms of diagnosing fascism. Also, a woman or a gay man within the movement could become the "great little" leader, and in fact, we have already been witnessing instances of such cases (e.g., Marine Le Pen's rise as a leading figure in France and Ben Shapiro's potential rise to a political leadership position in far-right movements in the United States). Of course, all these movements tend to be extremely misogynistic and homophobic, but they can also be pragmatic enough to go through some deceptive and superficial liberal motions if that makes them more popular in a certain place and time. Having a (perceived) minority member in the position of leadership is an effective strategy to sustain the status quo, a change in order not to change.

On the level of the individual personality of the followers, fascist narcissism is manifested as an irrational idealization of a father figure and some form of naturalized patriarchal moral criteria. The obsession with the father figure can result in any number of social and political expressions depending on the specific societal norms and political hot topics. The leader's role, almost like a job description, is quite literally determined by the movement itself in accordance with its anxieties and fears in that particular sociopolitical circumstance. Another disturbing part of fascist dynamics is that the democratic candidacy and selection processes function as a quest, a test, or a filtering device, so to speak, to determine who could best fulfill that role (in both the dramatic and the psychological senses of the word). In other words, the movement creates its leader democratically. If the leader is empowered as the country's leader, then their leadership will take the final step to undermine the very democratic means that brought them to power as they will translate the movement's totalitarian wishes into action whether through issuing executive orders, inciting insurrections, plotting an outright coup d'état, or triggering a counter-revolution to highjack society at a moment of crisis. However, any such sudden development is a sign of a well-developed fascist movement.

The Fascist Power Complex

Usually, every fascist takeover is preceded by long and gradual evolvement in terms of the popularity of exclusionary discourses and groups that had been permitted through passive enablers, many of whom might even identify as liberals. The problem is that these petit bourgeois and bourgeois enablers are not alarmed by fascism precisely because they do not perceive the magnitude of exclusionary physical and symbolic violence that takes place every day. The real habitat of fascism's growth is not the would-be leader's head, as so many Hitler biographers try to have us believe. In fact, reducing fascism to the personality of a leader is one of the worst methods of reductionism. The real habitat for the growth of fascism is the normal social environment under capitalism. There is arguably nothing more central to the ideological means of capitalism than depoliticizing and normalizing class violence, rendering it as anything else but class violence. Discursive strategies that reduce fascist violence to a problem of an evil genius (e.g., a bad leader), morality (e.g., bigotry), corruption (e.g., bad apples), or innocent ignorance about cultural differences are common strategies for masking class violence in order to deny it, often unconsciously. Fascist enablers are habitual denialists, and the reason behind denialism is not so mysterious when we take into account class relations and class politics. Also, it is understandable why so many people seem to be more concerned about the use of the word "racism" or "fascism" than the daily and systematic acts of violence and exclusionism.

The normalization of the exercise of power against the marginalized, the excluded, the silenced, and the othered is at the heart of fascist dynamics. Whatever the expressions of the obsession with the cult of power, the image of an enemy is essential. The enemy as an existential threat to "our" nation, culture, community, and so forth is needed not only to stimulate the urge for the exercise of power but also to glue the individual members of the in-group together. Capitalist relations of production tend to turn people into automated and alienated individuals, especially in the absence of a cosmopolitan project of resistance to negate the prevalent order as the best possible world. The isolated and alienated subjects become incapable of intimacy as such, so what brings them together is the common revulsion of the same object of hatred, which is essentially a projection of the suppressed powerless self-image. The very powerlessness and hopelessness when suppressed will end up making the subject hate the powerless and hopeless Other precisely because the subject senses in that Other their own defeated and suppressed self. At the same time, the subject fetishizes the vulgar exhibition of power (e.g., a leader who acts like a bully) and the apparatuses of pure violence (e.g., armed forces).

As an ideological form, fascism is centered around the exclusionary dichotomy of in-group versus out-group whereby the popularized collective self-image intensifies xenophobic and narcissistic peculiarities. For instance, an already marginalized minority would be depicted as the fatal threat to "our nation," and at the same time "the nation" is supposed to be the greatest nation on earth. The in-groups would be told "our nation" is the most powerful nation ever existed, yet groups of desperate refugees would be depicted as invaders who, if not stopped, will destroy "our nation" and "our way of life." In another fascist movement, massacring the men and enslaving the girls and women of a religious minority are considered not only permittable but also moral. The latest instance of this was the genocide of the Yezidis at the hands of ISIS. There are patterns in the stories told by surviving Yezidi women about certain behaviors of their torturers and rapists, and those patterns are invaluable in terms of studying the role and ramifications of ISIS's ideology. Certain reoccurring noticeable behaviors suggest that the perpetrators experienced a momentary sense of guilt prior to or after raping their victims, and it seems that in every case the perpetrator cited certain decrees that permit the act or even render it an obligatory duty. What becomes apparent in these behavioral patterns is that perpetrators immediately resort to ideological resources to gain approval of acts that otherwise might be impossible for them to commit. This is indicative of the role of the ideology in normalizing what otherwise most human beings would find repulsive.

Mob violence is more easily born and justified by the members of the mob, and this is sufficiently explained by both Gustave Le Bon and Sigmond Freud. A fascist ideology's role is far more essential before the mob is physically formed (i.e., for and during the mobilization process). It is also an essential symbolic capital for the follower to resort to when they are about to commit violence in a setting where the crowd is not present physically to lend the overwhelming moral support that may numb their sense of empathy for the victim. It is in such isolated settings where some sense of autonomous judgment, thinking for oneself as Kant would say, might creep back into the subject's world. Precisely because of this, a full-fledged ideological system, with catchy phrases, easily quotable assurances, sharp and visible distinctions between the in-group and the out-group, and absolutist moral decrees, is indispensable in any fascist movement anywhere.

FASCISM AND ANTI-PROLETARIAN PROPAGANDA

Ishay Landa's *Fascism and the Masses* (2018) convincingly argues against the common depiction of fascism as a "mass" movement. Landa explains how commonly, and falsely, historical fascism has been associated with the masses in most of the literature. His book is a valuable project that critiques the convention of blaming the underprivileged for the rise of extremist and violent movements including fascism. The masses, "the rabble," "the herd," were often openly looked down upon by the enlightenment philosophers in Europe, including liberal philosophers such as Kant and Mill, let alone others such as Nietzsche and Herder. In fact, Marx and Engels, and those who later followed their lead, are the only nineteenth-century European philosophers who adamantly and universally reject that pejorative bourgeois and aristocratic use of the term "the masses." Marx reversed the use of "the masses" from a derogatory expression to what signifies a revolutionary subject capable of leading human society into its ultimate historical emancipation. Of course, here we are speaking of Marx's "proletariat," but due to Marx's influence, communist discourses across the world adopted a very progressive use of "the masses."

"Mass politics" first emerged in Europe in the early nineteenth century (for more on this, see Hobsbawm 1996), and it was broadly speaking progressive because it was influenced by the French Revolution and the enlightenment. More importantly, mass politics was the kind of politics that insisted on the democratization of state and public affairs. Therefore, the privileged groups and classes, to which most writers and philosophers belonged, delegitimized mass politics. Authors played a crucial role in these campaigns simply because they were among the public opinion makers in the age of print and later technologies of mass communication. Of course, the bourgeois thinkers who advanced the enlightenment project played a key progressive role in evoking democratic mass politics, but the bourgeoisie as a social class quickly tried to solidify its own hegemony, so its political progressiveness steeply declined when the old aristocratic, monarchic, and theocratic hegemony started to fade away. Just as it is not surprising that mass politics came under hostile attack from the outset, it is also not surprising that it took a modern communist project to defend the masses and their potential cosmopolitan emancipatory role.

While the Frankfurt School émigrés did use "the mass" in an unfavorable sense, I think we should note that, unlike partisan Marxists, they did not use the term in reference to the disempowered, oppressed, and exploited majority under capitalism. Adorno, who is the most criticized Frankfurter for his (supposed) elitism, was concerned about the confusion the use of the term "mass" in "mass culture" might cause, so he decided to use "culture industry" (Löwenthal 1989, 49–50), which does not have any anti-egalitarian or anti-democratic connotations. Indeed, the culture industry is managed from above and does entirely fall within the capitalist modes of production. It is shaped around the principle of exchange, unlimited accumulation of capital, commodity fetishism, and so on. Moreover, the culture industry does feed into fascism through interwoven processes of standardization of perception, repetition of totalizing patterns of sameness, commodification of identity (as individuality, uniqueness, or difference), and fetishization of (national) oneness.

I would argue that even Arendt did not mean to use "mass" in reference to the working class even though Landa is completely justified to point to her ungrounded defense of Nietzsche and others. Arendt was not enthusiastic about the communist universal doctrine of standing with the working-class masses, and it is perhaps understandable why she would adopt the old language that is inherently biased against the marginalized majority. Nonetheless, Arendt's account of the term warrants a defensive argument.

Arendt's use of "the mass" is not only not interchangeable with the working class but stands in contrast to it. The mass is formed through *de-classing* people (Arendt 1979, 261). That is to say, the mass politics, for Arendt, is premised on the depoliticization of class; the worker is not mobilized as a member of the working class; the totalitarian mobilization entails the liquidation of class and its replacement with the mass (Arendt 1979, 311–23; see also, 323–24). Class is an objective social identity founded on actual material conditions and, hence, objective interests of people, whereas followers of a totalitarian movement are composed of alienated and automatized individuals mobilized against the universal interests of the working class.

Fascism is Counter-Revolutionary

Fascists viciously oppose universalist politics of egalitarianism even though, socially, large numbers of them may be coming from the working class. Fascists may be, and often are, against capitalist modernism and bourgeois liberalism, but they are nonetheless modern creatures of capitalism fanatically mobilized against every actual and potential cosmopolitan project of egalitarianism. They may follow ideological systems based on racist, culturalist, nationalist, patriotic, and/or religious foundations; they may be Pan-European or anti-EU, American or anti-American, Orientalist or anti-Orientalist, imperialist or anti-imperialist, Pan-Arab or anti-Arab, Russophile or Russophobe, monotheist or secular, Hindu or anti-Hindu, Buddhist or anti-Buddhist; they may be climate change deniers or ecologists, misogynistic or gender-pluralists, consumerists or minimalists, hedonists or stoics, soldiers or poets, athletes or philosophers. In all cases, historically and sociologically, they are outcomes of the capitalist social relations.

Fascists might and often do call themselves revolutionaries, but if for nothing else for the sake of anti-fascist revolutionaries, we should not attribute the revolutionary quality to any fascist movement. Fascist movements are counter-revolutionary in every sense. Primarily, as Žižek noted in his reading of Benjamin, it is precisely the failure of revolution that gives rise to fascism (Žižek 2008, 386). This was true of both secular and nonsecular first generation of fascist movements in the first half of the twentieth century, such as Italy's Fascism, Germany's Nazism, and Spain's Falangism. In most cases, whether in Europe or elsewhere, only when the communist movements weakened did fascist movements rise to power and manage to maintain their hegemony. As Traverso, among others, notes, anti-communism is one of the most common features of old fascism. To make his point, Traverso refers to Mussolini's own statement that fascism is a "revolution against revolution" (see Traverso 2019, 12). Even a right-wing scholar such as Ernst Nolte, who notoriously blames Bolshevik violence for the rise of Nazism and Asiatic cultures for Bolshevik violence, admits that fascism is "counterrevolutionary" (Nolte 1965, 31, 39, 45, 62). Nolte is also right in his observation that fascism is "bourgeois and populist, modern and antimodern" at the same time (Nolte 1979, 394). Fascist ideologues mobilize sections of the working class for anti-proletarian purposes and utilize modernism for anti-progressive purposes. By the same token, they may adopt revolutionary tactics for entirely anti-emancipatory objectives in order to totalize social and political domination (while communism, by definition, is a revolutionary doctrine to end social and political domination and hierocracy). Therefore, the revisionist accounts that attribute a revolutionary characteristic to fascism could not be more misleading just as their pairing of fascism with communism could not be more contradictory.

Fascism without Normal Symptoms

After fascism fell out of fashion following World War II, fascists in Europe developed discursive camouflaging to avoid immediate detection in the new public sphere (this does not necessarily apply to fascist movements and discourses outside Western and Central Europe).[3] For instance, most Western fascists do not openly express hatred toward Jews or affinity toward Hitlerism, and in some cases, they have simply shed that skin altogether when they realized Hitlerism had become a bad populist investment. Except for some small groups, they know that to gain popularity, they need affective mass appeal. Their strategists come up with discourses that correspond to their potential constituencies' current frustrations even though those strategies still feed on the same old collective phobias. For instance, to exploit xenophobia, anti-immigrant language proves to be more effective in a world where there are more and more refugees, and Islamophobic platforms pay off quickly when the Muslim Other appears more visible in Christian majority communities.

We will be witnessing a continual increase of fascist duplications of corporate models and commercial strategies. This also means more swift transitions from the business sector to politics; after all, thanks to the global triumph of consumerism in the post-Soviet era, market strategies can be used effectively in election campaigns to appeal to large numbers of de-classed and bourgeoisified people. Therefore, if an international movement does not emerge to reclaim democracy and social emancipation, we will witness more and more fascist exploitation of democracy leading to the ultimate end of the age of liberal democracy—contrary to the predictions of the prophets of neoliberalism, such as Francis Fukuyama (1992), who told us that with the fall of the USSR we had entered the end of history, crowned by the ultimate triumph of liberal democracy. We are living in the age of the decline of the bourgeois liberal state not in favor of something more democratic but in favor of something that is openly tribalist, sectarian, extremist, militaristic, and exclusionary, something that is and should be called fascist.

All that a fascist demagogue needs to do is to give the frustrated masses reasons to justify their impulses and redirect their potential anger against their oppressors who make their life conditions miserable to the imagined imminent threat of the invading and implanted Other, an enemy. As a rule, when there is no actual threatening enemy, fascism creates an enemy in the public imagination. The image of an outside enemy conspiring with collaborators among "us" is just a more satisfactory explanation for all the decay, weakness, and security threats, which in turn are believed to be the reasons why the miserable are miserable.

The Sociopsychology of Fascism

The psychoanalytic approach remains necessary not to reduce fascism to a psychological disorder but rather to avoid dismissing the dimension that has to do with alienation under capitalism. Fascism on the psychological level is a play on the human fear of separation from the original unity with the mother, the primordial peaceful oneness with the womb where security is absolute. Life, especially in the mechanized world of capitalist modernity, is a lonely undertaking. The alienation and reification that are built into the capitalist relations of production render a nihilist relapse into primordial tribalism extremely appealing. Therefore, in the absence of emancipatory movements based on a post-nihilist philosophy, the rise of fascism is always a real possibility (for more, see Ahmed, 2022b). The crisis of alienation does not have individual solutions, and on some level most people sense that something else more profound is needed. In the absence of a popular universalist emancipatory movement, fascist ideologues and movements have the best chance of attracting the millions of isolated and alienated subjects. Fascism speaks to the frustration of people and offers semi-religious and simplistic answers. On its fundamental level, fascism's answers are based on an easy dualism that stems from both pathological narcissism and primordial fear of the outside world. The dualism is, of course, composed of the clan versus the Other. The image of the Other may change from one place or time to another, but its continual reproduction is essential for every fascist enterprise. Like most mythical traditions that were later reappropriated in the Abrahamic religions, the role of the evil demon is absolutely essential for both making the role of God indispensable and framing an identity on the basis of exclusion. The evil demon is both what glues the members of the in-group together and what ensures the internal power hierarchy. It is the fundamental source of the oppressive structure and absolutist order. Practically the in-group members trade their freedoms for a sense of certainty, autonomy for a sense of security, and intellectual potentiality for a sense of belonging.

As we learn from Erich Fromm's famous *Escape from Freedom* (1965), the state of freedom is scary because it requires autonomy of thought and full responsibility for the future. Also, as the existentialists of the twentieth century, like Albert Camus and Jan Paul Sartre, realized, freedom necessarily entails never-ending anxiety.

The *mobomassdividual* would do anything to keep that existentialist anxiety at bay.[4] The first technique to eradicate it is to submit to an authority, a father figure, whether found in religion or the tribal/national leader. Only if one submits does the father figure have the psychological power of eradicating anxiety. Therefore, the fertile soil of fascism is the *mobomass* mentality itself, the antipode of autonomous thought. In the absence of emancipatory movements, the more suppressed individuals become, the more likely they are to join a fascist crowd, and the larger the crowd becomes, the faster we fall into a dark age.

In our contemporary age, the vast majority of people inevitably experience forms of alienation due to an array of reasons that have to do with both lifestyles, which are drastically different than what we as a species have been used to for many thousands of years, and life conditions, including working circumstances and their psychological consequences. When the compound sense of alienation, absurdity, individual insignificance, and purposelessness reach a certain point among people of any society, a societal change must take place. The agents of that change are people themselves. The difference is whether the change they bring about will amount to (A) the invention of a progressive way forward toward more emancipation from all that is irrational, toward the realization of both individual autonomy and the universality of one's humanity or (B) a fall back into primordial tribal space defined by the desire to return to the purity of the mythical origin. In the absence of an international emancipatory project, fascism in one way or another prevails, making total barbarism a reality. Once a fascist coalition becomes popular enough to seize the political ruling institutions, it will certainly create actual enemies through its own antagonistic policies. When the antagonized Other reacts, which is inevitable, fascism will have already placed us in its fatal reactionary cycle that will continue to eat away lives to reproduce itself.

Everywhere, fascism begins its campaigns of hatred against the most marginalized and defenseless groups. Fascists identify with the powerful precisely in order to reject all that subconsciously resembles their own sense of insignificance, weakness, and powerlessness. In dissolving themselves in the shadow of the powerful, the fascist finds a strategy to abolish their paralyzing sense of purposelessness in life. When modernism destroys the collective myths and rituals, and the critical faculties of reason are not enhanced within emancipatory social projects, fascism becomes the new collective religious refuge to provide the suppressed and confused individual with a realm of meaning. The fascist space needs its own image of evil and never-ending sacrifices. First the most vulnerable will be targeted. As the madness of the ritual elevates and fascism totalizes its will over the society, more and more people will be perceived as enemies. If it is not stopped, eventually nobody will be safe even when and if the fascist world collapses inwardly.

Conclusion

If there is one thing we must learn from ideology critique, it is the fact that ideology does not present itself as ideology, that is, as a way to perceive the world. In fact, it does not *present* itself at all insofar as its followers are concerned. It merely *describes* what it purports to be the truth and what it would have us believe is reality. Once one buys into the fascist version of the *truth*, only fascist action makes sense. True to their religious roots, today's dominant ideologies stand on the corpse of epistemology and point to the shining starts in their metaphysical space. If one looks in the direction where an ideology points, one had already fallen under the ideological spell. For instance, the moment one enters a debate in which the center of the dispute is whether Black people have equal mental capacities as White people, even when one adamantly rejects the racist position, one is already crediting the racist worldview and reproducing its linguistically codified false logic. This is precisely the problem with the common anti-racist discourses that merely rely on the moral refutation of racism or other fascist claims. When anti-racists depict the problem of racist discourse as a mere moral wrong, as opposed to factual distortions, practically they continue to see the human world and every individual as if "race" had a biological weight, and, thus they reproduce racism, albeit unintentionally. Therefore, we need to refuse to make racism something debatable by refusing to engage with racist discourses for the same reason any reasonable person would consider a debate about whether the earth is flat as intellectually offensive. Of course, respecting everyone's right to freely express their beliefs, we can still tolerate flat-earthers, obviously not as opinion leaders or educators. However, forms of denialism that cast doubt on the universal entitlement of all human subjects to human rights are not merely a matter of "free speech," as some naive liberal arguments wants us to believe; rather, such denialism is polit-ical through and through. It distorts truth in order to justify otherwise unjustifiable inequalities and forms of dehumanization against populations who are already silenced and marginalized by the existing relations of power and knowledge production. By the same token, historical revisionists will continue to cast doubt on genocides and will do so in the name of reason and freedom of thought and speech, but if for nothing else, for the sake of reason and freedom of thought and speech, genocide deniers must be denied platforms in the public sphere while critical problematizations of discriminatory ideologies should be supported in all the arenas of knowledge production and opinion-making.

The norm is naturalized even if it is pathological. It is the marginalized who are named to be demarked, to be further othered and pathologized. A dominant ideology does not hesitate to name everything other than its own assumptions, and of course it does not want to be classified as an ideology among other ideologies precisely because its legitimacy is based on its supposed metaphysical superiority, its presumed objectivity. There is one way to see the truth and many ways to interpret it, we are supposed to believe; thus, the ideologue merely makes the truth visible, and their political and moral judgments then follow logically. Racists, for instance, are genuinely unaware of the fact that racism is an ideological feature—let alone a completely flawed one that was devised to legitimize the interests of ruling groups. For racists, to give voice to racism is simply to speak the harsh truth. Polite racists try to avoid using racist speech forms, at least in public, but they nonetheless continue to endorse the same distorting worldview.

The same applies to sexists in their perceptions of sexism. This is precisely why so many racists and sexists are adamantly opposed to liberal political correctness. Another common complaint of racists is that certain minority members habitually label the actions of majority members as racist.

Sexists, likewise, frequently complain that feminists see everything as being sexist. The critical account we all need to hear in response to such objections is something along the following lines: *Yes, what is normally uttered is more likely to be racist/sexist because the entire history behind the value system we inherited had been shaped by racism and sexism. We are born into a social world that is deeply racist and sexist, so being non-racist and non-sexist necessitates a process of unlearning, which takes much more than good intentions.* In a similarly dismissive way, leftists have long been accused of carelessly throwing around the word "fascist." It does not occur to the accusers that fascism might indeed be all around us; even some self-proclaimed leftists can fall into their own forms of fascism, which they usually envelop in superficial rhetoric borrowed from Marxism or feminism.

If we classify ideologies according to their forms, as opposed to contents, fascism would be a form of ideologies, indicating some that go back to even before Mussolini, some that are contemporary, and potential ones that could emerge in the future. Two fascist ideologies could be completely opposing each other in terms of their political conflicts, nationalist and religious discourses, and any number of other specifications. Some fascist movements are Aryanists, others are not. Some identify themselves as Christian, Islamist, Hinduist, Buddhist, or Shamanist while others proclaim secularism. Some fascist movements have antagonistic relations with each other while others have both ideological kinship and strategic shared interests. However, none of today's fascist movements that are worth noting in terms of their relative popularity identify as fascist. Then, the immediate question that arises is whether there are any good reasons to use the term "fascism" to refer to the particular phenomenon we intend to designate.

Fascism, as a concept, is needed for the purpose of naming and problematizing a phenomenon that is global but has local variations. Because chauvinism is a characteristic aspect of these movements, each one of them necessarily adheres to its own distinct ideology, with particular specifications such as the image of a perceived enemy. Chauvinism necessarily imposes bold particularities on each fascist movement, and in this sense, fascist movements have more differences than similarities. However, what they have in common is precisely their exclusionary, xenophobic, absolutist, and irrational way of perception, which result in various forms of violent discourse, politics, policies, and platforms. The rise of such movements is indeed a global phenomenon. "Fascism" captures the form of this class of ideologies better than any other attempted term including populism, authoritarianism, or extremism, each of which is either too narrow or too broad. Fascist

movements are tribalist anti-communist, modern anti-modernist, instru-
mental-rationalist irrational, and totalitarian automatist. Whenever possible,
they make use of democratic means pragmatically to attract the maximum
number of people to reach state power, and once in power, they have little
regard for democratic institutions and practices.

The formation of an international/internationalist anti-fascist front is
long overdue. The new internationalist force can be inspired by the formulas invented by resistance movements that have been struggling against
multiple forms of oppression without falling into a nativist, chauvinist,
nationalist, fundamentalist, or capitalist trap. It is simply not true that the
age of movements that are at the same time cosmopolitan, egalitarian, and
inclusive is over. The social inequalities and political crises that gave rise
to the communist and anti-fascist movement about a century ago have
only intensified, so it is only rational to expect the persistence of such a
movement but of course with new strategies and in other places. What
the international left needs to do is to pay closer attention to the margins
of the margins to recognize, stand with, and be inspired by such creative
movements.[5]

Chapter 3

Mobomass Mentality, Culture Industry, Fascism

This chapter, like the previous one, addresses the issue of fascism. However, it is mainly focused on proposing the concept of "mobomass" as an alternative to the problematic concept of "the mass." Mobomass is meant to capture the mob psychology of fascist followers and at the same time allude to the role of the bourgeoisie in mobilizing members of the working class precisely in the sense of de-classing their views and politics and thus recruiting them for anti-proletarian politics and in favor of the privileged groups. While fascism has been described as a mass movement, as Ishay Landa (2018) shows, blaming the so-called masses for the rise of fascism is misleading and based on inaccurate historical assumptions. I argue that neither Arendt nor Adorno meant to use "the mass" in the elitist way it has been used. However, the term's ambiguity understandably allows for its anti-democratic (mis)uses. Therefore, theorizing an alternative concept without that problematic ambiguity and with better analytic potentiality is necessary especially for further advancing a critical theory of fascism and aiding us in identifying fascist ideologies and movements wherever and whenever they may appear.

Class versus "the Mass"

To claim that fascism is a mass movement is only the beginning of the problematization, not the end. In his *Fascism and the Masses: The Revolt Against the Last Humans, 1848–1945,* Ishay Landa does an excellent job both showing how the masses have regularly been blamed for fascism and refuting that assumption (2018). It is, therefore, an indispensable contribution to fascism studies. This along with Paxton's assertion that "the only route to power available to fascists passes through cooperation with conservative elites" (1998, 16), and Polanyi's pioneering work on the capitalist crises and fascism, suggest a picture of fascism that is radically different from the typical accounts that define fascism as a "mass movement."

For a long time, terms such as "masses," "rabble," and "herd" were used to denigrate the marginalized majority, and this view was reproduced widely in Western philosophy. Often Nietzsche comes to mind when this kind of elitist myth of superiority is mentioned, but the truth is that even the liberals, including Mill, Kant, and Hegel, used terminologies such as "masses" and "rabble" to degrade ordinary people. One of the revolutionary aspects of Marx's writing is precisely his intentional use of "the masses" in a favorable sense. Not only that, but Marx also turned the table around by designating the working-class populace as the revolutionary subject who takes it upon themselves to emancipate us all and put an end to the prehuman history, which is the history of class society.

Arendt emphasizes that totalitarianism entails the liquidation of class and its replacement with the mass (1979, 311–23). This is of crucial importance to distinguish between "the mass" as a modern political force and the ordinary meaning of the word as it is used in reference to the supposedly uncultured majority. In Arendt's work, and the works of the critical theorists of the Frankfurt School, "the mass" is certainly not used as a reference to the working class. The mass is in fact formed through de-classing people (Arendt 1979, 261). Class is an objective identity based on actual material conditions and, hence, political interests of people, whereas "the mass" is a mobilized collective, composed of alienated and automatized individuals, acting against the interests of the working class despite the fact that large numbers of the collective socially come from a working-class background. Describing the structure and nature of "the masses," Arendt writes:

> Totalitarian movements are mass organizations of atomized, isolated individuals. Compared with all other parties and movements, their most conspicuous external characteristic is their demand for total, unrestricted, unconditional, and unalterable loyalty of the individual member. . . . Such loyalty can be expected only from the completely isolated human being who, without any other social ties to family, friends, comrades, or even mere acquaintances, derives his sense of having a place in the world

only from his be- longing to a movement, his membership in the party. (1979, 323–24)

In addition to her description of the composition and nature of "the masses," Arendt's allusion to the psychology of the individual members of a "mass" movement is useful and in agreement with the Frankfurt School thinkers' relevant accounts. Arendt even draws a line between the emergence of "atomized, isolated individuals" and the social relations of production under capitalism. She tells us about this democratically dysfunctional subject who is alienated and isolated. Also, she convincingly argues that this subject is the social basis of totalitarianism. She is prepared to admit that this supporter of totalitarianism is a child of capitalism (Arendt 1979, 232, 261, 308–17).

Arendt's fellow émigrés on the left, including Leo Löwenthal, Friedrich Pollock, Herbert Marcuse, Erich Fromm, Wilhelm Reich, Max Horkheimer, and Theodor Adorno, not only recognize the Marxist thesis of alienation but also set out to discover other aspects of capitalism that rendered such a swift rise of fascism possible. Each of the critical theorists worked on a wide range of questions spanning multiple disciplines. Even in their approaches and methods, there was hardly any collective agreement, but the thread that connects their works to loosely form a school of thought is what I call *the dialectics of hope and hopelessness*, which had also been central to Marx's philosophical project. On this broad yet decisive level, the unsettling (and therefore motivating) question has to do with what Horkheimer and Adorno called "dialectics of enlightenment" (2002), the crossroad between the potentiality of an emancipatory revolution and the threat of absolute barbarism. The critical theorists witnessed what was much more devastating than the failure of the 1848 revolutions and the 1871 Paris Commune; they looked back at the crossroad between universal emancipation and fascism from the age of fascism. Therefore, to them, the fascist metamorphosis of capitalism was not a hypothesis about an anticipated future that could be prevented but a bitter reality that had to be comprehended, not through abandoning the Marxist critical project but precisely through taking it more seriously both as a philosophy of history and a philosophy of social sciences.

Perhaps, Adorno more than anyone else, even among the Marxist émigrés, was aware of the fact that the abyss is bottomless, that anticipating light after the darkest point is a myth, that fascism could continue to create what would become the darkest point of history, that even most of the revolutionary hope is false hope, that the true scope of the unfreedom imposed on us under capitalism and the bourgeois hegemony must be comprehended to stand a chance to be able to stop the fall down into the abyss. In a lecture delivered in 1978 on Adorno, Löwenthal said, "Adorno's work and life in post-Hitler Germany serve as eloquent testimony to his historical sensitivity and his knowledge that only by a determined no, which he so admirably practiced, could historical progress and regression be kept alive in critical consciousness" (1989, 57). Löwenthal adds:

> The point here is unmistakable: capitalism will not provide the emancipation that, according to every good Marxist, including Adorno, would technically be possible every day, since "the productive forces" would allow the termination of misery and domination. In contrast to his critic, Adorno remained rather melancholic, if not desperate, about the seemingly unresolvable—for the time being at least—intertwining of the establishment and its nonautonomous subjects (in the true sense of the term *subjection*). This is the opposite of a "retraction" of the original thesis of "enlightenment as an instrument of rationalized domination and oppression." (Löwenthal 1989, 57. Italics from original)

It is no secret that Arendt had little sympathy for Marxists. Arguably, she had more sympathy for Heidegger, even after the latter refused to repent his Nazi association, than for any Marxist thinker of her era, except for Walter Benjamin—still not so much as the Marxist Benjamin saw himself to be. In fact, she did not have much esteem for Marx's original work either. Nonetheless, what is clear in her account is that "the masses" that serve the totalitarian political agendas are not the same (working class) masses that are despised by philosophers and revered by Marx. She makes clear that only when workers are "de-classed" will they become the kind of masses who serve totalitarianism (Arendt 1979, 261, 315). Arendt's conceptualization of "the mass" is not quite developed, but it is helpful for concretizing a new concept to denote or problematize a modern sociopolitical entity that seems to play a central role in reactionary, including fascist, movements across the world. Describing this new entity, "the mass" in this new sense, Arendt writes:

> Masses are not held together by a consciousness of common interest and they lack that specific class articulateness which is expressed in determined, limited, and obtainable goals. The

term masses applies only where we deal with people who either because of sheer numbers, or indifference, or a combination of both, cannot be integrated into any organization based on common interest, into political parties or municipal governments or professional organizations or trade unions. Potentially, they exist in every country and form the majority of those large numbers of neutral, politically indifferent people who never join a party and hardly ever go to the polls. (1979, 311)

Confusing Arendt's use of the term with its common use causes the most ironic fallacies in interpretation. The Frankfurt School thinkers also used the term "the masses" as an anti-working-class entity that is rallied on irrational bases and for reactionary objectives. Unfortunately, neither Arendt nor the Frankfurt School critical theorists offered a concrete conceptual grounding for their new use of "the mass." They should have come up with a different term to refer to this new sociopolitical species to avoid the anti-democratic and anti-egalitarian language that has a long history from Plato to Weber. I think at least partly this confusion between the two senses of the term has been a major reason behind accusing Adorno of elitism. I will revisit Adorno's work in more detail, but for now I wish to draw attention to the distinction, or rather *contrast*, between "the mass" in the new and old senses.

As a matter of fact, and contrary to the common assumption, "the mass" in the new sense of the term is wholly a bourgeois creature. This bourgeois creature has played a central role in the perpetuation of fascism in different parts of the world. In the meantime, it is the main anti-proletarian and anti-communist mobilized social force whether in the Indian subcontinent, the Middle East and North Africa (MENA), Europe, or the Americas. Despite my extensive use of the works of (first-generation) critical theorists of the Frankfurt School, who habitually use the term in its new sense, I suggest a different term to avoid the ironic confusion that results from the ambiguity, which is of the worst type simply because the two meanings are exact opposites. I propose "mobomass" to refer to the new meaning.

A New Concept: Mobomass

"Mobomass" is meant to allude to "**mo**b," "**bo**urgeois," and "**mass**," to suggest that it is a reference to neither "the mass" nor a mob per se, but rather it denotes bourgeoisiefied people from different social classes. In terms of size, mobomasses are larger than a mob and smaller than the mass in the traditional sense. Also, their mobilization involves political agenda even though, like mobs, they are the least interested in politics in the true (i.e., broad) sense of the word. They are politicized in ways that effectively further depoliticize their consciousness, rendering them a mere instrument of force qua a large and utilizable number of people. Thus, Arendt is right to emphasize the "sheer numbers" (1979, 311), but their political indifference is inseparable from their mobilizability by demagogic discourses and leaders. To take one example, Donald Trump could not have gathered millions of followers had Americans not been depoliticized for decades. This is not a tautological proposition because mass depoliticization is not the same as political massification; rather the former precedes the latter. In other words, the gullibility of tens of millions of Americans was itself produced over decades of depoliticization, but that gullibility was exploited politically by the extreme-right demagogy to produce a highly utilizable (because of near-complete lack of political awareness) and overwhelming force (because of the sheer numbers). Used as a political force, the movement further depoliticized the consciousness of the *mobomassified* individuals. As a whole, the movement of course de-democratized American politics almost to the brink of the collapse of the state institutions. The mobomassification has not stopped and the worst is yet to come.

Mobomassness is a kind of collective yet regressive identity that is formed around phobias, irrational tendencies, compulsive attitudes, and aggressive, mafia-like beliefs. Yet at the same time, mobomass individuals are extremely pragmatic in terms of their own individual interests, and they represent the average automatized men and women who cherish conservative values and are fanatic advocates of the institution of the family. The mobomass, therefore, is a relatively large number of people who form a collective bloc in the name of politics but with a mafia-like mindset, that is, the mindset centered around unconditional allegiance to the leadership and full commitment to the unity of the group regardless of what the group's father figure may or may not decide at any given moment. In the course of this chapter, the intended meaning of the term shall become clearer, but let us keep in mind that "the mobomass" is intended to be an alternative concept for "the mass" in its new sense. Of course, the mass in the new sense, and therefore the mobomass, still need further explication in way of conceptual clarification. Down the road, mobomass will help in various other conceptions, theorizations, and analyses. For instance, we can already gauge why "mobomass culture" instead of "mass culture" or "mobomass mentality" instead of "mass mentality" would make more sense especially to avoid the confusion between popular progressive platforms formed around the interests of the majority, including the underrepresented *versus* populist platforms that are inherently discriminatory whether on nationalistic, racist, patriotic, or religious bases. "Mass politics" could be read in terms of either of the above opposing meanings, whereas "mobomass politics" leaves no room for such ambiguity as it has a clear connotation of irrationality, reactionism, and aggressiveness.

The mobomass, as I have begun to argue, is a product and production of capitalist social relations. The mobomass individual, contrary to what the common term "mass individual" might suggest, has more affinity with the bourgeoisie on several levels. We are never short of examples of accounts that blame democracy for the desecration of "high" culture and moral values. Even in the age of liberal democracy, more often than not, the average populace, the uneducated or undereducated men and women, are blamed for the fall, and there is always a fall. It can be the fall of the national, patriotic, civilizational, religious, or some other fictional glories. And yes, according to the typical moralistic narrative, whether in the Islamic Republic of Iran or the United States of America, it is the ignorant, weak, impure, vulgar, majority, empowered by democracy, who is responsible for the fall and the abyss into which we are descending. The accused in these discourses are of course the working class, the mass in the old sense. Therefore, blaming "the masses" for fascism does indeed run the risk of elitism, and more importantly, it is a false charge. The mobomass, or the mass in the sense used by Arendt, Adorno, and Horkheimer, is genealogically affiliated with the bourgeoisie, not the working class. I do not claim that this is what the aforementioned thinkers argued, but rather my proposition can be defended using their works. For instance, rejecting the anti-democratic assumptions, Arendt maintains, "the masses, contrary to prediction, did not result from growing equality of condition, from the spread of general education and its inevitable lowering of standards and popularization of content" (1979, 316). Then she goes on, adding:

> It soon became apparent that highly cultured people were particularly attracted to mass movements and that, generally, highly differentiated individualism and sophistication did not prevent, indeed sometimes encouraged, the self-abandonment into the mass for which mass movements provided. Since the obvious

fact that individualization and cultivation do not prevent the formation of mass attitudes was so unexpected, it has frequently been blamed upon the morbidity or nihilism of the modern intelligentsia, upon a supposedly typical intellectual self-hatred, upon the spirit's "hostility to life" and antagonism to Vitality. Yet, the much-slandered intellectuals were only the most illustrative example and the most articulate spokesmen for a much more general phenomenon. (Arendt 1979, 316)

Going by this, we could conclude that the social protagonist of totalitarianism is not the worker but the bourgeois elite. Even more important is Arendt's proposition at the end of the same paragraph stating that "social atomization and extreme individualization preceded the mass movements (Arendt 1979, 316). "Social atomization" and "extreme individualization" are certainly most characteristic of the capitalist relations of production. Based on Arendt's own account, we can already establish that the mobo-mass is an immediate outcome of the dominant mode of production (i.e., capitalism). In fact, Arendt gets even closer to making this very point: "The decisive differences between nineteenth-century mob organizations and twentieth-century mass movements are difficult to perceive because the modern totalitarian leaders do not differ much in psychology and mentality from the earlier mob leaders, whose moral standards and political devices so closely resembled those of the bourgeoisie" (Arendt 1979, 313). Thus, the affinity between this new phenomenon, that is, "the mass" including its mob (gangster) mentality, and bourgeois politics must be kept in mind when we read Arendt, not to mention the critical theorists whose work is unapologetically Marxist. In the following passage, from an article originally published in 1945, Arendt makes the connections between the mob/mass and the bourgeoisie even clearer: "The mob man, however, the end-result of the "bourgeois," is an international phenomenon; and we would do well not to submit him to too many temptations in the blind faith that only the German mob man is capable of such frightful deeds. What we have called the "bourgeois" is the modern man of the masses, not in his exalted moments of collective excitement, but in the security (today one should say the insecurity) of his own private domain" (Arendt 1994, 130). Having clarified these crucial points,[1] it is time to move forward to discuss fascism in relation to the culture industry, mobomass mentality, and fascism. To start, let us remember that Adorno was keenly aware of the anti-egalitarian tendencies of the elitist uses of the term "the mass." He was also aware of the ambiguity of the term "the mass," which is why he preferred to shift from the expression "mass culture" to "culture industry."² His opposition to the elitist and classist antagonism against "the masses" is evident when he points to the main difference between Freud's approach to "mass psychology" and Le Bon's approach to the same field of study. The following passage by Adorno is worth quoting in its entirety because in addition to the appropriation of the term "the mass," it also contains crucial allusions to Adorno's own approach to the question of fascism:

> The method of Freud's book constitutes a dynamic interpreta-
> tion of Le Bon's description of the mass mind and a critique
> of a few dogmatic concepts—magic words, as it were—which
> are employed by Le Bon and other pre-analytic psychologists as
> though they were keys for some startling phenomena. Foremost
> among these concepts is that of suggestion which, incidentally,
> still plays a large role as a stop-gap in popular thinking about
> the spell exercised by Hitler and his like over the masses. Freud
> does not challenge the accuracy of Le Bon's well-known charac-
> terizations of masses as being largely de-individualized, irrational,
> easily influenced, prone to violent action and altogether of a
> regressive nature. What distinguishes him from Le Bon is rather
> the absence of the traditional contempt for the masses which is
> the *thema probandum* of most of the older psychologists. Instead
> of inferring from the usual descriptive findings that the masses
> are inferior per se and likely to remain so, he asks in the spirit
> of true enlightenment: what makes the masses into masses? He
> rejects the easy hypothesis of a social or herd instinct, which for
> him denotes the problem and not its solution. In addition to
> the purely psychological reasons he gives for this rejection, one
> might say that he is on safe ground also from the sociological
> point of view. The straightforward comparison of modern mass
> formations with biological phenomena can hardly be regarded
> as valid since the members of contemporary masses are at least
> *prima facie* individuals, the children of a liberal, competitive and
> individualistic society, and conditioned to maintain themselves as
> independent, self-sustaining units; they are continuously admon-
> ished to be "rugged" and warned against surrender. Even if one
> were to assume that archaic, pre-individual instincts survive, one
> could not simply point to this inheritance but would have to

explain why modern men revert to patterns of behaviour which flagrantly contradict their own rational level and the present stage of enlightened technological civilization. This is precisely what Freud wants to do. He tries to find out which psychological forces result in the transformation of individuals into a mass. (Adorno 2001a, 134–35)

Thus, there is nothing interesting in blaming the masses for the rise of fascism as if "the mass" were a metaphysically or biologically determined species, a species that is hopelessly stupid and therefore self-destructive. The main question is, as Freud put it and Adorno re-emphasized it, "What makes the masses into masses?" (qtd. in Adorno 2001a, 135). Because "the mass" is not an ahistorical given, the question of "the transformation of individuals into a mass" is what is worth investigating (Adorno 2001a, 134–35). Far from looking down on the working class and blaming them for the rise of fascism, to Adorno what must be inquired about is fascist propaganda's role in turning people into an irrational social force. In the same article, Adorno states:

The term "rabble-rouser," though objectionable because of its inherent contempt of the masses as such, is adequate in so far as it expresses the atmosphere of irrational emotional aggressive- ness purposely promoted by our would-be Hitlers. If it is an impudence to call people "rabble," it is precisely the aim of the agitator to transform the very same people into "rabble," that is, crowds bent on violent action without any sensible political aim, and to create the atmosphere of the pogrom. The universal purpose of these agitators is to instigate methodically what, since Gustave Le Bon's famous book, *Psychologie des Foules* (1895), is commonly known as "the psychology of the masses." (Adorno 2001a, 132–33)

Nationalists, including fascists, almost entirely rely on the mobomass to overwhelm societal structures and state institutions in the interest of "the nation." Attributing the problem of fascism to "human nature" or to the working class's alleged political apathy and intellectual laziness amounts to the depoliticization of the question, which is itself a symptom of intellec- tual laziness. There is nothing easier than blaming the "stupid majority" for everything that might be disappointing politically. We have all heard of some variation of the elitist argument that blames the abstract "people." The argument is usually presented as something along the lines of, People will always bring about injustice, violence, and so on, so I am not so naive and utopian as to hope for an egalitarian world. Such an argument implicitly attributes stupidity to the majority of ordinary people while at the same time the arguer assumes some sort of unique wisdom to themselves. The arguer assumes that somehow they have unique access to an ultimate truth about humanity, a truth that is beyond and above history itself. Not only that, but they also want us to believe that that metaphysical truth about humanity, or the human nature law they haddiscovered, does not apply to them. The problem is that behind the proclaimed wisdom there is nothing but the stupidity that is falsely attributed to the masses. For it is precisely that kind of self-exceptionalism that justifies committing all kinds of political actions (or inactions) that clearly go against the basic premises of universal emancipation. Bourgeois nihilism comes in handy for not only the moral justification of selfishness but also for perpetuating ignorance in the name of some sort of ultimate wisdom. In fact, there is nothing more characteristic of the mobomass individual than the bourgeois nihilism and the bourgeois aspiration to total privatization of everything, including public space. This is exactly what explains why even when massive amounts of information are available, which is the case in this epoch, the bourgeois nihilist as an example of the bourgeoisiefied individual insists on choosing ignorance.

Marx's Democratic Stance with the Masses

The proletariat, to Marx, is the subjugated subject, the dehumanized human, the propertyless in a society ruled by private property, the laborers whose personhoods are increasingly diminished not despite but because of their continual labor. As the living embodiment of the inherent irrationality of capitalism, the proletariat is historically conditioned to abolish subjugation, and with that, they will put an end to not only their class status but the entire class society as such. Marx, therefore, is the first philosopher who tries to establish a counter science, a negative system of knowledge that goes directly against the dominant as such. Marx breaks up the duality of power-knowledge in an unprecedented way establishing a system of truth that fundamentally opposes the hegemonic regimes in the social and epistemic arenas. Of course, there have been other thinkers who tried to defend certain oppressed groups and produced knowledge accordingly, but one can easily argue that no other figure has established such a comprehensive theory of history so adamantly grounded in systematic critical research and so unconditionally universalist in its egalitarianism and egalitarian in its inclusivity. In other words, Marx should be credited for setting up the most wide-ranging knowledge system aimed at the negation of domination in its totality. In the meantime, the perpetuation of capitalism renders communism as *the rational* objective continually relevant. In other words, it is the absence of communism that makes the doctrine of communism continually present even if that presence is at times marginalized due to the weakening of the communist protagonist, the Marxist revolutionary subject. It could only be expected that Marx's communist doctrine would unsettle conservative forces across societies because the privileged almost intuitively realize how threatening such a doctrine is to their interests.

From anti-Marxist points of view, including fascist ideologies, the working class must be derailed from the track of class politics and put in the service of something else, something that does not represent a threat to but rather perpetuates social hierarchy.[3] This is not some sort of ideological technique or even strategy but the most decisive objective of the capitalist class politics. The exploitation of many by a few can never be sustained by sheer force, so in every epoch the dominant's capacity to maintain domination is mainly dependent on the effectiveness of the ideological means deployed to compel the exploited to act in accordance with what the exploitation system requires as opposed to what their own freedom might require rationally. In the age of capitalism, therefore, what determines the continuation of bourgeois domination, or simply capitalism, comes down to the extent to which the working class is kept off the political stage. This is where the bourgeoisie had to invent democratic ways to establish and sustain its totalitarianism. Namely, the bourgeois invention allows for the political participation of workers if and only if the workers do not act as members of their social class. Hence, the social and political domination of the bourgeoisie is inseparable from nationalism, religious fundamentalism, and ultimately, fascism. Since proletarian consciousness is inevitably universal, and proletarian politics is universalist, bourgeois domination, on both local and global levels, necessitates the tribalization of the working class. Nationalism, patriotism, religious fundamentalism, racism, and culturalism are indispensable tools for such a tribalization. Put shortly, the popularity of tribalist ideologies allows for the continuation of capitalist totalitarianism, or the unlimited exercise of power by the bourgeoisie. Of course, national bourgeoisies have antagonistic relationships among themselves, and various imperial conflicts continue to shape much of international politics, but capitalism continues to be the dominant mode of production, and the dominant class across societies and regions continues to be the bourgeoisie. Considering both its vertical hegemony and horizontal scope, this bourgeois domination is the most totalitarian form of domination in human history.

Culture Industry and Fascism

It is now time to take Critical Theory to a new level. Namely, we should be prepared to depict the links between the culture industry and fascism. That link runs through the totality of sameness, which is also the ultimate aspect of mobomass mentality. This will enable us to demystify the affair between fascism and the mobomasses on the one hand and further analyze the relationship between totalitarianism and fascism on the other.

Horkheimer and Adorno could hardly be any clearer about the following two propositions:

1. The alienated and isolated subject is the immediate outcome of the capitalist relations of production.

2. This alienated and isolated subject is further disempowered and de-individualized through the culture industry.

For a critical theory of fascism, there is another crucial proposition that could and should be added:

3. This subject, whom I call the *mobomassdividual*, is the main protagonist in every fascist movement.

In terms of the first proposition, Horkheimer and Adorno write:

Through the mediation of the total society, which encompasses all relationships and impulses, human beings are being turned back into precisely what the developmental law of society, the principle of the self, had opposed: mere examples of the species, *identical to one another through isolation within the compulsively controlled collectivity*. The rowers, unable to speak to one another, are all harnessed to the same rhythms, like modern workers in factories, cinemas, and the collective. *It is the concrete conditions of work in society which enforce conformism—not the conscious influences which additionally render the oppressed stupid and deflect them from the truth. The powerlessness of the workers is* not merely a ruse of the rulers but *the logical consequence of industrial society,* into which the efforts to escape it have finally transformed the ancient concept of fate. (2002, 29. Italics added)

As for the second proposition, Horkheimer and Adorno state, "The mentality of the public, which allegedly and actually favors the system of the culture industry, is a part of the system, not an excuse for it" (2002, 96). Then, moving toward the third conclusion, they add, "The relentless unity of the culture industry bears witness to the emergent unity of politics" (96). The capitalist basis of fascism has been largely dismissed, and this, not surprisingly, has led to widespread reductionism in fascism studies. Despite the variations of the non-Marxist approaches, there seems to be a general presumption that fascism is an ideology or a body of ideological fragments, a pathological deviation from liberalism. Ironically, non-Marxist and anti-Marxist scholars advanced their reductionist accounts in the name of rejecting economic determinism, or so-called Marxist reductionism. We usually assess theories by their accurate, not false, applications, but in the case of Marxism, some oversimplified applications have been taken as the ultimate proof of the invalidity of Marxism. A merit of the Frankfurt School's Critical Theory is that it rejects both disciplinary tendencies of reductionism and the anti-Marxist pressure in Western academic institutions. A critical theory of fascism remains desperately needed and the works of the Frankfurt School's critical theorists have indispensable significance in this respect. In the following fragment, for instance, Horkheimer and Adorno point to alienation under capitalism, the bourgeois pseudo-individuality, the bourgeois privatization of the public space, and the culture industry as areas to be problematized in searching for what forms fascism. Horkheimer and Adorno write:

> *The citizens whose lives are split between business and private life,* their private life between ostentation and intimacy, their intimacy between the sullen community of marriage and the bitter solace of being entirely alone, at odds with themselves and with everyone, *are virtually already Nazis,* who are at once enthusiastic and fed up, or the city dwellers of today, who can imagine friendship

only as "social contact" between the inwardly unconnected. The culture industry can only manipulate individuality so successfully because the fractured nature of society has always been reproduced within it. (2002, 126–27. Italics added)

Following Horkheimer and Adorno's example, the present work tries to offer a non-reductionist problematization of fascism as a phenomenon whose endless variations as an *ideological form* stem from other structural and ideological backgrounds. There can be no critical theory of fascism without a critical theory of capitalism, or as Horkheimer puts it, "Whoever is not willing to talk about capitalism should also keep quiet about fascism" (2005, 226).

The proliferation and internalization of fascism take place through the propagation and internalization of ideologies that capitalize on a chauvinistic collective identity, according to which the mere existence of "the other" represents a normative threat to the in-group. Potential fascists are the automated individuals whose alienation and incapacity to negate their conditions push them toward seeking some sort of identification that might open the gate into the festive spirit of one extended brotherhood and sisterhood under the absolutist authority of a father figure. In this sense, the phenomenon of fascism is an existential crisis of individualism that results from capitalist modes of production and is intensified by nationalism. For fascists, culture is exactly what "[gives] meaning to a world which makes them meaningless" (Horkheimer and Adorno 2002, 161). As an authoritarian personality, the mobomassdividual cherishes the oppressor and loathes the disadvantaged. Also, the mobomass mentality is sickly reductionist: it reduces all humans into a few types, whether races, faiths, nationalities, regions, or cultures.

The first main affinity between mobomassness and fascism can be located in this homogenizing mentality. Two fascist movements from two different places of the world might seem to be fatal enemies to each other, but their way of (not) thinking is similar as they have the mobomass mentality in common. To the mobomassdividual the very classification process of themselves under a certain collective identity is one and the same process as the classification of the othered Others under the opposite category. An Islamist, for instance, needs the existence of the "other" as the "infidel," in order for their image of the Islamist brothers and sisters to make any sense. Meanwhile, some contemporary fascists in the West need their own image of "the Muslims" in order for their brotherhood and sisterhood to function. It seems that this kind of reductionist attitude applies to fascism everywhere, and every group's culture, however loosely "culture" may be defined, provides fertile soil for the bifurcation of the world based on "us" versus "them."

Horkheimer and Adorno state, "Culture has evolved under the shadow of the executioner" (2002, 180). Even before the culture industry, culture has always been ideological and political. Cultures are xenophobic and exclusionary in different ways and to various degrees. Paranoia is the central theme in culture, and the established group is paranoid about the outside world because its members project their irrationality on the world. The world represents a constant conspiracy against the in-group (163). Culture provides the members of the group with patterns of stereotypes that are formed around the phobic stance, which is the group's main stance toward the outside world. Ultimately, "stereotypes replace intellectual categories" (166). Intellectually, considering every "individual" as a distinct subject with personhood is too demanding for a mobomass mind in the age of mass production. As the bourgeois standardization mentality becomes the norm, difference is abolished. It is as if the mobomass mentality is obsessed with creating a world in its own image: distinctly divided into classes, hierarchically arranged as types, and fully defined in terms of the exercise of power. That is a world that does not and cannot have a place for a defenseless Other. Therefore, the silenced, already oppressed othered Other is the ideal project for the fascist image of the enemy and for the pathological exercise of power. Since Jews have been historically among the most oppressed and geographically the most othered minorities across the world, various fascist groups from different parts of the world have anti-Semitism in common. There are antagonistic fascist groups that might differ in every aspect of the in-group versus out-group identities, but they hold similar anti-Semitic views. That said, as Horkheimer and Adorno insist, the capitalist system is inherently discriminatory, and anti-Semitism is an example of bourgeoisie's racist enterprise. They state, "Race today is the self-assertion of the bourgeois individual, integrated into the barbaric collective" (138).

Culture is the display that provides a predigested image of the world to the members of the established group. In our age, the culture industry's commodities are the homogenizing and oversimplifying lenses through which in-groups perceive the world. Also, as objects of enjoyment or entertainment, cultural commodities minimize the chore of thinking (Horkheimer and Adorno 2002, 109). As a result, they further transform subjects into mobomassdividuals with a paranoid reductionist mentality. This paranoiac reductionism has become global, integrating local so-called cultures into a global full-fledged climate of mobomassification. Therefore, the culture industry is at the heart of the rise of fascism.

In any particular case of the rise of fascism, the totalitarian scope of domination and the degree to which power is exercised are essentially contingent on the social structure that makes up the fascist force as a mobomass movement. While the discourse of unity might suggest a sense of collective cooperation among the members of a fascist movement, members of fascist movements are extremely self-centered. If anything, their affinity toward nationalist, patriotic, or religious movements is rooted in their overwhelming sense of loneliness and purposelessness. Joining a movement immediately provides them with a sense of significance and gives them the noble purpose they desperately need. In this sense, fascism is the fastest path to heroism. Merely joining a fascist movement means partaking in a historical mission as one of the nation's warriors.

Even the Führer principle should be understood in this vein. The fascist leader is fundamentally a mobomassdividual whose projection on the followers proves most effective. The leader is both the man of the people, who speaks their language, and the father figure who embodies the ultimate power hierarchy; therefore, mobomassdividual can both identify with and find the ultimate savior in the leader. This is the role of the "great little man," as both a down-to-earth fella and a cult at the same time.[4] Hate is the fascist glue for creating unity. What brings mobomassdividuals, who are otherwise automized individuals, together is their shared hatred of the marginalized. Any perceived Other who may remind a mobomassdividual of their suppressed sense of *vulnerability* and weakness would make a good candidate as the object of the common fascist revulsion.[5] Psychologically, the leader signifies this common hatred and thus a personification of the collective obsession with sheer power.

Adolf Hitler, Kemal Ataturk, Recep Tayyip Erdogan, Ruhollah Khomeini, Narendra Modi, Donald Trump, and Jair Bolsonaro have in common an admiration for other bullies and a pathological hatred against the most powerless. Notice Hitler's admiration for Ataturk and hatred for the stateless and socially marginalized, including Jews, gypsies, and physically challenged; Ataturk's obsession with military power and intolerance of Armenians, Alevis, and Kurds; Erdogan's admiration for Putin and brutal suppression of Kurds not only in Turkey but everywhere; Khomeini's anti-Semitism and brutal aggression against Baha'is, Kurds, and the socially oppressed groups; and Bolsonaro's respect for Trump and hostility toward the indigenous peoples of the Amazon rainforest and Afro-Brazilians. Fascists, including both leaders and followers, almost everywhere, in addition to their typical masculinist sexism, have in common xenophobia. These characteristics (i.e., the obsession with sheer power and intolerance of the marginalized) not only have the same psychological roots but are symptoms of the problem. The problem is the suppression of an overwhelming sense of weakness and masking it by the persona of a strongman. The strongman's neurotic hatred of the weak is unconsciously motivated as an act of demolishing every reminder of the "true" self. In eliminating the weak Other, the fascist desperately attempts to bury the mirrored image of what they deep down consider to be their real self. Writing on the victims of anti-Semitism, Horkheimer and Adorno state that "their powerlessness attracts the enemy of powerlessness" (2002, 138). Later, they add, "The marks left on them by violence endlessly inflame violence" (150). The point Horkheimer and Adorno emphasize could be generalized on the relationship between fascism and its already marginalized victims. Fascists are disgusted by powerlessness as much as they are infatuated by the vulgar exhibition and brutal exercise of power.

What once was art as a response to loneliness and alienation is now the culture industry, which is a main tool of mobomassification. Adorno emphasizes three main characteristics of cultural commodities: repetition, standardization, and predictability (2001c, 200). These features are fundamental to the structure of each cultural commodity, the culture industry's mode of production, and the experience of consumption. The mobomassifying results of the culture industry are accomplished through:

1. the transmission of mass subliminal ideological messages;

2. endless depoliticization of the political in everyday life; and

3. extreme flattening of the cognitive topographies of the consumers.

While each of these points deserves in-depth elaboration, which I will try to do in the context of this chapter, the third one might be the least self-explanatory and therefore most crucial to pause on. Let us start by taking a close look at the following by Adorno: "Regressive, too, is the role which contemporary mass music plays in the psychological household of its victims. They are not merely turned away from more important music, but they are confirmed in their neurotic stupidity, quite irrespective of how their musical capacities are related to the specific musical culture of earlier social phases" (2001c, 47).

He adds, "There is actually a neurotic mechanism of stupidity in listening, too; the arrogantly ignorant rejection of everything unfamiliar is its sure sign. Regressive listeners behave like children. Again and again and with stubborn malice, they demand the one dish they have once been served" (2001c, 51). The more we consume "predigested" cultural commodities, the more addicted we become to the passive-activity, the state of being entertained without having to conduct anything, including thinking. The important point here is not that the essence of cultural commodities is stupidity because that should be obvious. The entertainment industry might come across as an innocent sector that merely aims to amuse us and, hence, make everyday life more enjoyable for everyone, but this could not be further from truth. While the issue is certainly not that there is a political conspiracy against the public, the ideological and political consequences of the entertainment industry are far more effective than any old-totalitarian propaganda system. That is so precisely because the entertainment industry affects us as thinking beings, and we voluntarily grant its commodities access to our cognitive systems. Old-fashioned propaganda regimes could not successfully deny what they are: lying machines that aim to deceive us. Under a dictatorship, every time one sees images of the leader on TV, in the front pages of newspapers, or in public places, one is inevitably reminded of the deep chasm between oneself and the ruling regime. On the other hand, in an advanced totalitarianism, where the culture industry takes up the role of old-fashioned propaganda, one is unaware of the most effective means of deception, distortion, and ideological indoctrination. The culture industry is a refuge we seek to escape boredom, exhaustion, loneliness, and alienation, which are themselves the outcomes of the same system the culture industry fortifies. The culture industry's "amusement," in Horkheimer and Adorno's words, "always means putting things out of mind, forgetting suffering, even when it is on display. At its root is powerlessness. It is indeed escape, but not, as it claims, escape from bad reality but from the last thought of resisting that reality. The liberation which amusement promises is from thinking as negation" (2002, 116). Thus, the important point to emphasize is that the commodities of the culture industry have mass stupefying effects. Both the stupidity and stupefying influence have only increased since Adorno's time, or the early 1970s. In much of the American film industry and TV shows, for instance, the utterly apolitical has become the norm. Ironically, the stupidity Adorno speaks of as an effect of the culture industry is explicitly screened nowadays. The stupid protagonist has become a prototypical hero in the industry. There has been an extremely popular genre of movies that never fails to surprise its viewers by the heroes' stupidity. It is as if stupidity has become the secret of all amusement and entertainment, so the stupider the better. Much of the creativity in the movie industry has come down to finding new ways to stay utterly apolitical. It is, in an ironic way, amazing how the American television sitcom *Friends* (1994–2004) managed to run for ten years without ever failing to be utterly apolitical. Of course, the American TV industry also has produced a number of late-night shows, imitated in other parts of the world, that tackle political news. These shows have managed to attract many viewers who are interested in political affairs. They have also done a terrific job turning political news into jokes. Ultimately, everyone and everything is excluded through inclusion. "Something is provided for everyone so that no one can escape; differences are hammered home and propagated" (Horkheimer and Adorno 2002, 97). Precisely in this sense the culture industry is totalitarian.

Art within the frame of the culture industry is mere entertainment, and as such, it has to require as little thinking as possible. Adorno writes, "The pre-digested quality of the product prevails, justifies itself and establishes itself all the more firmly in so far as it constantly refers to those who cannot digest anything not already pre-digested. It is baby-food: permanent self-reflection based upon the infantile compulsion towards the repetition of needs which it creates in the first place" (2001c, 67). The cultural commodities compete in terms of minimizing thought, and the culture industry as a whole produces mobomassness, which is, in turn, essential for perpetuating the existing capitalist order.

It is crucial for students of Critical Theory not to be carried away too much by its descriptive account of the culture industry. While the culture industry's ideological function within the dominant modes of production is profound in terms of perpetuating that domination, dismissing the material relations of production will lead to a fallback into old-fashioned idealism unknowingly. Depicting the mobomass mentality as something innate, something characteristic of the majority qua human beings, is not different from the old aristocratic depiction of the working class as rabble. In theology, the sinful origin of the human fall into this world is one and the same as the hopelessness of the human condition. Something is fundamentally wrong with the human presence in the world, and therefore, as the theological argument goes, divine salvation is the only remedy. Even with the divine promises to save us, the curse is imprinted on the human project. The ultimate apocalyptic fate is metaphysically predetermined, so to speak.

In European bourgeois philosophy, the original sin is replaced with something no less damning for the entire human project, even as a secular historical project. The substitute is the so-called human nature. The assumption is that any philosophy that does not grasp that nature accurately cannot make a valid basis for any inquiry pertaining to history and society. For instance, we are told that humans by nature are competitive and selfish; hence, as the argument goes, a social and political system that does not take this fundamental premise into account is bound to fail. What is supposed to be realistic, true, right, and good is determined accordingly. The outcome of domination is used to justify and perpetuate domination. Material domination and ideological hegemony are hardly separable even though we may speak of them as separate notions for the purposes of conceptual problematization and critical analysis.

Mobomassification and Fascism

The mobomass is a modern phenomenon and the mobomassdividual is entirely a product of capitalist relations of production. Standardization and mechanization of production coupled with the extreme division of labor have endless totalitarian effects that run through the society under capitalism. Manufactured products and commodities carry the clearest manifestation of mobomassness. However, because our means of cognition and communication also fall under the dominated arenas, the social, ideological, and epistemic manifestations are difficult to detect without a critical theory focused on problematization and negation on both micro and macro levels of social relations of power and production. The modes of knowledge production are capitalist through and through. None of us lives outside the spheres of capitalist totalitarianism, so our modes of perception, interpretation, and articulation are hegemonized. Therefore, the total and perpetual negation of the capitalist mode of production is essential for making progress even in terms of being able to perceive the nature and scope of the crisis of unfreedom in which we live. Negation does not rely on a positive or a positivistic form of knowledge; rather, it amounts to the creation of new possibilities.

The philosophical framework for total and perpetual negation is what I call postnihilism (Ahmed 2022b). To put it briefly, the postnihilist act of negation entails the comprehension of the scope of the crisis of unfreedom, as the first dialectical moment. Only then will one be able to negate the existing reality and move beyond despair. Therefore, it is the move through and beyond hopelessness that makes the posnihilist who they are and their act of negation revolutionary. That is to say, the posnihilist starts from the impossibility to act outside the totalitarian system and accepts the inevitable lack of a prefigurative alternative while rejecting psychological solutions represented by false hope, such as forms of salvation offered by spirituality including theology and new-agism. Without rejecting denialism, we will not be able to create a possibility for moving beyond hopelessness. Without comprehending the magnitude of the totalitarianism and thus unfreedom, we will end up either acting nihilistically or appropriating an extra layer form of mythology to tolerate what is otherwise intolerable. In the act of posnihilist negation, the existing hopelessness is sublimated, a space for hope in the most realistic sense is created. Postnihilism, therefore, negates the system and processes that produce and reproduce totalitarian space, that is, the space of total exercise of power, of limitless gaze of power, where life can no longer leave a trace and living beings can no longer exist as anything but subjects and objects of control (Ahmed 2019d). The postnihilist negation is therefore an act for making a beautiful life, auratic existence, possible despite totalitarianism and the hopelessness it normalizes.

The mobomassification of workers is the immediate outcome of the totality of commodification. The dominant capitalist mode of production inevitably commodifies time and space, and by doing so it also renders the commodification of individuality a natural outcome of the social relations of production. Robbed of personhood, the alienated worker is faced with two options. The first is simply going on with the normalized everydayness under capitalism, which can only result in the ultimate commodification of the body as labor force, atomization of social existence, and parallelization of creative consciousness, including political awareness, artistic imagination, and unique discursive articulation. The worker, in short, will be forced to lead an auraless life and contribute to the reproduction of an auraless totalitarian space. In this case, the worker continually regresses as a unique subject capable of living meaningfully and beautifully. They become a mobo-massifiable human, a potential member of a bloc used as an instrument for trumping the marginalized, including the working class. The rise of fascism can be understood as the mobilization of increasing numbers of mobomassdividuals. However, under capitalism, in the absence of a universalist emancipatory movement gaining popular momentum, fascism will continue to be on the rise, and its ultimate takeover in any given society is merely a matter of time.

The second option for workers is to politically organize to strengthen the proletariat. Individually, this means the worker must immediately put an end to the normalized everydayness that continually and increasingly alienates her. She must, postnihilistically, negate the system that is actively denying every space of individuality and every sense of personhood. Such a process of negation, however, necessitates political action, which entails collective self-organization on the basis of class identity and in solidarity with all other projects that try to negate subjugation. In this case, the worker becomes a member of the proletariat, a revolutionary subject who is already emancipating herself and by doing so inching forward in the process of enlarging the universal space of freedom. Being a laborer does not inherently translate into a proletarian membership because the latter is a political project, just as being a woman does not automatically translate into being a feminist. Oppression is a social condition; it is the political choice of the oppressed that determines their actual political identity.

Under capitalism most workers may actively take the side of the bourgeoisie and retroactive forces, whether nationalist or religious, against the working class, just as under patriarchy most women may support the domination of men and men's institutions from the family to the state. These contradictions are inherent in domination itself. The moment most of the oppressed reject their normalized systems of oppression, whether in terms of the social and political institutions or ideological nuances of everydayness, the dominant start to lose ground and may eventually lose their means of domination. Therefore, saying that most workers support the existing bourgeois systems is tantamount to saying capitalism is the dominant mode of production. In the meantime, such a statement tells us nothing about the nature of working-class masses or the so-called human nature. "Nature" itself is a myth produced within the dominant modes of material and knowledge production. Whenever we are told something along the lines of "humans by nature are . . . ," we are simply in front of another daily instance of the reiteration of a dominant myth. And dominant myths have in common a fundamental characteristic. Namely, they are all depoliticizing of the political, metaphysicalizing of the historical, and eternalizing of the existing order of domination.

Ultimately, material domination and ideological hegemony are inseparable, so the fall of one will result in the collapse of the other as well.

Therefore, there is a straightforward answer to the question: how are the working-class masses made into fascist mobomasses? Namely, the working-class masses are made to act as something that is not the working-class masses. They are turned into an anti-working-class force. They are bourgeoisiefied and, as such, ideologically depoliticized and politically instrumentalized. The same formula can be applied to analyze the colonized-colonizer relationship: so many colonized are made to act as colonized, as opposed to anti-colonialists.

Under capitalism, the normal state of a worker is a state of total crisis because her own labor continually disempowers and alienates her. Therefore, without active involvement in proletarian politics, the worker always plunges deeper into bourgiousiefication, which could only mean further depoliticization of her consciousness and dehumanization of her being in the world. The automatized worker is not only deprived of an auratic existence but also incapable of articulating the loss. Under the dominant modes of perception, she is incapable of perceiving the traces of the loss, and as such, she cannot even mourn. She may be depressed but cannot be melancholic, may sense that something is wrong but be incapable of articulating the falsehood that envelopes her life. While she may swing between feelings of happiness and unhappiness, excitement and boredom, intimacy and loneliness, her worldness diminishes by the day, rendering her being in the world more and more devoid of subjecthood, more and more characterized by repetition, predictability, and banality. Unlike the bourgeoisie, the bourgeoisiefied worker does not even have time to actively engage in the production of cultural commodities in the name of art or anything else. Instead, her participation in the culture industry is that of a mere consumer. If she happens to produce something "rebellious," by the time we consume the product it has already been commodified by the culture industry.

Bourgeoisiefied workers cannot perceive the tragic in their reality, so they cannot be tragic beings. The dullness of everydayness renders the mechanization total and the totality of life banal. They are almost dead ontologically and become a social units that are manageable, calculable, disposable, and potentially utilizable by any system of mobilization or administration. It is in this sense that the mobomassdividual could become a typical fascist follower anywhere, anytime. As citizens, mobomassdividuals are indifferent to politics in the broad sense of the term, but precisely because of that they can be easily recruited by fascist movements who put a social spin on all that is political, turning the public space into an extension of a private space for patriarchal cultism. The new social space of the larger patriarchal family offers the mobomassdividual an immediate opportunity of intimacy, a sense of significance, and even a sense of heroism.

The military is a clearer instance of such a social space of perverted intimacy under patriarchal rules. It is no wonder that after their military service, often soldiers fall into paralyzing depression as they face the reality of their total alienation while lacking even the linguistic creativity to express themselves or the creative imagination to problematize their crisis. A good soldier executes the orders of superiors without questions. An excellent soldier is one that executes orders without even thinking any questions. Thus, the heroism corresponds to the total action, which requires total unthinking. The best soldier therefore is the total mobomassdividual, whose resistance to the leadership is almost zero, whose manageability and utilization is endless. The rule is the same in fascist movements both old and new. Hitler's motto, "Responsibility towards above, authority towards below" (qtd. in Adorno 2001a, 143), is the cornerstone of mobomassness and the mobomass production of social space.

Thus, as much as fascism is a pathological perversion on all levels from the personal to the societal, from libidinal to the behavioral, and from social to the political, it remains to be the natural outcome of the capitalist modes of production. To Marx, the proletariat represents the embodiment of the contradictions produced within and by capitalism. Therefore, in the absence of a proletarian revolutionary project to negate capitalism, barbarism will inevitably continue to multiply. Just as the individual worker is faced with two decisive options, the complete dehumanization through giving in to daily life under capitalism or the total negation of the dominant system through engaging in proletarian political organization, society both regionally and globally is faced with two possibilities: total barbarism or ultimate emancipation, fascism or communism.

As Žižek's writes, in reference to a statement by Benjamin, "Behind every fascism there is a failed revolution" (2008a, 386). Rosa Luxemburg, in a speech almost a century ago, at the early days of the rise of fascism in Europe, also alluded to the same duality when she said, "Socialism has become necessary not merely because the proletariat is no longer willing to live under the conditions imposed by the capitalist class but, rather, because if the proletariat fails to fulfill its class duties, if it fails to realize socialism, we shall crash down together to a common doom" (2004, 364).

From a Marxist point of view, the "common doom" Luxemburg mentioned cannot be avoided through moral approaches simply because capitalism cannot be lived ethically. When a violent system becomes dominant in any society and historical era, morality merely legitimizes forms of violence by normalizing them (i.e., by presenting systemic violence as something other than violence), by naming acts of mass murder something other than murder. Morality, in fact, is at the heart of the perpetuation of the catastrophe that is reproduced on a daily basis under capitalism. Therefore, negating the moral authorities, including the institutions of family, religion, and culture industry at large, should be considered a priority for any genuine emancipatory project aimed at realizing a new horizon of possibilities. Moreover, the negation of the dominant is a necessary condition for gaining the creative consciousness and will for realizing an alternative world, not vice versa.[6] That is to say, it is false to assume that we must first imagine an alternative world in order to negate the existing one. Negating the existing world opens a space for us to be able to imagine a different world theoretically, realistically, and practically. With every act of negation, we inch forward toward a new horizon. Reversely, with every act of nihilistic submission or submissive indifference we further the impossibility of imagining and creating an alternative world and, thus, an auratic space in which we could live as true individuals, as opposed to mobomassdividuals.

The Capitalist Destruction of Aura and Fascism

Walter Benjamin saw in the democratization of art an element of proletarian revolution, and he was optimistic about the mass influence of cinema. In the decay of the auratic distance of the work of art, Benjamin saw a progressive potentiality, as did Brecht who famously tried to eliminate the distance between art and the audience. Adorno repeatedly decried what he considered to be a bad influence of the Brechtian Marxism on Benjamin (2007, 126; 2001, 182). Instead of a promise of revolution, Adorno saw signs of manipulation in the system of popular culture and a decline of resistance that he thought had been retained in serious art (2007, 126). The totalitarian and the manipulative nature of popular culture threaten individualism and freedom of choice because popular culture overshadows art, and when it adopts a work of art, it will only commercialize it.

Benjamin's positions regarding the destruction of aura are not consistent. In his famous article, "The Reproducibility of Works of Art," Benjamin first mourns the destruction of aura, as he had done in other works since his early attempts to secularize and conceptualize aura (2006b). In the second half of the same article, however, he celebrates the destruction of aura mainly because of his equation between aura and the cultic value of works of art. The problem with this position has two sides. First, equating auratic distance with the cultic desistance amounts to undermining the entire project of the secularization of aura pioneered by Benjamin himself. Second, by associating aura with the cultic value of art, and opposing the latter to the exhibition value, Benjamin seems to also equate the exhibition value with democratization in a manner that is rather undialectical (i.e., identitarian, simplistic).

Benjamin did not consider a much more plausible relationship between exhibition value and cult value. Namely, instead of simple opposites, it is the exhibition value that transcends the cult value in *modernity*, the age of the domination of vision at the expense of the other senses (for more, see Ahmed 2019d, chapters 4 and 5). That is to say, when the divine was radically divorced from the sense of vision, in modernity what is seen more tends to gain more cultic value. What is seen everywhere gains the status of the omnipresent cult. The fascist play on visual repetition of symbols and images and the endless exhibition of flags represent the direct exploitation of the principle of the domination of the visual sense. Through the endless repetition of sameness, all distances between the ruler and the ruled are demolished, producing a flat and transparent world, a totalitarian space perfectly suited for fascism. Thus, it is precisely the destruction of auratic distance that leads to the totalitarianism that is at the heart of fascism. The abolishment of spatial aura is the same as the elimination of the most fundamental condition for unique experiences. Without unique spatial experiences the human subject is existentially denied identity qua difference. As such, the subject becomes a mobomassdividual, an endlessly repeatable and replaceable unit within visual ornaments and their corresponding mental patterns, stereotypes, or racially, nationally, culturally, and ethnically classified groups. Mobomassification, therefore, entails several simultaneous processes: the destruction of auratic spaces of subjectivity; the construction of totalitarian modes of perception according to which people are grouped and classified under meaningless and essentializing labels; and, on the individual level, the internalization and projection of mass-manufactured nationalist, racist, and culturalist identities.

Modernity gave birth to both the individual, as the universal right holder, and the mobomass, as a Frankensteinian leviathan. The potentiality for universal emancipation of the human subject everywhere came into being at the same time when the conditions for the ultimate submission, for totalitarianism, started to take shape. The enlightenment project and the project of the racialization of human societies belong to the same age. Immediately after the birth of the American Republic, slavery was institutionalized. As Horkheimer and Adorno put it, "With bourgeois property, education and culture spread, driving paranoia into the dark corners of society and the psyche. But as the real emancipation of humanity did not coincide with the enlightenment of the mind, education itself became sick" (2002, 163). All these contradictions indicate that in modernity the historical conflict between the primordial tribalist xenophobia, the pathological obsession with violence, on the one side and the aspiration for maximizing the horizons of the human possibilities on the other side reached the most decisive and direct point of confrontation.

One of the manifestations of this conflict was the clash between reactionaries who were nostalgic for the pre-enlightenment world and the progressives who defined themselves by the courage to go forward toward the full realization of human emancipation. In the first camp, there were the romantics and nationalists, whereas anarchists and communists, despite their bitter disagreements, can be seen as the main parties in the other camp. During the second half of the nineteenth century and the first quarter of the twentieth century, the universalist camp seemed to have a real chance of saving the enlightenment project, but that is also the period of the rise of nationalism, which matured to become fascism.

The age of democratization of politics could have gone the other way, the way of universalism, but by the 1930s it became clear, at least in the Western hemisphere, that the reactionary politics that was both based and dependent on mobomassification was about to knock off the proletarian revolutionary subject, the protagonist of universal emancipation. The last hundred years can be seen as a century of nationalism's evolution, the last stage of which is fascism. The culture industry and mobomass mentality have been at the very center of the prolonged rise of fascism for the last one hundred years. Yet, once again, we should not commit the idealist fallacy of eternalizing the existing order and metaphysicalizing mythical assumptions in the way of rationalizing the eternalization. Thus, it needs to be reiterated that mobomassness is both a product and production. As both a product and production the mobomass is inseparable from the capitalist mode of production. Negating capitalism through a progressive project centered around the movements of the margins of the margins will lead to the liberation of the mobomassdividual as well. What is hopelessly perceived as "human nature" will no longer be there, compelling the modes of perception to undergo an alteration as well.

The temporospatial world of everydayness is conditioned in such a totalitarian way that the social outcome is almost entirely predetermined. With a degree of social engineering and national unification of knowledge production, which for the most part amounts to the normalization of a nationalist mode of perception, the mobomassdividual becomes the standard product and actor of social relations.

The culture industry is inseparable from the capitalist modes of production, and as such, it produces a mentality of sameness, which in turn reproduces a totalitarian mode of perception. Ultimately the mobomass mentality is a product of the totalitarian regime of sameness and the basis for the production of totalitarianism. Even "difference" is predetermined under this democratized form of totalitarianism. On the most fundamental level, under capitalism, everything from aesthetics to politics becomes a realm of exchangeability through a single medium that is the pure and global commodity, money. Therefore, all spaces become dominated by the institution of the market. The market in this sense is not a space but a mode of spatial production, and it is centered around *exchangeability according to the pure commodity*.

Totalitarianism, the Market, and Fascism

In such a world, artistic difference is a myth because the ultimate aesthetic standard falls under the same principle of quantified value and, thus, exchangeability. The standard is an abstract value determined in terms of capital and on capital's terms. Capital exercises the unlimited power of quantification over everything whether material or cultural, human or nonhuman, so the institution of the market by definition is the highest authority as a form of absolutism, and it is totalitarian in the fullest meaning of the concept. Therefore, artistic uniqueness is a mere myth that serves the democratic facade of the totalitarian regime of sameness, further legitimizing the total domination of capital. The first casualty of the capitalist mode of production is aura, and the first aspect of the capitalist reality is the endless repeatability of patterns of sameness. Under the capitalist domination, therefore, there can be no aura of art or space.

Ultimately, the "free market" is nothing but another term for the dictatorship of the principle of exchange. Whatever cultural, artistic, material, and symbolic products may be produced, they are inevitably objects of quantification. A producer, whether a journalist, an artist, a laborer, or a theologian, is also placed within the power relations based on speculations of their value. Thus, every person is ultimately also an object of quantification. In fact, this bourgeois mode of perception is so dominant, even theologians are forced to convert God to currency in order to appeal to their fellow brothers and sisters in faith.[7]

Capitalist mass production entails maximum standardization, and the actual manufacturing process of any mass product depends on mechanical repetition. In the end, indistinguishability is an essential aspect of mass products. It is sameness that makes mass products what they are. This is crucial for the quantifiability and thus exchangeability of the products. Therefore, what is perfected within this mode of production is the destruction of aura. A produced item cannot possess any quality every other item does not have. Any dissimilarity, even if it does not affect the function of the item, is an undesirable abnormality.

Auralessness is not an accident but an essential condition of commodities. The process of mass production ensures total sameness. As for a product that is not mass produced, whatever its individual qualities, difference, uniqueness may be, it is quantified in terms of money just like a commodity that is mass produced is quantified. When a unique item, such as a work of art, is valued, the uniqueness itself is necessarily quantified in terms of money. Let us say a painting is estimated to be worth $100,000. Even those of us who have not seen the painting understand that the value of the painting is equal to the value of two items of a product that is worth $50,000, one thousand items of a product that is worth $100, or two hundred thousand units of a product that is worth ¢50. In short, this very language of "value" or "worthiness" is the language of exchangeability. Things that are not produced for the market must be quantified, priced, and made exchangeable all the same.

That is to say given the mere fact that the worthiness of any object is determined in terms of money, uniqueness cannot survive the totalitarianism of the market regardless of whether certain objects are sold and purchased. The market's unlimited authority, therefore, exceeds all institutional powers and is in fact a universal frame of reference. The market is an epistemic medium that is all-encompassing and yet invisible as an institution. Its effect is inherently flattening, quantifying, and totalizing. It eliminates the auratic potentiality of everything one could possibly think of. Even sacred and totemic objects, divinities, and mythologies must be converted into the language of banking, stock market, private property, profit, and so on in order to maintain their cultic value. Capitalism is a monotheistic religion with capital as its sole divine being; however, unlike other monotheistic religions, it exercises its power even on those who do not believe in it precisely because it is a totalitarian monopoly on the material conditions of life.

While the object-commodity is mass produced in accordance with specific engineered plans and fully managed processes, mobomassdividuals are produced within the social relations of production but without direct engineering plans and fully managed processes of production. To explain the material basis of social massification under capitalism, we may benefit from Marx's work directly. Marx focused on the alienation of laborers, whose very labor is the reason for their increasing alienation. For instance, in the *1844 Manuscripts*, Marx wrote:

> Thus the more the worker by his labour *appropriates* the external world, sensuous nature, the more he deprives himself of *means of life* in two respects: first, in that the sensuous external world more and more ceases to be an object belonging to his labour—to be his labour's *means of life;* and secondly, in that it more and more ceases to be *means of life* in the immediate sense, means for the physical subsistence of the worker.
>
> In both respects, therefore, the worker becomes a servant of his object, first, in that he receives an *object of labour,* i.e., in that he receives *work;* and secondly, in that he receives *means of subsistence.* This enables him to exist, first, as a *worker;* and, second, as a *physical subject.* The height of this servitude is that it is only as a *worker* that he can maintain himself as a *physical subject,* and that it is only as a *Physical subject* that he is a worker. (2010b, 273. Italics from original)

Also, by virtue of being forced to sell their labor force, laborers are, under capitalism, forced into what is essentially prostitution. Again, in the *1844 Manuscripts*, in a passing but extremely important footnote, Marx stated, "Prostitution is only a *specific* expression of the *general* prostitution of the *labourer*, and since it is a relationship in which falls not the prostitute alone, but also the one who prostitutes—and the latter's abomination is still greater—the capitalist, etc., also comes under this head" (2010b, 295). Here, Marx alludes to the totalitarian nature of the capitalist massification as he indicates that the prostitution is not limited to workers but necessarily exceeds the boundaries of classes. The capitalist is of course the exploiter but existentially cannot escape the equation. By virtue of being a party of the quantifying conversion (of what is human into what is unhuman), the capitalist cannot come out with their own subjectivity unaffected. This is the mildest possible way to put it. The truth is that the capitalist is the major party of the quantification enterprise, and as such their own subjectivity must be sacrificed a priori. For the worker, the quantification is real but not necessarily comprehendible as such, and when it is comprehended objectively, it is not necessarily acceptable internally. In other words, if the worker perceives the contract as essentially dehumanizing and admits that to themselves, they might conserve a subjective space for their potential freedom given that they would be aware of the fact that external reasons compelled them to accept the terms of the contract. On the other hand, for the capitalist, the quantification of what is human had already been assumed as a premise and prerequisite for entering the contract with laborers simply because, unlike laborers, the bourgeoisie chooses the arrangement freely as far as exploitation is concerned. Just assuming the quantifiability of human subjecthood as a premise is sufficient to de-subjectify the bourgeoisie, so the bourgeois subject is the first and the standard case of thingification. While homogenization is imposed on the exploited, for the bourgeoisie homogeneity is internalized (dehumanizing the bourgeois self), objectified (denying the exploited any entitlement to subjecthood), and imposed (as dehumanizing conditions on the exploited) at the same time. Therefore, homogenization, or "massification" in the Arendtian sense, is a bourgeois project in the fullest sense of the word. Now, it should be clear why mobo-massness first and foremost applies to the bourgeois personality, hence the "bo" component of the term, which is also key in the imposition of the "mob" mentality on the alienated masses.

We may go on to further explicate the *prostitutional* nature of the bourgeois space. In addition to being the main social party that represents mobomassness, the bourgeoisie imposes mobomassification on the members of other classes. Also, the bourgeoisie embodies prostitution in the sense of its historical representation of the hegemony of vision. The capitalist age is the age of the dictatorship of vision par excellence. The exhibition value is at the center of all commercialization, advertisement, marketing, or in one word, "persuasion." Shop windows are inseparable from the ultimate social and political bourgeois triumph at the end of the nineteenth and beginning of the twentieth century in Europe. The exhibition value is at the core of exchange value, the dictatorship of which is of course the ultimate core of capitalism.[8]

We should keep in mind that shop windows and fascism spread in Europe simultaneously. Mass production (i.e., commodification of objects) and mobomassifiaction (i.e., objectification of humans) are two inseparable aspects of the capitalist modes of production. Moreover, the dominant mode of perception cannot be formed but around the same, that is, capitalist, epistemic frame of reference. The market is the bourgeoisie's space of the unlimited exercise of power, and at the same time it is the all-encompassing institution in terms of value distribution and social relations of power.

The bourgeoisie embodies prostitution in the temporal sense as well. Universally, time is quantified in relation to the production of value (i.e., accumulation of surplus value) and, thus, capital. Marx and many Marxists have done justice to the subject matter of the commodification of time (of special significance is Marx's *Capital*). However, what is worth mentioning here is a more specific aspect of the *prostitutional* nature of the bourgeoisification of time. Unlike the laborer, the capitalist is not forced to sell their own personal time to a second party in order to survive. Assuming that only a portion of their time is spent managing labor and wealth, they are left with a great deal of time to engage in creational and entertainment activities. For the most part, the cultural commodities of the culture industry are the result of the bourgeoisie's boredom and self-indulging art. The bourgeoisie has the capacity to realize in cultural products what it finds entertaining and potentially profitable, that is commodifiable. Ultimately, the production of cultural commodities, that is the culture industry, has two main objectives: (1) profit, just like the material industry and (2) the ideological bourgeoisiefication of the world. The first simply reinforces the dictatorship of money and further empowers the bourgeoisie through more accumulation of capital. The second objective is far more subliminal precisely because it concerns the ideological aspect of bourgeois hegemony. It does not have to be prefigurative in the way propaganda is. Rather, it is simply the universalization of the bourgeois mode of perception and the externalization of the bourgeois worldview, taste, and so on.

In "Culture Industry Reconsidered," Adorno writes, "The masses are not the measure but the ideology of the culture industry, even though the culture industry itself could scarcely exist without adapting to the masses" (2001b, 99). He also states, "The entire practice of the culture industry transfers the profit motive naked onto cultural forms" (98). Thus, Adorno did not miss the connection between the principle of profit and the ideological aspect of the culture industry. Building on this relationship is crucial for pinpointing the structural connection between the capitalist mode of production and the formation of the social environment in which fascism may spread swiftly.

Also, recalling Gramsci's concept of hegemony is of great help to understand how the system of culture industry functions in relation to the mobomass mentality. What is effective in the culture industry is not the simple process of "control"; rather, it is the dialectical case of hegemony. Gramsci writes:

> The "Popular Study" is mistaken at the outset (implicitly) by presupposing that the great systems of the traditional philosophies and the religion of the high clergy, that is, the world conceptions of the intellectuals and of high culture, are opposed to this development of an original philosophy of the popular masses. In reality these systems are unknown to the multitude and they have no direct effect on their modes of thought and action. This certainly does not mean that they are without any historical effect: but this effect is of another kind. These systems influence the popular masses as an external political force, as an element of force binding together the leading classes, as elements, therefore, of subordination to an external hegemony which limits the original thought of the popular masses negatively, without influencing it positively, like a vital ferment of inmost transformation of what the masses think embryonically and chaotically about the world and about life. (1957, 90–91)

Again, the first objective of the culture industry is quite straightforward. Whether they are great works of art or literal garbage labeled as art, in the end everything is utilized within the same totality under the unlimited power of capital. We may have songs about revolution, movies about anti-capitalist revolt, and novels about socialism. Regardless of their artistic and philosophical value, they are all cultural commodities produced by the same industry to be sold and consumed within the same totalitarian space. Therefore, products of the culture industry should not be interpreted in terms of the old distinctions between "high" and "low" cultures. In addition to all the problematic assumptions behind the hierarchical value system of aristocracy and the elitist ideology of the bourgeoisie that reproduced its own hierarchy, the high-low classification is simply irrelevant in the age of the culture industry. Adorno was unfairly accused of elitism because most of his critics read his work through lenses of nineteenth-century literary and art criticism. The ultimate target of Adorno's attacks is the culture industry, the boundaries of which by far exceed all traditional classifications of culture, value theories, aesthetics, and so on.

Behind the plain principle of exchangeability/profitability, there is a much more nuanced factor that ensures the proliferation of the bourgeois massification, and this will take us again to the second objective of the culture industry. The culture industry, in its function as an ideological instrument for hegemony, "limits the original thought of the popular masses negatively," to use Gramsci's words (1957, 91). As Adorno insists, "The customer is not king, as the culture industry would have us believe, not its subject but its object" (2001b, 99). In effect, the marginalized consumer of cultural commodities voluntarily allows the ideological hegemony to take place bit by bit and settle in while they are supposedly free and enjoying themselves. The primary and most effective parts of mobomassifcation process take place when the marginalized subject least expects ideological indoctrination (e.g., when watching a movie on Netflix, listening to music, etc.).

While the bourgeoisie has the means to universalize its mode of perception, the culture industry allows, and in fact encourages, the participation of the marginalized masses. However, whatever cultural items the marginalize masses produce will have to submit to two crucial criteria in order to make it as cultural commodities. First, the product must prove its own quantification, or exchangeability, so it is born auraless. Second, it must be appealing to the dominant taste. That is to say, the success of every producer of a cultural item is dependent on their speculation in terms of the dominant, that is the bourgeois, mode of perception. The degree of success the product accomplishes, the level of popularity, and thus the profit it provides are indications of its contribution to making the dominant more dominant. This is where Gramsci's concept of hegemony becomes indispensable in terms of making tangible the link between the bourgeoisie's domination and the age of fascism.

Through the commodification of cultural products, the bourgeoisie continually reproduces the bourgeois character, so the consumption of cultural commodities results in the ideological and structural bourgeoisification of the consumers. Whatever cultural items the bourgeois produces, the production itself is centered around the personal, which has an internal uniformity that can only result in totalitarianism as long as the culture industry remains dominant. Again, Horkheimer and Adorno put it profoundly well when they state that "every bourgeois character expressed the same thing, even and especially when deviating from it: the harshness of competitive society," and it is precisely through the bourgeois individualism that individuality has been abolished (2002, 125). In a relevant line of critique, Benjamin noted the bourgeoisie's narcissistic obsession with privatization of space (1999, 20). At the heart of the privatization of the public space and public sphere is what can be called the emotional prostitution. The perfect example of such emotional prostitution is the type of poetry in which the self is so pathologically inflated it is incomparably larger than the universe. The reader is reduced to a traveler in the poet's muses of feelings from a moment to the next. The expectation that the rest of us should be interested in such emotional prostitution should itself raise serious concern about the state of public health, let alone art, in the age of bourgeois domination.

Ultimately, the culture industry is a relentless campaign for total depoliticization of all that is political, so it is no wonder that the paradigm of culture has become so dominant since the 1960s that today even physical elimination of peoples, such as the aboriginals of Canada, is habitually dismissed precisely by putting all the emphasis on "cultural genocide"! Culturalization as a condition of fascism is the subject of chapter 4 of this book. Here, it is worth emphasizing that Gramsci and the Frankfurt critical theorists were among the first who pointed to the ideological essence and uses of culture.

Culture is far more political than any political manifesto precisely because culture tends to present itself as something other than what it is, which is the most essential aspect of ideology. The apolitical appearance of culture is, in turn, what makes culture even more political as an ideological apparatus. Chapter 4 focuses on the racialized sense of "culture," which has been predominantly applied to the Other of the White self (Essed 1991; Wright 1998; Lentin and Titley 2011). There is of course another sense in which culture is used, namely within the European/ized contexts. In this case, it is a reference to refined aristocratic taste and manners (appropriated by the bourgeoisie) and, of course, arts as a broad category. Nobody can miss or deny the overwhelming presence of art in fascist spaces. In one of his brilliant insights, Benjamin described fascism as the aestheticization of politics (2006b, 269).[9] The transformation of the public space into a space of consumption and exhibition of the personal has also contributed to the totalitarian mobomassification, which in turn reinforces and normalizes fascism.

Chapter 4

It Is Political, not Cultural

Problematizing culturalism is essential for exposing the degree to which exclusionary thinking has been normalized through the good yet false intentions of the elites who popularized the notion of "culture" in place of "race" following the horrors of World War II. To put it briefly, the dominant paradigm of "culture" created a norm that is deeply, but covertly, racist. More often than not, those who commit cultural racism do so unintentionally and without being aware of the act. The norm in question is the mental depiction of all non-White populations as homogeneous cultural communities. Culture, when it is used in this covertly racist way, anthropologizes and essentializes the political currents and individual members of entire societies. Fascist movements have exploited the spread of such false culturalist assumptions about the non-White Other to make fear-mongering cases among European and North American youth about the alleged cultural threat to the West. Not surprisingly, fascist movements in the Third World also seized the opportunity to pragmatically pick up the essentializing paradigm of culture to popularize their chauvinistic views. Thus, emancipatory movements in, say, the Middle East and North Africa (MENA) region are further marginalized globally thanks to oxymoron expressions such as "Islamic human rights" and "Islamic feminism." No wonder very few outside the MENA region are aware of the fact that some of the most militant secular movements of emancipation, including feminist movements, are actually located in the MENA region.[1] The Kurdish movement in Turkey, Syria, and Iran is just one example of such a movement. In this chapter, and throughout the book, I argue that effective anti-fascist awareness requires much more than a mere moral rejection of fascism. To raise anti-fascist awareness, it is absolutely necessary to problematize false beliefs and assumptions about the Other. It is equally essential to clearly falsify the premises on which fascist discourses rely. One of these premises is directly borrowed from culturalism. Today's fascist movements use the same false premise of culturalism, according to which people are classified in terms of their perceived cultures. Hence, invalidating such a premise and paradigm is one of the central objectives of the book and this chapter.

Culturalism and the Rise of the Far Right

With conservatism in its various social and political forms on the rise in many parts of the world and egalitarianism increasingly withdrawing from political and social life over the last three decades, there are important questions concerning the reasons that have led to the current global situation. While it is obviously by no means possible to easily list the reasons that led to the current decline of democratic and egalitarian movements around the world, I try to identify some of the defused ideological paradigms and mechanisms that sustain the contemporary climate of opinion, which is premised on the impossibility of the realization of a non-capitalist world. The fallback we are witnessing is first and foremost exemplified in the absence of a popular international egalitarian worldview, which has its roots in false but widely indoctrinated assumptions about the world. Each racially and nationalistically perceived society is assumed to hold a "culture" that prioritizes values other than the enlightenment ideals. In other words, this covertly racist worldview has contributed to the liquidation of the old leftist (cosmopolitan) goal regarding universal equality and progressive emancipation of humanity. The term "culturalization" can be used to indicate this phenomenon of homogenization and essentialization.

Culturalization of societies is the contemporary form of tribalization, and culturalism is today's common form of tribalism. At least in the English-speaking world, this tribalism is expressed in a myriad of discursive formulas depending on the orientation of each political platform. For instance, in liberal-leaning discourses it may be called "cultural relativism" or even "multiculturalism," while in the far-right discourses the nativist tone of "culture talk" usually comes across somewhat more explicitly. The culturalist mode of perception, according to which human society is divided and people are classified, is necessarily fictive and fictionalizing, inherently false and falsifying, because it is a form of idealism that directly mythicizes real social relations of severe inequality among actual breathing human beings. This mode of perception is meant to fundamentally reverse materialism through dismissing the material conditions of life and metaphysicalizing what at best amounts to an oversimplified outcome of the material conditions.

As Slavoj Žižek frequently reminds us, the norm among leftist intellectuals up until the 1980s was to question the material roots of problems anywhere they appeared in the world. Now, in the age of neoliberalism, however, the general perception is a culturalist one, according to which the world is seen as different cultures and religions we cannot hope to understand but can only "respect" from afar, in the best cases. This deeply but covertly racist worldview normally assumes culturalist lenses to look at not only violence and despotism but also poverty. A late 1800s to mid-1900s anthropological conception of "culture,"[2] as a collectively applicable "way of life," has been widely adopted. It functions in culturalization as the ideal paradigm to homogenize, essentialize, de-subjectivize, and thus marginalize entire populations and demographic groups within a population. It is as if "culture" has become the magical, all-encompassing concept able to transmit understanding of the entire state of affairs to "experts" and nonspecialists alike.

If "race" had become the most poisonous pseudoscientific term before and during World War II, "culture" is today's genealogical offspring and ideological equivalent of "race" (Essed 1991; Wright 1998; Lentin and Titley 2011). Particularly since 2001, as a means of and due to the unprecedented Othering of perceived Muslims in the aftermath of 9/11, culturalism saturated the discourse of policy makers, media elites, academics, and thus ordinary people. Culturalization has infected all veins of everydayness not only in openly racist discourses but also (or perhaps especially) in multicultural discourses. The underlying claim here is that racism has in fact grown more after World War II partly because of the naive optimism of liberals and leftists and their impartiality toward, if not adoption of, "culture" as a neutral paradigm. Its instrumental use for Othering must be de-normalized through more critical research informed by what Alana Lentin (2005) refers to as "the story of how the potentially liberating, political tool of culture was harnessed in the aim of bypassing 'race,'" (395) thus preserving the racist power structures of Western nation-states. Likewise, projects such as multiculturalism that were essentially constructed upon the paradigm of culture must also be seen as the facade of the enduring relations of domination rooted in colonialism.[3]

Culturalism as New Racism

The term "culture" was introduced to anthropology in 1871 by Edward B. Tylor, who famously defined it as "that complex whole which includes knowledge, belief, art, morals, law, custom, and any other capabilities and habits acquired by man as a member of society" (2010, 1). Since then, the applicability of the concept has been the subject of extensive debate in anthropology. Still, the term has been generalized, oversimplified, and mystified to the degree that even some anthropologists (Eriksen and Nielsen 2001, chap. 7; Wallerstein 2006, chap. 1; Said 2000) became highly critical of its use as a fixed set of traits to define groups of people.

As Žižek also notes, "culture" is commonly used in two almost opposing senses (2008b, 141)—first, to indicate sets of leisure, aesthetic canons, artistic taste, and simply methods of enjoying life, and second, to refer to a collective set of absolute norms and rules that are considered definitive and determining with regard to all social values, practices, and moral principles. Žižek writes, "The basic opposition on which the entire liberal vision relies is that between those who are ruled by culture, totally determined by the lifeworld into which they are born, and those who merely 'enjoy' their culture, who are elevated above it, free to choose it. This brings us to the next paradox: the ultimate source of barbarism is culture itself, one's direct identification with a particular culture, which renders one intolerant towards other cultures" (2008b, 141).[4] When it is used in reference to Europeans, as a racial category, it denotes the old meaning, civility, palate, fine education, aesthetic appreciation, courteousness, and so on. When it is used in reference to non-Europeans, it has collectivizing and essentializing implications. "Indian culture," "Chinese culture," or "Arab culture," for instance, immediately invokes mental images that have to do with traditional clothes, so-called ethnic food, and so on. It, in one word, *anthropologizes*. Contrary to the individualizing sense in which "culture" is used in reference to the White, this anthropological sense is inherently collectivizing, de-individualizing, and essentializing. It de-persons the individual Other by depicting her as a unit identical with endless other units within the group of people in question (i.e., people who supposedly share the same culture). In the European case, the referent is *character* in the full sense of the word (i.e., as the uniqueness of individual personality in terms of everything from taste in the arts to political views, from style in utterance to personal philosophy). Whereas in the second sense, "culture" simply demolishes every possibility of perceiving whatever could fall outside the denoted total, almost in the same sense of the definitive totality of an animal's nature—it is certain that a deer does not act as anything but as a member of the species of deer, a duck as duck, a fish as fish, and so on. Žižek makes this point as well, stating that "such negative characterizations of animals (speechless, worldless, etc.) engender the appearance of positive determinations which are false: animals as captured by their environs, etc. Do we not encounter the same phenomenon in traditional Eurocentric anthropology?" (Žižek and Gunjevis 2012, 313). The referent of "culture" in the non-European context is in fact the "nature" in the sense of the old duality of culture versus nature. No wonder the typical stereotypes of the non-White Other include intensity, quick emotional (read as *instinctive*) reactions, and some sort of rawness (read as manners that lack cultivation or civility), although often, especially in the liberal end of the culturalist spectrum, these presumptions are expressed in less negative terms or even as, albeit problematically, positive adjectives (e.g., straightforward and generous) to suggest some sort of primitive innocence unspoiled by civilization.

From reading Kroeber and Kluckhohn (1952), we can see the evolving usage of "culture" in anthropological studies beginning in the late nineteenth century from the humanist or evolutionist "culture as civilization" (most closely aligned with the first definition above), to "cultures" (that is, ways of life) of human groups. It is this second variation of "culture," applied unreflectively, oversimplified, and homogeneously generalized, that is at the heart of culturalism as new racism. All kinds of strange, irrational, over-simplified, contradictory, and mythical views are imagined about different peoples under the assumption that these are part of their "culture," implying that culture is something the Other is born with, like skin color. If mentality X attributes categorical differences to different groups of people based on Y and Y is assumed to be natural, ahistorical, and/or metaphysical, then X is a racist mentality. Obviously, Y does not have to be skin color or "blood" in order for X to be racist.

The shift away from the overtly biological racism of the past and toward less tangible (often imagined) differences is the subject of a good deal of research output, particularly throughout the 1990s. Étienne Balibar theorized "racism without races" in relation to decolonization and immigration in "the absence of a new model of articulation between states, peoples and cultures on a world scale" (1991a, 21). Others have classified the shift away from biological racism to "laissez-faire racism" (see Bobo and Smith, 1998), "colorblind racism" (see Bonilla-Silva 2010), and "cultural racism" (see Razack 2001; Rodat 2017; Wright 1998), among others. Often in reference to the contemporary situation of Blacks and Latinos in the United States, these contributing theories are essential to understanding the nature of new forms of racism, and they also document the use of "culture" (particularly the so-called culture of poverty) as a means of dismissing racial inequity. Nonetheless, more critical research on the pseudo-concept of culture as it functions in culturalization is badly needed to account for systemic and everyday Othering as an additional pillar of new racism.

The culture that is assumed, that is attributed to the Other, by way of culturalizing the Other (as a homogeneous group composed of similar units) has little to do with the Other's actual "way of life" or the individuals' beliefs. It is rather an anthropologizing stamp imprinted on the Other in the same way that biological racism racializes the Other. Meanwhile, the culturalizer is situated within a *culture* that is deeply racist and imperial, a *culture* that proclaims itself not only superior but also invisible by virtue of aculturalizing itself. Much like the liberal ideology that depicts itself as above ideologies (as objective truth) and accuses leftist criticism of the existing order of being ideological, racist culturalizers who habitually commit culturalization of the Other depict themselves as the rational and neutral subjects in possession of civilization and universal judgment. Indeed, in the dominant discourses, White/European "culture" is normally assumed to be the assortment of values taken to represent the pinnacle of human civilization: reason, freedom, equality, democracy, and so on. In other words, the fundamental prerequisite and parameter of culturalization is Eurocentrism, which is based on the belief that the ideals of the enlightenment are uniquely European values.[5] By implicit comparison to the universal (White/European) ideal, the non-White Other, who has a different culture, is depicted as irrational, weird, primitive, uncivilized, violent, fanatic, and/ or both non- and anti-individualist.

Culturalization and Politics

Žižek calls the phenomenon of culturalization "the Huntington's disease of our time" (2008b, 140), in reference to Huntington's thesis of "the clash of civilizations": "The Velvet Curtain of culture has replaced the Iron Curtain of ideology" (Huntington, 2010, 10).[6] Describing the phenomenon of the "culturalization of politics" in what he calls the "liberal multiculturalist's basic ideological operation," Žižek states, "Political differences—differences conditioned by political inequality or economic exploitation—are naturalised and neutralised into 'cultural' differences, that is, into different 'ways of life' which are something given, something that cannot be overcome" (2008b, 140). This culturalization of politics took currency among former leftist Marxists when attacks against the orthodox, economist interpretation of Marxism became extremely popular after the fall of the socialist states in Eastern Europe. The popular form of this critical attack, however, has now lapsed into the other dogmatic pole: dismissing the material conditions of life entirely in the "new" worldview. Now, "culture" is expected to be behind all social and political phenomena, especially when people from the third world are the subject of concern. Although this culturalizing view has become more popular in the last few decades, its roots go back centuries, as Said's *Orientalism* (2003) illustrates.

The important point to be made is that "culture" carries with it no substantial designation that could aid us in understanding the fundamental features of any human being anyway. In the best cases, this pseudo-concept, culture, would indicate a set of very general attitudes and superficial appearances, by way of loose approximations, that could give us a hint about a society's social manners and customs, which would be admired or despised to various degrees, or indifferently ignored, by the individuals. On any more serious level, culture is inevitably and deeply political. It is beyond thoughtless naivety not to see the politicality of, for example, the religious roots of casteism in India or of Islamic laws under Islamist regimes. To pause on the latter example, the official charge against some political opponents of the Islamic Republic of Iran is *Moharebeh,* by which is meant "enmity towards God" but is of course merely a way of justifying the persecution of those individuals who oppose the state. However, casteism and Islamism are often treated as pure cultural phenomena, meaning that culturalizers also ignore the tremendous degree of opposition to casteism and Islamism within the same societies, respectively, because these forms of opposition have no place in the homogeneous images culturalizers hold about those societies.

In addition to being too insensitive to account for popular acts of dissent and progressive politics of resistance in its view of the Other, the culturalizing mentality also mistakes even what is openly political (such as the discourse of political Islam) as culture. Hence, it is even more improbable that this mentality could be sensitive to the more diffused levels of ideological arenas whereby political agendas are put forward most effectively precisely by masking them with nonpolitical claims, such as moral, metaphysical, or spiritual justifications. Even if we take "culture" to mean a set of common beliefs, values, rituals, practices, and customs, even the most supposedly metaphysical or natural cultural component among them is still deeply political. This metaphysical or natural (ahistorical) facade is exactly where ideology lies because ideology functions qua ideology by disguising itself and thus presenting itself as neutral. In short, "cultural interpretations" amount to the de-historicization and apoliticization of sociopolitical phenomena.

Similarly, Said's work on Orientalism is particularly helpful to better understand the politicization of culture. Although it has almost become a matter of political correctness to avoid the word "Orient" in English due in large part to the impact of Said's work, this style of thought based on a clearly divided line between "Orient" and "Occident" is still extremely common, even among Eastern academics. Essentially, what Said claims about the nineteenth and early twentieth centuries is that the forms of knowledge produced about the Oriental Other by European thinkers, writers, and scientists, who had conscious and distinct beliefs about "race," was crucially imperial and served imperialism. Therefore, Orientalism was in fact a process of racializing knowledge that functioned within a broader political project, the aims and methods of which have changed very little in the decades since *Orientalism* was first published in 1978.

The most successful forms of distortion and deception are often conducted not despite truth but via the ideological recontextualization of truth. Truth is a currency that can be manipulated in all kinds of ways, and usually it is used most effectively by those who control the means of knowledge production, and that is precisely what makes "power and knowledge directly imply each other," as we have learned from Foucault (1984b). Likewise, discourse is the locus of the ideological agenda, and as such it emphasizes a truth only to deliver an untruth obliquely. While the ideological purpose is concealed in the oblique part, the argument is structured around the obvious part, the truth. That is to say, the racist's aim is never to communicate facts, and the moment we begin to engage in a debate on the factuality of what the racist claims to report in their discourse, we immediately fall into the trap. New-racist arguments do not rely on what have now been proven to be false premises, such as the biological notion of race. Nonetheless, the arguments put forward by new racism are unsound as a whole, and their persuasive power lies solely in diverting our attention to proving or disproving their claims. As Žižek (2008b, 100) concludes, the aim should instead be focused on falsifying the racist's motive. Hence, whether what the liberals and conservatives claim about the headscarf and burqa as symbols of oppression is true or not is irrelevant; the point to emphasize is that there is a racist aim concealed within this well-structured discourse that strategically relies on the politicization of the cultural and culturalization of the political.

Culturalism and the Denial of Personhood

Culturalist uses of "culture" can generally be distinguished by two primary factors: the social and political consequences of its use and the ideological implications of applying the cultural label. To begin with the former, whenever the cultural label ultimately functions to homogenize individuals and attribute the actions or values of an entire group of people to a shared culture that is assumed to override each individual's political, economic, or social milieu, culturalization will inevitably result. With regard to ideological implications, culturalization is, first and foremost, a means of Othering. Whether motivated by a desire to present other groups as dangerous threats or by a less overtly racist need to comprehend seemingly incomprehensible other groups in a politically correct fashion, culturalism presupposes and culturalization reinforces an atomistic view of the world. Culturalists attribute "culture" to the Other as an oblique means of discrimination, which necessarily reinforces an "us" versus "them" social dynamic in a new, superficially less racist way.

It should go without saying that the complexities and nuances in Western societies that necessitate the rigorous production and interdisciplinary application of knowledge in all fields of the sciences and the humanities are present to the same degree in the rest of the world. Yet the common attribution of "culture" as a sort of unifying umbrella to non-White societies and demographics dismisses the necessity of studying and understanding the historical, sociological, economic, and political dimensions thereof. The existing order in which the Other is marginalized and oppressed on the bases of oversimplified and racist generalizations is thus sustained as well. The culturalized is denied the minimal recognition of personhood or even the potentiality of personhood. The non-White Other is systematically denied individual agency (i.e., the ability to think independently and the will to make choices autonomously) on the basis of the ideological assumption that her personality is determined by the "whole." Hence, the Other is never seen as a subject; she is rather a repetitive unit, an "it," the abstract animal Derrida (2002) refutes as a category.

Just as a species of animals is usually defined by their nature, the culturalized individual is defined by her "culture." Even when committed out of sheer ignorance, culturalization is rooted in a larger ideological worldview sustaining White domination and pigeonholing Other peoples into biological classes with identifiable collective traits and predictable behaviors. This explains the tendency of culturalizers to equate familiarity with one non-White person to an insider's understanding of that person's entire "culture." For instance, if a culturalizer happens to know a Chinese person, she can speak in the comfort of having firsthand knowledge about Chinese people because she automatically considers one Chinese person representative of all Chinese. The same goes for virtually all acquaintances of non-European descent. The Other is seen as a flat being without history or complexities. Thus, she is often regarded as either good or bad and little in-between. Again, this has been the human conception of animals since mythological times. While some animals are simply evil and they have been so for thousands of years in the human imagination, other animals are inherently good, peaceful, cute, useful, and so on.

Since 9/11, culturalization has been more visible in depictions of what has been dubbed "the Muslim world." This form of culturalization amounts to the imposition of Islam as the definitive identity upon nearly two billion people, including the estimated 23 percent of the world's population (Pew Research Center 2012). These include those who practice Islam as well as those who are considered Muslims due to their skin color, language, name, or ethnic origin. I call this phenomenon Muslimization—not to be confused with the term used to convey the belief grown out of Islamophobia that the West is becoming increasingly Islamic—and it is by no means new.

Writing in the late 1980s, Balibar notes the differentialist traces of anti-Semitic discourse in what he termed Arabophobia since it carries with it an image of Islam as a "conception of the world," which is incompatible with Europeanness and an enterprise of universal ideological domination, and therefore a systematic confusion of Arabness and Islamicism (1991a, 24). Today's Islamophobia carries with it the same underlying presumptions that Islam is much more than merely a system of belief and that it is just as natural and irrefutable as one's "race," for a racist mode of perception.

The homogenizing, flattening effects of Muslimization have become increasingly absolute both at the theoretical level and in everyday social interaction.[7] For a culturalist, a Middle Eastern person cannot be, for instance, a nonbeliever because the freedom to choose to be an atheist or agnostic belongs solely to the White, who alone is an individual. It should not have to be said that just as Europeans cannot definitively be identified as

Christians, Middle Eastern and North African peoples cannot automatically be identified as Muslims.

To make matters worse, because of the oversimplifying, flattening effects of culturalization, Islam has come to be viewed as a unified world-view without regional, let alone individual, variations, in spite of the vast geographies encompassed by the so-called Muslim world. Thus, whatever stereotypes come to be associated with Islam as such are automatically applied to "Muslims" at large. Edward Said, in a lecture entitled "The Myth of the 'Clash of Civilisations,' " said:

> In today's Europe and the United States what is described as Islam . . . belongs to the discourse of Orientalism, a construction fabricated to whip up feelings of hostility and antipathy. . . . Yet this is a very different thing, than what to Muslims who live within its domain, Islam really is. There's a world of difference between Islam in Indonesia and Islam in Egypt. By the same token, the volatility of today's struggle over the meaning and definition of Islam is evident, in Egypt, where the secular powers of society are in conflict with various Islamic protest movements and reformers over the nature of Islam and in such circumstances the easiest and least accurate thing is to say, "That is the world of Islam, and see how it is all terrorists and fundamentalists and see also how different, how irrational they are, compared to us. (1998)

In itself, and in a less culturalized world, this association of Islam with violence is not necessarily a racist problem, but the ensuing association of "Muslims" with violence is. Therefore, counterclaims that Islam is a religion of peace fail to address the most dangerous aspect of Muslimization, which is its denial of personhood to individuals perceived to be "Muslim." It is this same culturalizing setup that explains why the wrongdoing of a Muslim individual is treated as the wrongdoing of the entire "Muslim world," which is more or less the case for all non-White individuals and minority groups. The wrongdoing of any number of individuals from the majority, however, remains an exceptional wrongdoing of individuals. If the perpetrator of a public shooting happens to be from a non-White background (regardless of nationality), the immediate presumption is that we are facing a cultural conflict (e.g., in the form of a religious fanatic/terrorist), whereas if the shooter happens to be White, the presumption is that the shooter (as an individual) had somehow been failed by society. That is to say, if the criminal is White, opinion makers turn to psychology for an explanation. A non-White criminal, however, only further validates mainstream White fears of the alien Other who can never be assimilated into Western society.

Multiculturalism is New Racism

This uncritical process of culturalizing the Other is undertaken by conservatives as well as many liberals. In both cases, what we end up with is an erroneous depiction of the world backed by knowledge authorities in academia (and thus various specialists who help shape public opinion) and manufacturers of mass belief in the media. The only noticeable difference between conservative and liberal culturalization is that conservatives frequently seek to demonize the Other, while the liberal spectrum of culturalization extends from tolerance to superficial romanticization. In terms of policy approaches, conservative culturalization is typically anti-immigration oriented due to a belief that the non-White Other cannot be assimilated, whereas liberal culturalizers often ascribe to the multiculturalist view that "different" cultures ultimately enrich the host (White) society.[8] In either case, the unspoken motivation and result is Othering. Yet because the racist motives of conservative culturalization are typically more visible, I will focus on the liberal variety, which has been enshrined as the politically correct means of relating to the non-White Other.

What liberal proponents of multiculturalism fail or refuse to see is that in response to their desire not to speak about "race" amidst the breakdown of geographical and linguistic boundaries that previously served to isolate Europeans from non-Europeans, they have merely erected new racist boundaries on cultural bases. Thus, the privileged is able to continue to discursively segregate themselves from the Other while purporting to be living in a new age of harmony alongside each other. Conveniently, the belief that all people belong to unique cultures from which they draw their identity is the perfect preventive antidote to the cross-societal political alliances that could be fostered in this age of heightened connectivity. Regardless of the knowledge, beliefs and values, or citizenship of the racially Othered, her skin color, name, or ethnic ancestry will continue to be taken as an indication of her Otherness in the form of a perceived/assumed culture. The Other, who is implicitly raced, can essentially never regain the personhood that culturalization denies her. Moreover, because culturalizers simply fail to ascribe personhood to any Othered person, even their "love" for the Other is demeaning, and their "respect" is intrinsically disrespectful.

Multiculturalism gained legitimacy as an alternative to policies of assimilation and discriminatory practices against underprivileged and racialized groups. Therefore, what gave rise to the doctrine of multiculturalism was first and foremost the imperative to recognize diversity and reject homogeneity both as an assumption and as an objective, simply because homogeneity is factually false when it is taken as a premise and morally wrong when it is set as an end to be attained. Equally important was the need to reject the prejudices that are rooted in the nineteenth-century myths of racial hierarchy advanced by social Darwinism and nationalist ideologies. Thus, especially after World War II, the public sphere in the West became politically more sensitive to racist language (Essed 1991; Wright 1998; Lentin and Titley 2011), but the Eurocentric mindset, for the most part, failed to change its deeply normalized racist mode of perception. While explicit racism began to lose the normalcy it enjoyed for nearly two hundred years in the Europeanized and colonized parts of the world, the same worldview and logical frame of reference continued only through the non-demeaning paradigm of "culture."

Multiculturalism has always been opposed by adherents of exclusionary ideologies of various types. Nonetheless, I do not think it is a valid pluralist doctrine. Despite the good democratic intentions that gave birth to multiculturalism, not only does it fail to recognize plurality of identities, but it also contributes to the existing homogenizing and essentializing racist ideologies. Like biological racism, it implicitly denies the Other autonomous agency by essentializing her identity as a mere member of a larger homogeneous collective.

The "multi" part of the term "multiculturalism" is supposed to designate a pluralistic philosophy, but it is only pluralism of an identity that is no less homogenizing than "race." That is to say, when it comes to the doctrine of "multiculturalism," the intended plurality is nulled by the homogenizing worldview of culturalism, which considers culture as the most determining factor of identities. We have focused for too long on the positive connotation of "multi," while ignoring the false assumptions of homogeneity inherent in the very idea of "culturalism." Culturalism has amended and masked, as opposed to negated, racist discourses. Also, "multiculturalism" is necessarily an oxymoron, just as "multiracism" would be an oxymoron.

What is at stake is more than a blind spot in multiculturalism; the multiculturalist worldview inevitably denies pluralism by using plurality as an attribute of something that is inherently homogenizing, which is "culture." As a result, it reproduces the very problem it set out to solve. Culturalism, in all its forms including multiculturalism, denies every individual what constitutes her intrinsic individuality or "unpredictability," to borrow Hannah Arendt's term for describing what she considers to be the highest human activity (1998). Instead, culturalism assumes that perceived homogeneous cultural practices are ontologically definitive of the identities of all the members of an entire population, depicted on the basis of their perceived national, religious, and/or ethnic identity. A multiculturalist merely assumes a positive attitude toward the fictional mass identity of the Other.

Essentially, both ultra-right White supremacists and their liberal rivals assume that the Other's difference is a cultural one, thereby ruling out the Other's individual identity, her ability to make autonomous decisions based on, say, her political and moral judgment. The difference between the White supremacist and liberal multiculturalist, therefore, is sentimental, not philosophical. Both sides commit the same fundamental fallacy, of de-individualizing the Other, of failing to assume a space for the Other's personhood.

Personhood should be a premise not a conclusion. That is to say, I do not need to know anything about a person to recognize her personhood. In fact, it is precisely the privacy of a person's innate space, in the sense of nontransparency, that I need to recognize unconditionally and universally. The private space of uniqueness is the condition of identity, in the same sense time and space are conditions of experience per Kant. Therefore, failing to recognize the individual space of uniqueness necessarily entails denying the person her identity.

As a matter of fact, a genuine recognition of a person's humanity is recognition of her individual space of uniqueness. Intrinsic in the notion of "person" as a "subject" is the capacity of being different from every other subject in the world. Therefore, pre-assuming any person's identity (based on a notion of culture or whatever else) is not necessarily rooted in a particular prejudice but in a mentality that systemically objectifies other subjects, and consequently it forms prejudices, which may or may not become sensible in speech or other acts. This is why political correctness can be frustrating for all the concerned parties in public sphere. Prejudices cannot be problematized, let alone solved, by speaking "properly." If anything, false political correctness could merely prolong prejudices by virtue of preventing their exposure to critical reasoning necessary for diagnosing and undoing the deeper ideological mode of cognition. There is no mystery in this claim. Because Eurocentric-dominant ideologies for centuries attributed humanity exclusively to the European, the dominant mode of cognition is simply incapable of operating on the assumption that a non-European can be a subject.

The minimal condition of genuine respect necessitates the treatment of a person as the only authority of her identity—socially, politically, and "culturally." That is to say, assuming a person's identity on the basis of her appearance, background, or name means not perceiving her as someone entitled to personhood. Making an assumption about a person's identity that is not based on her own self-description is a sign of prejudice, which is in turn indicative of an essentialist ideology such as racism or sexism. The essential condition for genuine respect is to meet everyone on the ground zero of sensibility. Apart from what all humans have in common, all that we can know about a person's identity is what her utterances and other acts may signify personally and politically.

If I do not assume that essential space of uniqueness, that basic dimension of human existence, the moment I come into any social contact with any person, even if for the duration of an elevator ride, it is more likely I will insult her regardless of my true intentions toward her (or the category through which I conceive her). Racism had been part of the dominant mode of perception long before anyone who is alive now was born, so the norm is racist. Therefore, what needs to happen is a process of negative education. Culturalism and other forms of essentialist modes of perception must be unlearned. Without meticulous unlearning, it is pointless to try to be moral, polite, tolerant, and so forth. This is precisely why those who see racism merely as a moral problem cannot imagine how widespread racism is and how they habitually partake in racist behavior through living their normal everyday lives whatever the social settings may be.

While the paradigm of "culture," unlike "race," does not entail hierarchy, when it is used in the quasi-anthropological sense to classify identities of the Othered, it is tantamount to "race." As the dialectical negation of "race," "culture" in fact preserved racist de-individualization and essentialization while at the same time transformed the whole racist discourse to a more advanced ideological level whereby it is less detectible as a subject of critique in today's dominant ethos. The insensitivity to personhood makes multiculturalism discriminatory and alienating.

What is treated as the culture of X people is, at best, symbolic representations of the patriarchal value system of a ruling group. At worst, the perceived culture is the product of a few mental images drawn from the travel logs and diaries of tourists, which essentially anthropologizes millions of people, reducing them to a few outfits, rituals, and dishes. Of course, there are cultures of resistance in every society, but by virtue of being marginalized they cannot be detected by the superficial sensory perception of the multiculturalist.

Even going by the basic principles of liberalism as a philosophy, every individual is entitled to the right to personhood. The social world is composed of persons, not cultures. The culturalist mode of perception culturalizes people not to recognize their diversity but precisely to collectivize them and thereby deny their individuality. The move is a taxonomical one, aimed at classification for the sake of grouping and thus de-individuating individual human beings.

In reality, whatever my mental representation of any culture might be, I will never meet a culture. I only meet persons. In every society there are endless cultures, most of which are constantly changing based on living conditions, power relations, social interests, political conflicts, political associations, and so on. Still, every person in the world has an intrinsic ability to endorse, modify, or reject any worldview or value system. A genuine recognition of diversity necessitates leaving the mentality of culturalism behind. In principle, ensuring inclusivity is utterly easy: all individual human beings should be treated as individual human beings. There must be a zero-point ground of no prejudices applied to all.

An anticipated objection may be that since the universalist view of individual autonomy is an outcome of the enlightenment, assuming its universality is itself a form of Eurocentrism. This is at the heart of the cultural and moral relativist theories. Indeed, the universalist doctrine of individual autonomy is an outcome of the European enlightenment, but it is inherently egalitarian and universally applicable insofar as human individuals everywhere are essentially subjects. According to implied logic in the relativist argument, all ideas regardless of their apparent rational universality and cosmopolitan applicability bear the stamp of their discoverers or founders and their validity is contingent on their original cultural context. By that logic, Europeans should quit the act of writing and instead return to what is authentically European. For writing is not a European idea. Mesopotamians, Chinese, and Egyptians invented the first systems of writing in ancient history.

The same argument of singularity of authenticity drawn from the doctrine of multiculturalism could be made against the use of algorithm because it is not European. In fact, it is named after the polymath and astronomer Muhammad ibn Musa al-Khwarizmi, also the founder of algebra, who was born in Khwarazm in 780 AD and died in Baghdad in 850 AD. The universal use of zero, whether in mathematics or any applications of mathematics, makes the world Endocentric because zero was discovered by the Indian mathematician Brahmagupta in 628 AD and first put into use by Indian mathematicians. One could also use the monadic logic of multiculturalism to say all societies that use legal codes are under the influence of the native peoples of what is now Iraq because legal codes are Sumerian and Babylonian inventions.

The list can be much longer, but this suffices to refute the multiculturalist argument and other similar anti-enlightenment arguments of cultural relativism and tribalism in all its forms including nationalism. Once and for all we need to comprehend the fact that drawing such metaphysical lines between societies can only lead to more fallacies in both theory and practice. The enlightenment is universal not only because it represents a historical stage of human progress but also because like all great projects it was rooted in such a plurality that is impossible to break down to pure ingredients as fancied in nationalist false consciousness. Egyptians, Sumerians, Hans, Mongols, Nobis, Mores, Slavs, and Nordics are everywhere and nowhere. Europe itself had long stopped being a secluded place by the time of the enlightenment. When it was secluded, it was a place of barbarism. Any time an attempt was made to take it back to purity, there was barbarism. The same is true for Baghdad. When it was a place for great research and discoveries, it was cosmopolitan. The moment the myth of national culture infected the region, it started to fall into barbarism.

Not the enlightenment values but the mentality that depicts non-Europeans as cultural communities and attributes the enlightenment exclusively to Europeans is a Eurocentric mentality. What is needed is critical education for detecting subliminal racism in culturalist discourses and, more generally, tribalism in discourses of national identity. A Kurd or a Darfuri does not sacrifice her life for so-called cultural rights. That is completely a European myth. No human being would be prepared to fight a bloody regime merely because she is not allowed to wear certain clothes. The opinion makers who reproduce the ideology and discourse of culturalism, and national and religious identities, are perhaps too homogenized by the anti-enlightenment reactionary ideologies to realize how their position is Eurocentric, but it should be less difficult for them to realize that they exemplify liquid sentimentalism to the degree of ethical nihilism. Perhaps they are not Eurocentric, but they are certainly tribalist of the worst kind, namely the kind naively used in the perpetuation and legitimization of fascism. By the same token, the Kurdish anti-jihadi fighter knows too well how universal the enlightenment values must be. Multiculturalist, anti-enlightenment moral-relativists should at least ask themselves the following basic question: Outside the West, who is most adamant on emphasizing cultural uniqueness? Certainly not most political prisoners, human rights activists, communists, or feminists. It is most fascistic regimes and movements who insist that human rights and individual freedoms are Western values and as such not viable in the societies they want to silence.

Undoing Culturalism

Mystification, naturalization, and racialization of culture have contributed significantly to the global decline of a universalist vision of humanity. As universalist ideologies and philosophies began to lose ground in the social and political world in the late 1980s, religious and nationalist waves began to accumulate more populist force. Today, no world heroes exist because the world lost its worldness qua one world. Nations have their own heroes whose visions are dreams for some and nightmares for others. Capital alone is fully globalized, which embodies the objectification of human relations and the humanization of relations among objects, as Marx predicted (1990, 166).

Of course, this is not to say the world should be conceived in terms of monadic individualism without any plausible collective political will. The point here is to overcome the politics of Othering on the bases of differences that should not have any political significance, such as differences in skin color, ethnicity, gender, and imagined social values. Instead, we should realize and capitalize on collective wills that would emerge as soon as pseudo-identities collapse into a more critical view of the question of human liberation. Though race and gender relations are political now, the subsequent response should not be internalization of those constructed differences as natural and metaphysical; rather, it should be a struggle against the conditions that sustain such inequalities. As for class relations, the old Marxist goal of abolishing class society is still as legitimate as it was in the 1950s and 1960s regardless of how unrealistic it may sound.

One of the most central conclusions of Marxist philosophy is that humans create their own history whether they are aware of it or not and whether through activity or passivity. enlightenment from the Marxist point of view, one could argue, is the awareness of the human potentiality to determine history, and to be enlightened would thus mean to work consciously toward the liberation of humanity by leaving behind the prehuman history in which humanity is the object, not the subject, of history. That is to say, universal equality and freedom will never be realistic as long as we fail to see history as the product of our own actions. By the same token, the more human societies are perceived and treated as naturally and fundamentally different from each other, the more impossible the realization of a freer humanity will become by virtue of people's own actions. The dominant belief in equivalents of "human nature" (such as "race" or racialized "culture") amounts to the self-fulfilling prophesies of the Hobbesian war of all against all in the form of exploitive multisided (class, race, gender) domination. What differs is the amount and the forms of oppressions different groups of people have been subjected to throughout their histories, not their natural entitlement to or (cultural) appreciation of equality and freedom. A key point in undoing the history of oppression is to cease taking today's "cultures" as natural and absolute determinates of people's identities. Even nature itself, and all that is natural, has a history, and humans alone are capable of living, thinking, and acting in accordance with that historical awareness. It is the belief that reality is above and beyond our will that sustains and prolongs the existing state of affairs.

If we continue to limit ourselves to what we are made to think are realistic options, the history we are creating will only grow bleaker. The alternative to the existing world and its relations of power is not even conceivable for a mindset that habitually perceives humanity in terms of some cultural identities. A mindset that is incapable of imagining an international worldview sharing foundational concepts of human equality and freedom while grounding its struggles on local circumstances and histories cannot expand the limits of the possible. In a world where the most dominant is an ideology of domination, a true alternative cannot even theoretically be constructed if first the dominant ideology is not de-normalized. Accordingly, deconstructing the current paradigms of the dominant ideology is the prerequisite for emancipatory movements both theoretically and on the level of day-to-day political struggle against exploitive multisided dominations. Moreover, we should not be afraid to at least reject the depoliticization of relations of domination that are defused and legitimized under the name of multiculturalism. Individuals and groups of people should be empowered to be able to cultivate forms of political communication capable of expressing the universal extensions of their identities. As long as oppressed groups are fitted with cultural lenses to view the collective self and the collective Other, fascism will continue to gain popularity.

Appendix: The Case of the Indigenous *Pueblo* of Hueyapan

When Judith Friedlander moved to the indigenous *pueblo* of Hueyapan in fall 1969, the village was still a relatively isolated community.[9] Tucked away in the northeast corner of the State of Morelos, under the majestic volcano Popocatepetl, the village had a population of about three thousand people. Although very few tourists had discovered the village at that time, it was already well known to anthropologists and other non-Indians. Tourists or no tourists, the residents already knew what outsiders expected to see when they came to the village. Be they non-Indian peasants living in neighboring *Mestizo* towns, members of Mexico's urban elite, or American anthropologists, the villagers knew that their visitors had all come to Hueyapan looking for the same thing: confirmation that the villagers were Indians and still practicing indigenous traditions that supposedly dated back to pre-Hispanic times. But for the residents themselves, what made them Indians had less to do with the few remaining traces of their indigenous past than with the crushing socioeconomic reality of their everyday lives. Despite the disconnect, the villagers were gracious hosts and "played Indian" for their visitors with the hope that they would look kindly upon them and leave a little money behind.

When the villagers spoke about their indigenous identity among themselves, they talked with self-hating bitterness about what made them Indians, summing up their condition with the expression "our lack of culture" (*nuestra falta de cultura*), a vague and unstable notion whose meaning changed with every passing year. As Friedlander put it:

> Since colonial times, the villagers have faced the formidable task of filling in the void of their Indianness, something, it seemed, they could never do. Every time they tried to overcome their condition by adopting traditions associated with members of the non-Indian elite, the ruling classes introduced new cultural markers to keep the two groups apart, demoting their old outmoded practices to the lowly status of Indian. As a result, the villagers stayed Indian by virtue of the fact that they continued to lack what Mexico's elite continued to acquire. (2006, 67)

The villagers, in other words, saw their Indian identity "in a static, ahistorical way, which accurately reflected their social status in Mexico, but ignored the historical processes involved in keeping the villagers marginalized and poor" (2006, 67).

Although the villagers defined their Indian-ness in 1969–1970 more by what they lacked than by what they had, they did practice a number of "exotic customs," which set them apart from non-Indian Mexicans, most of which were first introduced to the village during colonial and postcolonial times. Still, a few "authentic" customs dating back to pre-Hispanic times had survived as well, in addition to the the Náhuatl language, the lingua franca of the Aztec Empire that older, illiterate, members of the community used almost exclusively, unable to speak Spanish well. Other customs with traces of pre-Hispanic Mexico included their traditional weaving technology and the cultivation, preparation, and consumption of a number of foods, for example corn tortillas, tamales, and mole. But no matter what the origins were of these so-called indigenous traditions, they were all unambiguous class markers, evidence of the villagers' lowly place in the social hierarchy of the country.

Complicating the matter further, since the Mexican Revolution of 1910–1920, the nation's elite had a double agenda vis à vis the country's Indians. For decades, the one-party authoritarian government passed legislation upon legislation to address the so-called Indian problem, introducing programs to assimilate the inhabitants of remote indigenous villages into the dominant culture of the country and turn the Indians into modern Mestizos. At the same time, Mexico's leaders paid tribute to the indigenous heritage and called upon Indians to serve as living symbols of the country's pre-Hispanic past. Ideologues took great pride in describing Mexico as a Mestizo nation, both Indian and Spanish, whose citizens were the descendants of a painful history that mixed the blood and tradition. Since the 1920s, school teachers have been instructing the children in indigenous villages to celebrate their Indian heritage on patriotic holidays, particularly when government officials visited their communities, placing the Indians in a double-bind: on the one hand they were supposed to abandon their backward indigenous ways and become modern Mestizos, while on the other they were supposed to continue playing Indian for others.

Friedlander interviewed dozens of villagers about what it meant to be Indian, recording the many deprecating ways the villagers described being "Indian." After leaving the field, Friedlander continued doing archival research on the early history of Huyeapan community, which had been conquered by the Spaniards between 1522 and 1524 (2006, 53–54). What the conquistadores failed to destroy with their swords, the Catholic missionaries annihilated by baptizing the Indians, turning them into faithful servants of God and of the land-hungry colonists of New Spain. The Dominican priests, who settled in Hueyapan, preferred to learn Náhuatl rather than teach the

Indians Spanish, keeping the villagers dependent on them to communicate with the outside world. While they kept the Indians monolingual, they also diminished the value of Náhuatl, refusing to recognize it as a real language. According to the priests, Náhuatl was a dialect, not a language because, they explained, it did not have a written grammar (2006, 80–81).

Yet, in spite of all the persecution and humiliation, the Indians of Hueyapan embraced Christianity—at least those who survived the brutal conquest—taking great pride in praying to the same God as the elites in Mexico and sharing in the same religious heritage: "During the year I lived in Hueyapan," Friedlander noted, "I learned more about [the villagers] ties to medieval Europe than I did about prehispanic Mexico" (2006, 182). In the years following the Mexican Revolution, a sizable minority of villagers converted to Protestant Evangelical sects as well.

As Friedlander traced the cultural history of Hueyapan, from colonial times to the present, she described a steady stream of outsiders arriving in the village over the years to teach the Indians how to stop being Indian. Then others came to teach them how to be more Indian and proud of it, and still others with a double message instructing them to do both at the same time: stop being Indian at home but play Indian for others. Most recently, since Mexico has adopted the international language of multiculturalism, we often see proponents of cultural diversity turn a blind eye to the material conditions of life and circumstances of exploitation that have preserved the existence of Indians in the country for over five hundred years. Like the privileged tourists who go to India in search of meaning and spirituality, Hueyapan's visitors have been too busy enjoying the product of their cul- turist ideology to pay attention to the devastating impact poverty has had on people identified as "Indian" by the descendants of confused Europeans who landed by mistake in the Americas at the end of the fifteenth century while they were looking for a new route to India.

What Friedlander saw in Hueyapan kept challenging this ideological turn, leading her back to the same unpleasant realization: it mattered little where non-Indians stood on the political spectrum or what relationship they had with indigenous Mexico. Be they mainstream government officials, political activists—on the left or the right—religious missionaries, anthro- pologists, or pro-Indian nativists, they were all chasing the same illusory dream and pressuring the most downtrodden in the country to embrace the non-Indians' romantic idea of an enduring indigenous culture, with deep ties to pre-Hispanic Mexico. So, what is this culture? I would argue it is nothing more than an image imposed on those who survived a long process of genocide.

Chapter 5

A Critique of Positivism

Building on the Frankfurt School's Critical Theory, and in particular Max Horkheimer's insights, this chapter points to multiple similarities between the positivist regime of truth and religious metaphysics. There is nothing new about a regime of truth that claims absolute objectivity in order to impose its own falsehood on the world, but a critical theory of society is essential for exposing the means the ruling system uses to achieve such a hegemony. Positivism has constructed its own metaphysics, aiding capitalism to universalize tribalism, thereby normalizing violence against the marginalized whose struggle for universal emancipation is in turn tribalized. In addition to a critique of positivism as a form of idealism, the chapter conducts a critical analysis of the ideological mechanisms that are used to distort class politics and class consciousness, replacing the potential for progressive change with idealist means of mystification precisely in order to perpetuate the existing order of inequality and unfreedom.

Critical Theory's Fidelity to Materialism

The Frankfurt School's Critical Theory for the most part has been substantially gentrified in terms of its power of negation and fidelity to the marginalized. The line of critique that is attributed to the first generation of the school has always been less concerned with abiding by the norms of conventional scholasticism and more interested in critiquing the dominant ideology and confronting the mechanisms of power. If anything, Horkheimer, Adorno, and the rest of the theorists who were associated with the school, such as Herbert Marcuse and Erich Fromm, made a point of rejecting institutionalized philosophy, defying the authorities in the arenas of knowledge production and challenging the bourgeois public sphere in all its domains of opinion-making. Some of them were faced with marginalization and occasionally with demonization. This antagonistic reaction toward the Marxist, German, and racialized Jewish thinkers was characteristic of not only the academy but also journalism and not only the right but also the left, albeit in various degrees and ways. These issues have been repeatedly revisited by a good number of philosophers, historians, commentators, and journalists. What I aim to do in this chapter is to offer a critique of positivism that is both true to the aforementioned line of Critical Theory and relevant to the present moment.

It is the idealist, not the materialist, camp that attributes absolutism to human reason, albeit unwittingly and in a roundabout way. One of the ironies neglected in philosophy is that the ontological argument of the absolute is inherently contradictory because on the one hand it is premised on the finitudeness of human reason, yet it claims knowledge about the absolute. Even reasoning against human reason is nothing but an unwitty assertion of the fact that human reason is the only category of reason. Reason is always human reason, and awareness is already irrefutable evidence for subjectivity existing in historical and social particularities. While idealism presupposes Idea as an a priori, materialism, in Horkheimer's words, "always understands thinking to be the thinking of particular men within a particular period of time. It challenges every claim to the autonomy of thought" (2002, 32). In materialism, history is a process of truth-making by the human actor. On the other hand, "In idealism, history is not a process of interaction between nature and society, already existent and emerging cultures, freedom and necessity, but is the unfolding or manifestation of a unitary principle" (51). Horkheimer makes Critical Theory's position explicit with regard to "the struggle for a better order of things" and materialism as "the theory appropriate to the struggle" (22).

Idealism is not only enduring but also hegemonic in the academy and the larger public sphere, which is as disturbing as the position of the flat-earthers. This idealist hegemony takes place through both positivism, in which metaphysics has persisted, and religious dogma, which is the main hub of metaphysics. The former fanatically equates between empirical facts and knowledge as such, conceiving the world as a mere aggregate of facts. The latter puts its emphasis on the absolute truth that supposedly resides outside time and space. Virtually, there is a conflict between positivism and religious belief systems, but, as I will argue, the duality of theology versus positivism is a false one. The two camps have in common what could be called the idealist fallacy. Politically, both camps serve ideological hegemony of the dominant, and they are certainly anti-revolutionary. Some of the bad forms of postmodernism, such as those that supposedly advocate cultural relativism, along with false interpretations of postmodernist criticisms of modernity have contributed to a type of nihilism, or the assumption that truth is merely a claim and a truth claim is just as good as any other truth claim. Religious dogma benefits greatly in such a nihilist ethos, which does away with not only syllogistic validity and rational soundness but even reasoning altogether. An intellectual hell is where all beliefs are deemed to have equal value, but the problem of nihilism is more than that. What is typically normalized and thus justified in such a world is precisely social inequality. In the post-Nazi era, cultural diversity is asserted *in order to* ensure the preservation of racial oppression and class inequality. It is typical of idealism to allocate total value to ideas and at the same time render humans, as concrete beings, valueless. The Other's perceived culture, religion, costumes, and so on are celebrated in the multicultural West, but the Other herself is treated as a threat to "Western civilization." The Other's perceived world is commodified and commercialized as mass-produced objects for mass consumption, but the Other is seen as a potential intruder who must be kept away at any cost or left to drown in the sea.

In the works of the Frankfurt School émigrés, materialism is considered to be the embodiment of reason in terms of rational validity, historical progress, and social emancipation. Today, as various forms of nihilism continue to be on the rise, we desperately need to revisit Critical Theory as a Marxist school of thought that is faithful to negativity in the face of a coercively and ideologically maintained irrational and violent order. Critical Theory rejects both superstitions and positivism at the same time without submitting to the easy position of no alternative. Thought in this emancipatory project rejects all regimes of truth that naturalize or metaphysicalize domination. Such a liberating thought has fidelity to the silenced, and the thinker is part of the struggle for negating the existing reality in favor of truth and history from the perspective of the marginalized. Thinking, Horkheimer maintains, "is less like a sentence spoken by a judge than like the prematurely interrupted last words of *a condemned man. That latter looks upon things under a different impulse than that of dominating them*" (289, italics added). Historical materialism reflects the struggle's history and presents the theoretical formula of the struggle as a revolutionary movement that progresses reason and realizes the conditions for a different reality at the same time (22; Benjamin 2006).

The discovery of materialism in its Marxian version is indeed a Copernican turning point in the history of knowledge and the theory of history. Yet religion is only one of the main idealist opponents of materialism. Another, no less fatal, idealist rival of materialism is positivism. As revolutionary and Marxist materialists, the Frankfurt School critical theorists such as Horkheimer, Adorno, and Marcuse found the critique of positivism to be more worthwhile of their time than the critique of religious belief systems and superstitions. Positivism's brand of idealism does not, and cannot, take issue with religion because positivism cannot even raise the question (Horkheimer and Adorno 2002, 19). Positivism does not provoke the immediately exposable illusions of theology, and this renders it more eligible to assume the official platform as the spokesperson of the dominant groups whose democratic facade is preserved to a great degree. This is precisely the reason for Critical Theory's focus on the critique of positivism.

We witness a similar tendency in Marx in terms of his focus on the critique of utopian socialism, bourgeois thought, and even the kind of materialism that unknowingly committed the idealist fallacy of treating ideas as superhistorical entities. Marx's critique of Feuerbach is centered around this problem, namely the latter's assumption that a rational invalidation of the religious doctrine would bring an end to religious myth. For Marx, of course religion is a myth formed around illusions, but the myth is nonetheless a social institution that is rooted in actual conditions of life historically perpetuated and reproduced through suppressive social relations of production. The falsehood, in other words, is first and foremost in the social reality, and the revolutionary historical materialist is one who confronts the sociohistorical conditions that have necessitated the institutionalization of the myth of religion, whereas other materialists, including Feuerbach (2008), seem to assume that the problem is solvable in the realm of ideas, that, for instance, if people realize that *man* created God in his own image, if the logical fallacy at the heart of religion is exposed to people, religion will collapse. Thus, while this kind of philosophy is materialist vis-à-vis theology, like religion, it belongs to the category of idealism.

The Problem with Positivism

A definitional clarification of "positivism" from the perspective of Critical Theory is in order. To borrow from Stanley Aronowitz's introduction to Horkheimer's *Critical Theory*, for positivism, "the world of appearances constitutes the structure of reality and man can only know that which is given in experience (or representations of experience through linguistic communication)" (xiii). In his account of Horkheimer, Aronowitz goes on to denote "positivism" and "metaphysics" as "the two sides of bourgeois thought" (xv). They are "the unified world view of the bourgeoisie, split according to the prevailing division of labor between science, which serves industry, and religions and secular spiritual ideologies, which serve social domination" (xv). In Horkheimer's own words: "Since the turn of the century positivism has seemed, in comparison with the reigning metaphysics, not to be "concrete" enough, that is, really, not spiritualist enough. But in fact positivism and metaphysics are simply two different phases of one philosophy which downgrades natural knowledge and hypostatizes abstract conceptual structures" (2002, 40). Aronowitz rightly identifies this critique as the most crucial aspect of the Frankfurters' entire project. He goes on to state:

> On the one hand, positivist thought denies the relevance, if not the existence, of universals. It asserts the rationality of the given surface reality and documents its permutations. On the other hand, metaphysics abolishes the positivist enslavement to the concrete and searches for a teleology to give meaning to human existence. Science offers no transcendent meaning to men; it simply asserts facts. Its immanent viewpoint is the unity of thought with outer reality. Metaphysics is the other side of positivist nominalism. Its universals are abstract. If not God, then the absolute idea informs its search for purpose so resolutely denied by empirical science. (Aronowitz 2002, xv)

Indeed, this is precisely the point this chapter emphasizes: namely, the distortive positivist objectivity and the bourgeoisie's false claim to objective knowledge. What makes this critique even more urgently needed, and at the same time more challenging, is the fact that the American version of positivism, which is American pragmatism, went much further than English dull empiricism. As Aronowitz argues, it is "the explicit reduction of reason to its instrumental value, carrying the utilitarianism of liberalism to its logical conclusion" (xvi). Aronowitz then writes, "In its most sophisticated form, pragmatism asserts the truth of any proposition in the agreement of qualified scientists about a particular phenomenon. The test of truth is its practical value for the achievement of human ends. Reality itself becomes an object of manipulation through human practice. Since the object of cognition is none other than humanly organized sensations, the question of external reality has no meaning. Thus, the problem of the difference between subject and object is thoroughly subjectivized" (2002, xvi). As committed Marxists, the Frankfurters saw in positivism not just miscomprehension of materialism but also a fundamentally anti-materialist, that is an idealist, frame of reference with serious counter-revolutionary and oppressive implications. In terms of the sociology of fascism, the critique of positivism is inseparable from the critique of bourgeois domination of society and thus from the rationalized irrationality that actualizes and normalizes mass murder committed scientifically, efficiently, and pragmatically. In so far as technique is concerned, there is no difference between manufacturing candies and wiping out entire populations. Technological rationality, therefore, is a characteristic aspect of fascism as a ruling regime that is mandated with managerial responsibilities. The more disturbing fact is that social engineering under the bourgeois rule is essentially a fascist enterprise precisely because it subjugates human subjects to a strict and efficient regime of quantification, rendering them calculable, reducible, exchangeable, displaceable, exploitable, and dispensable in a variety of ways and for whatever purposes deemed necessary by those who carry out the social engineering from the first stages as a proposal to the final end as a realized social landscape. The last outcome is prefigured during the planning stages, and its goal expressed mathematically or in similar "practical" terminology (e.g., more than 20 percent of immigrants in each neighborhood; complete elimination of X ethnicity; deportation of the X group; assimilation of X, Y, and Z into the national fabric; etc.).

As Horkheimer shows, positivism turned the enlightenment into another form of metaphysics. In metaphysics the dualism of truth and untruth is absolute. Therefore, the metaphysician's task is to discover the dividing line. Truth is assumed to be something out there independent of the truth claimers (i.e., the metaphysicians) and their history and space. Therefore, contrary to one of the most powerful critical theses of both modernism and postmodernism, in metaphysical modes of thought, neither "truth has a history" (Foucault 2000, 2) nor knowledge is an invention (Foucault 2002, 13; 1984, 95; 1998, 273; Nietzsche 1982, 450). Marx's materialism is a vigorous expression of all that is emancipatory in the enlightenment project and the critical pillar of postmodernist philosophies, including poststructuralism and feminist epistemology, precisely for its groundbreaking theoretical formula according to which our frames of reference are rescued from a fundamental falsehood that had been imposed on our very way of looking at the world and ourselves. This falsehood is idealism, according to which history is subjected to Truth (the assumed unchangeable principle of the true) and knowledge, to metaphysics (the assumed realm of the principles of truth). Marxist materialism is the turning point as a project that contextualizes the theory of knowledge within a critical theory of history and value theory within a critical theory of society whereby the concept of production is key in the dialectics of materialism, which in turn is inseparable from the revolutionary praxis for changing the world. Marxist materialism discovered that knowledge in any particular space and time and in every sense, including validity, legitimacy, utility, objectivity, ethics, and aesthetics, is produced within and in accordance with the mode of production that has been dominant in that particular space and time. Of course, this materialist awareness is itself knowledge, but only in the negative sense. It is a negative theory that rationally rejects the existing order's rationalized irrationality. It is a revolutionary theory that not only discovers the historicality of truth and the producibility of knowledge but also uncovers the very formula according to which historical forces in their continual conflicts determine social relations of power in their continual antagonism. The ultimate truth is not a superhistorical principle; it is movement, change, or the fact that there is no such thing as a non-changing truth. Marxist materialism has discovered that the ultimate actor, the most powerful (and only) subject, is not a metaphysical entity (Idea, Spirit, God, Brahma, etc.), but the human. This sole subject of history is of course also an object of history, and an object that can and should be aware of her historical subjecthood in this particular dialectical sense. This is an essential discovery for a true historical emancipation of that which we call humanity. Thanks to the bourgeois mystification of the reality and the bourgeois domination of the material and ideological domains of the contemporary world, every favorable mention of Marx/ism, even in terms of accreditation for these Copernican discoveries, is extremely rare outside texts that are openly Marxist, which is, needless to say, in the minority in the English-speaking public sphere.

Labeling the Frankfurt School as "cultural Marxism" is extremely misleading because, if anything, the Frankfurters further validated the Marxist formula of historical materialism by radically refuting the assumed autonomy of "culture" and its alleged, as it were, supermaterial power over societies and individuals. Through various projects of sociological, sociopsychological, and philosophical research, they showed that culture itself is meticulously produced in order to further perpetuate the existing relations of material inequality and exploitation. This is the fundamental thesis of "the culture industry," which further reinforces the theory of historical materialism. Contrary to the vulgar-realist assumptions about the failure of the Marxist project and its revolutionary subject, historical materialists from Karl Marx and Friedrich Engels to Frantz Fanon and Walter Rodney and all the millions who were killed, whether at the hands of fascist or Stalinist states, have always succeeded in changing the world. The belief in a magical transformation of the world is typical of idealist, non-materialist notions of change. Historical materialism in itself does not change the world, but it does show that the world and its truths are indeed changeable and already always changing, and every human subject is already taking part in the historical conflicts. The difference is whether one in any particular point in space and time is part of the oppressive or the emancipating social forces, whether one is standing against or with the silenced in whose struggle a different reality for all is in the process of realization. The velocity of the progress depends on (1) the scope and the degree of the project's negativity and (2) the number of those who join the revolutionary movement.

The positivist defenders of the enlightenment did the anti-enlightenment camp, the heirs of the Dark Ages, a great favor by subjecting the enlightenment to metaphysics. In fact, Horkheimer and Adorno repeatedly problematize the enlightenment's fallback into mythology and absolutism at the hands of the bourgeoisie. Without comprehending their Marxist and progressive stance, their critique of modernity will be not only undervalued but also easily confused with nihilistic and retrogressive, if not outright antagonistic, tendencies toward modernism as a potential project for human emancipation (see Horkheimer and Adorno 2002, xvi; Horkheimer 285–86).

For the metaphysician, the reality is a fixed manifestation of particular approaches to *the* superhistorical truth. The possibility for another reality is contingent on access to another world, a world with entirely different premises. Thus, to the idealist, all we can aspire to accomplish is an ethical life in this world that is doomed anyway. From the theological-idealist point of view, for instance, justice is not even a possibility within the social, political, and historical realms. The only just world is the one that has already been created, which is to say, spatially speaking there is nothing to be done or undone in the way of actualizing the alternative world. This means theological-idealism is utopian in the unpolitical sense of the word, in the sense of taking myths for ontology, taking fictional beings for supernatural beings with absolute metaphysical and moral authorities, a mental invention for a spatial world perfectly formed to exist eternally and independently of what humans do and do not do in their personal and societal histories. Believers do not take their alternative world in the sense of not-yet-existent. Rather, for them, such a world has always existed and will always exist. It is just inaccessible until after death. Ironically, only death renders access to the alternative world of justice and higher truth possible (this alone should be sufficient to anticipate what kind of politics a "pro-life" politics would be from such a perspective). Given that the theological conception of the alternative world cannot be a historical one and that spatially is already complete, theological-idealism is utopian in a fundamentally counter-revolutionary way.

Spatial Utopia versus Historical Utopia

Religious utopia, therefore, could not be further from socialist utopia, which is utopia only in the sense of *not-yet-realized*. In terms of rationality, it is not utopic at all. In fact, it is a world in which reason too is realized. The socialist world, therefore, is true in the sense that freedom or equality is true: truth as a rational value judgment. Such a truth may be unrealized, but its unreality does not make it untrue. Reason's inherent task is to realize truths such as equality and freedom, and historical materialism is the theoretical realization of communism as an actualizable world in which equality and freedom would become true in the sense of reality as well, that is a rational world where reason would be at home. Thus, the communist utopia is utopia in the rational and material sense, which is the sense of realizability and actualizability through the revolutionary praxis that negates the prevalent irrational and oppressive order. From this perspective, it is pointless to morally speak of justice, and even impossible to rationally speak of justice, in a world in which the real is irrational and therefore only partly true. The communist utopia, therefore, amounts to the negation of the existing dystopia. Rationally there is more truth in communism than capitalism; the conditions for the actualizing the truth of freedom and equality are meant to be brought about historically. We cannot conceive of the spatial construction of the alternative world except through the actual realizations of the conditions under which the socialist conception is possible within our theoretical reach. The latter can only take place through the negation of the prevalent regime of material and knowledge production.

Therefore, we should differentiate between two opposing types of "utopia." The first type, what could be called *spatial utopia*, is a fiction that is meant to mystify social and political space and further disempower the oppressed. It is anti-revolutionary and oppressive. The denial of historical truths and the truth of historicity is an implicit position entailed in spatial utopia such as the kingdom of heaven. Nihilism is the ultimate political stance that results from spatial utopianism. Spatial utopianism entails historical denialism, which amounts to sacrificing the potentialities of reason for the finalities of metaphysics.

Even in cases where the oppressive nature of spatial utopianism is not immediately apparent (e.g., Christian and Islamic theologies of liberation), the nihilism is immediately apparent, so the marginalized should not be deceived by assurances of apologists who often like to maintain their allegiance to regressive forces and institutions under the pretext of democratic tolerance. As we have seen repeatedly in various parts of the world, especially during the last four decades, democracy is the first thing to be cried by adherents of religious politics when they are not in power and the first thing to be mocked when they take power. The different Other maybe tolerated by theologians, but when circumstances are favorable, theology is the fastest route to imposing despotism.

The second type is what we may call *historical utopia*. This is "utopia" in reference to a rationally plausible state of social and political affairs that can be realized through dialectical thinking and should be actualized through social organization and political mobilization aimed at constructing an alternative world by humans and for humans. The historical utopian, therefore, affirms history and rejects the reality. To a historical materialist, as a historical utopian, there is nothing to be denied. The dialectics is a movement between affirmation, negation, and transformation. As a matter of fact, historical materialism does not deny even religion, God, and religious utopia, for religion is indeed an institution with effective social, political, moral, and economic powers. It exists because there are existing social classes with real and continued antagonisms. God is an illusion, yes, but an actual illusion, that is, an illusion that is held by real human beings with real brains. As long as the conditions of suffering persist, God and other irrationalities will continue to stick to hopeless minds of the helpless humans stubbornly resisting every philosophical argument.

Two Opposing Senses of Idealism: Culturalism as Bad Idealism

Having differentiated between two opposing uses of the term "utopia," a similar distinction between the opposing uses of "idealism" is in order.

While Marxist thinkers use "idealism" to mean the philosophical approach opposite to materialism, we should note that "Idealism" is also used in the revolutionary sense of being motivated by ideals, such as freedom and equality. The idealist in this sense is used in reference to someone who refuses to accept the reality precisely because it is imposed on us, because it is refutable, negatable, and changeable.[1] This should not be confused with idealism as a non-materialist or anti-materialist philosophy that adopts a metaphysical notion of truth, as something above and beyond history and societal activities. In fact, one should be aware of the clear contrast between the two usages of this ambiguous term. Horkheimer puts his finger on the issue when he writes that Critical Theory is in agreement with German idealism insofar as the latter "insisted on the dynamic moment in the relationship and has protested against the adoration of facts and the social conformism this brings with it" (2002, 245). Later in the same book, he makes the distinction between the two meanings of idealism clear: (1) "that it is possible to introduce reason among individuals and among nations" versus (2) "it is sufficient to set up the picture of perfection with no regard for the way in which it is to be attained." The he adds, "In modern times, loyalty to the highest ideas has been linked, in a world opposed to them, with the sober desire to know how these ideas can be realized on earth" (270). This is precisely the sense in which Marxism, as an anti-utopian and a utopian philosophy at the same time, affirms and rejects class society simultaneously. It adamantly rejects nihilist utopianism while it conceives a different world on the very materialist basis it theorizes dialectically. Philosophy, for Horkheimer, is precisely that "methodical and steadfast attempt to bring reason into the world" (268). Reason, in turn, "exists in the whole system of ideas, in the progression from one idea to another, so that every idea is understood and applied in its true meaning, that is to say, in its meaning within the whole of knowledge" (266). To Horkheimer, "only such thought is rational thought" (266). Marcuse too insists that "reason is the intellectual faculty to understand the facts and the factors which make the facts" (2016, 481). Then, empirically showing "facts" and rationally referencing them do not necessarily represent rational thought.[2] Nor does the presentation of facts in isolation from their historical *factors* and social circumstances amount to truth.

Parallel to its refutation of the enlightenment as a totalitarian enterprise of the bourgeoisie, Critical Theory defends the enlightenment as a project of *bringing reason into the world*. In doing so, it confronts not only superstitions but also scientific authorities that reproduce irrationality and unfreedom through a positivist regime of knowledge production. Critical Theory's struggle, therefore, is a struggle to rescue the enlightenment project itself from the oppressive social forces that have impaired its emancipatory potential and manipulated its mode of knowledge production for advancing a world order that is totalitarian and irrational. The enlightenment of the bourgeoisie furthers unfreedom and deepens domination through furthering the means of privilege and sophisticating the methods of the exercise of power. Because in the struggle for emancipation the true revolutionary subjects cannot appeal to any gods, whether dead or alive, their sole path remains that of *bringing reason into the world*. This is to say, the project of emancipation needs to be emancipated before it can have emancipating effects. The project of emancipation has to be true to reason in order to bring about freedom—irrational systems of belief may actualize some appearances of liberation, but they are inevitably oppressive. The existing order needs to be negated in order to make materializing a rational alternative world possible. The alternative world is a world where existing human beings (as opposed to imagined abstracts such as citizens, the nation, the children of God, the *umma*, etc.) can be truly free (i.e., materially and philosophically, both of which imply each other). It will not be a positively describable alternative until the conditions for imagining it become available. Until then, critical reason can only know it negatively, that is through negating the existing relations of oppression. This is why Marxist communism is a negative doctrine; it is the dialectical transformation of capitalism.

The enlightenment is by no means the first project to claim access to ultimate truth symbolized by universal illumination. At the same time, its potential significance is precisely in its rejection of absolutism. During the Dark Ages and the other eras and canons of the hegemony of metaphysics, true knowledge, objectivity, and ultimate truth, symbolized by "light," were of course claimed by distinct and unmistakable institutions of power. The enlightenment is the historical moment that creates a departure from such absolutism, yet the project quickly becomes infatuated with its own glamorous triumph, resulting in the reproduction of another system of absolutism, mythology, and unfreedom. The very class that claimed victory over superstitions and absolutism licensed itself as the democratic delegate of universal civilization and mistook its own strive for exercising unlimited power universally for the essence of universal liberty. This is what can be called the bourgeoisification of the enlightenment. Like other absolutist projects, the enlightenment's departure from darkness was suppressed by a new mode of the production of unreason and unfreedom in the name of the legitimacy of the ultimate truth as denoted by the positivists. In what became the social sciences, the ideology of the ruling groups was sanctified and naturalized in the name of science. For instance, since the ruling groups needed slavery to expand the boundaries of exploitation and to globalize their hegemony, they had to legitimize slavery by appropriating the enlightenment's ethos and regime of knowledge production. Since they already believed in race, their regimes of knowledge production manufactured race as a scientific truth using an emerging science but one that was most suitable for absolutizing their racist doctrine. Even before biology's validation of the term "race" in relation to subclassifications of the human species, anthropology was prepared to finish the job creating the right phraseology to establish a racist regime of knowledge production both discursively (i.e., in terms of ideological means) and socially (i.e., in terms of material means). Since the late nineteenth century, the race language has undergone several drastic shifts, the most significant of which is the racialization of the word "culture" and then the culturalization of the racist discourse, but the mode of perception has hardly changed. In fact, the purpose of the cosmetic amendments that were conducted on the dominant discourse was precisely to camouflage the racist worldview, which, in turn amounts to perpetuating social inequalities in the interest of the European ruling groups. Today, the racialized notion of culture is simply the dominant paradigm across the social sciences, and therefore the culturalized discourse of racism is hardly problematizable. Religious sectarianism and prehistoric senses of tribalism and xenophobia have only been further facilitated, reinforced by endless semantic supplies thanks to the social sciences. In the Middle Ages, religious institutions were the centers of knowledge authority, and thus the ideological power to sustain a reality formed around mythology. Today, instead of the Church, it is the social sciences that play that role at least in terms of maintaining what is fundamentally a tribalist worldview based on an in-group versus out-group dichotomy such as the American-European "way of life" versus the collective representatives of cultures; the liberal West whose individualist and liberal values are universally rationalizable and rationally representative of a universal civilization versus the West's Other whose world is collectively experienced, culturally determined, and only locally meaningful, at best. Of course, this dichotomy of the West versus the rest is a fictional one, which is precisely my point.

A fictional separation is metaphysicalized in order to justify and eternalize the material discrimination. A culturalist mode of perception is perpetuated in order to normalize a mode of material production that otherwise could be considered neither rational nor natural. In the Dark Ages, for most European urban centers, God was the arbitrator of the in-group versus out-group. Within that religious frame of reference, the Christian and human are used interchangeably by those under Christendom, and similarly under the Islamic hegemony the Muslim and the human are used interchangeably. A similar bifurcation of the world continues to be at work under the secular bourgeois hegemony, and what has made the endurance of such a tribalization possible is the bourgeois regime of knowledge production. What makes the challenge for the disadvantaged especially difficult, in addition to the fact that they are silenced, ideologically hegemonized, marginalized, and so on, is that, very much like religious beliefs, the beliefs held by social scientists cannot be invalidated through any rationalist or empiricist methods. That is so simply because if the object of a belief is X, even if X is a myth, then there is no way to prove that the belief is false; the belief will always be true insofar as the subject truly believes that X is true. Arguing with social scientists about the fictionality of the notion of "culture" (in the essentializing, homogenizing, anthropologizing, and de-individualizing sense typically used across academic fields and public spheres) is very much like arguing with religious believers about the fictionality of the object of their belief. The believers will always argue back about the truth of their belief, and they are correct in making such a claim (they truly believe that . . . , etc.). For every attempt to reason against the object of a belief, the belief reasserts itself, which, at least cognitively for the subject, is all that is needed to *reassert* the metaphysical truth. In Identitarian or conventional theories of knowledge, the existence of boundaries between truth and untruth, the rational and the irrational, subject and object are presumed, so the disputes concern the exact placement of those boundaries (of exclusivity and identity) as opposed to the broader ethos within which the methodological formulae are selected. Critical Theory, on the other hand, adopts the Marxist dialectical method whereby contradictions are analyzed together in their very relational dynamics, whereby rationality and irrationality, or reality and fiction, are interpreted in their sociohistoricality as opposed to some ontologically determined signifiers or attributes with metaphysical values. That is to say, within an irrational frame of reference, particular irrationalities are rational. Put differently, the irrational in a false world is completely rational, commonsensical, and even factual. Of course, "the irrational" should not be read to mean arbitrary irrational propositions. On the contrary, the rationalized irrational is always specific to the nuances of the broader irrationality that frames it along with the rest of the order of things. In fact, the problem is far more epistemological than moral and historical than phenomenological. How we perceive and the perceived are necessarily locked in a cyclical relation of production and reproduction. Each side is both a product and a production of the other side.

Revolutionary Negativity

Adorno's statement "wrong life cannot be lived rightly" (2005, fragment 18) should be interpreted in this sense (i.e., that an irrational frame of reference generates what would falsely be considered rational by those who are stuck in it and do not have access to another ethos). Fabian Freyenhagen uses the term "epistemic negativism" to encapsulate Adorno's position that we can only know what is wrong, that "we cannot know what the good life is prior to the realisation of its social conditions" (2013, 4). He also argues that Adorno was a "substantive negativist" because he held that the "world is fundamentally wrong, bad, even ill and pathological" (4). Freyenhagen goes on to demonstrate that the above two positions are not incompatible within Adorno's practical philosophy. In my view, "epistemic negativism" and "substantive negativism" are not only compatible with but also necessary for the critical consciousness that aims to negate the existing order. For analytic purposes, I posit that the opposite of what Freyenhagen terms "epistemic negativism" and "substantive negativism" would be "epistemic positivism" and "substantive positivism," respectively.

To assume epistemic positivism, to maintain that it is possible to know what is right in a wrong world, is both false and paralyzing. It is false for the same reasons that make idealism so problematic: consciousness can be conscious of itself and history, but it cannot be extrahistorical, superhistorical, or ahistorical. Of course, imagining that which does not exist is possible, but practical philosophy can only be grounded on actual historical circumstances, the same circumstances that shape consciousness. Epistemic positivism is paralyzing to progressive action because it leads to the false assumption that the realization of what is right is a prerequisite for the rejection of what is wrong, that in order to reject what is wrong, we must first know what is right. However, this common assumption is inherently false because imagining an alternative is an ability we can only obtain through the process of negating the existing order.

Substantive positivism, the belief that the world is fundamentally right, could very well lead to passivism or retroactive politics, as in the case of various religious movements. It is despair, not hope or faith in some form of metaphysical justice, that motivates truly progressive revolutions. Only after realizing that the world is Godless and fundamentally chaotic can we enhance the ability to free ourselves from psychological constraints and repressive social norms. Functioning as a psychologically protective cocoon, such constraints are precisely what prevent the subject from developing subjectivity, which functions as a resilient shell capable of facing the reality and changing it when it becomes unbearable. As we learn from atheist existentialists including Camus and Sartre, without being aware of the Godlessness of the world, freedom is unobtainable even as an abstract value. Freedom, thus, is inseparable from the existentialist awareness of the absurdity of existence. In other words, the grand philosophical focal point of freedom is necessarily existentialist. Politically, the historical materialist's capacity to be an emancipating subject within an emancipatory historical movement is contingent on her negativity. For this revolutionary subject, the following are imperative (1) radical unlearning of positive thought formulae that draw their premises from the indoctrinated dominant ideologies, which have already naturalized oppression, and (2) undoing of hierarchical social relations that have gained the status of metaphysical (unalterable) truth.

In Adorno's words:

> As long as domination reproduces itself, the old quality reappears unrefined in the dissolving of the dissolvent: in a radical sense no leap is made at all. That would happen only with the liberating event. Because the dialectical determination of the new quality always finds itself referred back to the violence of the objective tendency that propagates domination, it is placed under the almost inescapable compulsion, whenever it has conceptually achieved the negation of the negation, to substitute, even in thought, the bad old order for the non-existent alternative. (2005, fragment 152)

This is also why there is arguably nothing more deceiving in a philosophy of revolution than the typical supposition that a preconceived alternative is imperative for changing the world. A world that is not there yet cannot be perceived. Moreover, the existing order makes another mode of perception materially impossible. That is to say, the reasoning has to be faithful to the negative dialectics: for perceiving an alternative world to be possible, the existing world must be altered. This is what makes the negativity thesis materialist. By the same token, the positive, identitarian method, which imposes the necessity of preconceiving an alternative, is inherently false. It is a clear case of the fallacy of idealism: the reversal of causality, unknowingly placing the world on its head. A philosophy of revolution based on the negativity thesis, or a postnihilist philosophy, still has a tangible account of revolution as a real possibility.

While the falsehood and the irrationality, or the false consciousness and the wrong world, are indeed interlocked in a cycle of endless production and reproduction, revolutions can take place when the normal(ized) cycle is interrupted. In fact, as Walter Benjamin argues, the historical materialist tasks herself with creating an interruption in order to create new possibilities (2006, Thesis VIII). Since the normal state of the world is a state of emergency for the oppressed, the oppressed must comprehend this negative truth about the falsehood of the reality and act accordingly. Acting accordingly necessitates historical intervention, which by definition transforms the oppressed who is denied a space for a proper life into a revolutionary subject par excellence—not only a potentially emancipated but also an emancipating subject, a subject historically mandated to liberate humanity as such from the falsehood that pulls down individuals and societies into a state of utter barbarity, of which the current moment of multiple crises (ecological catastrophes, wars, ongoing genocides, economic sanctions and the resulting destruction) is an example.

Because thus far the history of human society is a history of unfreedom, what can be (and is) proven empirically is the facticity of unfreedom. To Marcuse the only worthwhile form of art is, therefore, negative art, which falsifies the reality through showing fidelity to a different truth, the truth that is not a mere reaffirmation of empirical facts. As mentioned earlier, reason in Marcuse's definition is "the intellectual faculty to understand the facts and the factors which make the facts" (2016, 481). Dull empiricism does provide useful information, but the knowledge production it serves is inherently irrational and oppressive. As Marx notes in his critique of capitalist political economy, bourgeois thinkers take what they observe around them and induce from the facts of their times and spaces metaphysical principles and laws. Even in registering the "facts" they habitually ignore the "factors," which are necessarily historical and material, as opposed to metaphysical. Marcuse states, "Social relations concealed the meaning of truth. They formed a horizon of untruth that deprived the truth of its meaning" (2009, 110). Negativity is the most defining aspect of Critical Theory as a philosophy because, as Marcuse states, "truth that is more than the truth of *what is* can be attained and intended only in opposition to established social relations" (110, italics added).

Long before the enlightenment, religions and other mythical systems of belief had adopted the dichotomy of enlightenment versus ignorance. In fact, even before the Abrahamic religions that typically adopt metaphysical dualism, from which everything else is drawn, Zarathustrianism was directly constructed around the symbolism of light in opposition to darkness. As well, Buddhist philosophical schools describe knowledge in terms of the epistemological ability to discover the various levels of truth, with absolute truth being at the highest level, which is literally associated with "enlightenment." For instance, Nagarjuna writes, "The teachings of the Dharma by the various *Buddhas* is based on the two truths; namely the relative (worldly) truth and the absolute (supreme) truth." Then, he adds, "Those who do not know the distinction between the two truths cannot understand the profound nature of Buddha's teaching" (1970, 146).[3] Buddhist philosophy is far more sophisticated than the metaphysical systems that grew out of Abrahamic theology because in Buddhism the ultimate truth is in fact the outcome of the relativization of the reality, as opposed to subduing the entire human reality to metaphysics. This is a more accurate philosophical interpretation of the multiplicity of the levels of truth in Buddhism. Santideva, for instance, writes, "It is agreed that there are these two truths: the conventional and the ultimate. Reality is beyond the scope of intellection. Intellection is said to be conventional" (1995, 115). Finally, Plato's metaphysics and corresponding epistemology, best described in *The Republic*, especially the allegory of the cave (1992, Book VII) and the divided line (Book VI), places *light* at the center (also see Plato 1961, *Meno* 81d). In Plato's system, the sun symbolizes the highest truth, and entire epistemological hierarchy is explained in optic terms (e.g., brightness, shadows, and reflections). At the very top of the pyramid, there are no objects to be illuminated; rather there is only light in its purist and absolute form, rendering even time and space irrelevant. Platonic Truth is homed with the gods in a metaphysical realm. Thus, in the Platonic universe, even within its social realm, there is no such thing as knowing. There can only be recollection because the soul is already endowed with absolute truth. That is to say there is knowledge without a knower. Even the philosopher does not discover anything new. Rather, she merely understands and elevates above the temporospatial obstacles, deceptions, and distortions that pull down the soul to the lower realms.

The Abrahamic universe is a reincarnation of the Platonic divorce between knowledge and the knower, truth and the social conditions of human reason, only with taking the absolutism, vertically, downward, and horizontally within the top level of the pyramid, to its utter absolutist limit, to the point of totalizing oneness and universalizing sameness. Essentially, all the Platonic forms and the Greek gods become victims of a coup by an intruder who declares himself the absolute Absolute. In John:12, Jesus says, "I am the light of the world," and he goes on to promise guidance through the darkness of the world, dismissing a rather sound counterargument that points to the fallacy of (the pseudo-proof of) self-referencing (see John:14–20).[4] In fact, in Aramaic there is a unique word to refer to the light that is property of God, *noohra*, which not only has a clear philological link to the Arabic word *noor*, but it is also still used in its original form as a relatively common female name across societies and languages in the Near East and North Africa.

As we move from Christianity to Islam, absolutism takes metaphysics to its logical end of unlimited power by removing even the holy family from the top center of power, whereby the Absolute is in fact defined by oneness, who has neither been parented nor will ever parent, who has never had anyone at all, as a Quranic verse *Al-Ikhlas* "enlightens" humanity using the most definitive forms of speech via the messenger who, in turn, is told to "tell," *qul*, in Arabic, which is the first word of the verse. Not surprisingly, Islam diverges from Christianity in the sense of being more Christian than Christianity in both the absolutism of authority and the metaphysics of power. That is precisely why the admission or conversion to Islam is conditioned around the monotheistic confirmation. If this account sounds tautological, it is so because it describes a proposition that cannot be anything but tautological. To become a Muslim, the person must announce: "There is no God but (the) God, and Mohamed is the messenger of (the) God." A person, any person, is not considered a Muslim until she utters that statement. The Quran, according to an even more bluntly self-referential testimony, is composed of divine messages, communicating which is Mohammed's primary task. These messages from the Absolute repeatedly emphasize that God is a light, *noor*,[5] for all the peoples, *lil-alameen* (i.e., a universal light).[6]

Western philosophy after the demise of the Greek civilization has also become a search for the enlightenment, the true truth, if you will. Theology almost entirely occupied the philosophical space throughout the Dark Ages, from antiquity all the way to the Italian Renaissance. The breathing space for Western philosophy that had been key to its survival was the cities that were located outside Christendom, especially Baghdad and to some degree other metropoles such as Damascus, Samarqand, and Qurtuba. That said, in the final analysis, the Christian and Islamic theology reappropriated Platonic idealism and turned it into an entirely mythical system, thereby subjecting the human agency and her world, including the philosopher and philosophy, to the absolutist authority of the religious institution. The Dark Ages, with relative historical and geographic exceptions, was the era in which those who claimed absolute light and ultimate universal truth ruled. It was the era of the metaphysical duality, and the era of a universe in which God was the only source of light as truth, goodness, and beauty. Wherever and whenever the ignorant, sinful, helpless, and hopeless were not wise enough to accept the universal wisdom or not good enough to accept the universal kindness, death and/or enslavement would be imposed on them. Therefore, it is not a mere rhetorical generalization to suggest that the age of absolute light was indeed the same as the age of absolute darkness. We need to keep in mind that, of course, thinkers from the Dark Ages did not see their ages that way. Similarly, for the most part, those who speak in the name of the enlightenment are neither socially nor epistemologically qualified to realize the prevailing unfreedom, let alone realize their own role in prolonging the unfreedom.

Engels called the fanatics of empiricism, or positivist heirs of the enlightenment, "inductive asses" (qtd. in Bloch 2018, 97). He and Marx were under no illusion when it came to the unfreedom that was about to be totalized over human society not despite but because of the bourgeoisiefication of the enlightenment project. That is also why they spent more time critiquing idealist socialists and bourgeois liberals than critiquing theologians. They were well aware of the fact that a new tyranny had been taking shape, and most of the knowledge-production establishment was pushing ahead with this new regime of absolutism. The enlightenment as an emancipating project, by definition, had to be a project of those who were continued to be subjugated, dehumanized, and silenced—those who have always lived under the threat of elimination. Their enlightenment, along with their truth and history, was at a turning point in 1848, 1871, and the following decades, so to Marx and Engels between carrying on the enlightenment revolution and writing down a theory of history, there was no time to waste. They were philosophers of crisis par excellence. The dialectical theory of history, or what became known as historical materialism, is also a theory that exposes the historicity of truth, knowledge, morality, and aesthetics. Most importantly, it is a critical theory written from the perspective of the silenced who had always been pushed outside history and history books. These two antagonistic outsiders who turned against every institution from family to state, every establishment from the academy to the imperial courts, forcefully extracted bits and pieces of time and space to produce a negative form of knowledge. In that spirit, one of their disciples, namely Walter Benjamin, at another moment of crisis, as fascism was literally eliminating every last corner for his existence, wrote that the "state of emergency" is the perpetual state of the oppressed and the struggle against fascism must be conceptualized with that in mind (see Benjamin 2006, Thesis VIII). "The subject of historical knowledge," Benjamin wrote, "is the struggling, oppressed class itself. Marx presents it as the last enslaved class—the avenger that completes the task of liberation in the name of generations of the downtrodden" (2006, Thesis XII).

Going Beyond the False Dichotomy of Positivism and Superstition

The facticity of facts is inseparable from the totality of truth, so when facts are (re)presented in separation from the sociohistorical background, they necessarily serve untruth even if scientific knowledge, as opposed to distortion or deception, is intended as the primary objective. The positivist representation of truth is produced through isolating fragments of "what is" from the history and the social relations that have shaped the current state of things. It presents the product as absolute truth and dismisses the production as if it never existed. Thus, positivism metaphysicalizes bits and parts of what is essentially social and historically spatial. No wonder, then, positivists speak with the confidence of theologians but without the spiritualistic touch, for good or ill. Historical and spatial reductionism, however, is only half of the problem of the positivist metaphysics. The other half has to do with the overwhelming tendency to universalize and eternalize the perspective of the dominant. Once a positivist truth is established in the name of science, the second political phase of its universalization starts, which is the more direct, administrative, phase. In this way, positivism constantly establishes a future reality that is untraceable to the prior historical and spatial conditions of production.

The antipode of the positivist claims of objectivity is not superstition. Rather, superstition is merely a more primitive version of what positivism represents. This is to say, nihilism is the framework, not the antipode, of positivism. Speaking in the name of objectivity does not make the speaker's worldview valid, and in fact, more often than not, it is a mere discursive strategy to distort the reality through fragmentation, abstraction, reduction, and idealization. Positivism, like premodern truth-regimes, is centered around particular social privileges of power, and it is actively engaged in eternalizing the relations of inequality. However, unlike those prior truth-regimes, which relied on all-encompassing mythology to rationalize existing social conditions of life, positivism's strategies for the production of knowledge utilize empirical facts, fragmented and rearranged discursively, to produce a universal myth. Theological metaphysics is a top-down structure with the universal myth securely placed at the top of the pyramid of power in the form of the symbolism of the sacred. Positivism, on the other hand, has reversed the metaphysical structure by moving from empirical facts to the construction of a universal myth. At the end, both modes of knowledge production claim objectivity precisely to mystify the objective and claim apoliticality to eternalize the prevalent state of affairs. In both worlds, the miserables' only hope for redemption is total submission to morality, an authority that has used metaphysics to secure the "houses of power," so to speak. Monotheism has always claimed true knowledge and speaking in the name of truth. The supposed detachment from politics in both cases, religiosity and positivism, is nothing but a political tool instrumentalized for the purpose of inching toward total control, and as such it renders both religion and bourgeois objectivity hopelessly biased and fanatically utopian, and it is as ideological as a totalitarian worldview can be.[7]

However, once more, the dichotomies are not always depicted accurately by those who assume a pro-enlightenment position. Pier Paolo Pasolini's statement about life as "the fearless exercise of reason" (1987, 13) could have been uttered by Voltaire and become the enlightenment's maxim, but reason is not as self-evident as positivists want us to believe. At the same time, it is next to impossible to convince a positivist that their conception of reason is a reductionist one, and it is even more challenging to have them conceive the ideological distortions they reproduce in the name of objectivity. If a positivist gains awareness of the bourgeois reductionism, which has normalized instrumental rationality as the only, and eternal, notion of reason, they may simply cease to be a positivist. Contrary to the common assumption, ideology is most effectively present when it is least tangible, when it is already a dominant mode of perception, a non-problematizable aspect of the common sense. It is easy to point to partisan politics and label it as ideological, or condemn, say, the guards in the Nazi concentration camps or the train operators. The bigger challenge, however, is to be able to problematize the unspoken and the accepted practices as they take place, as the victims suffer, or even better before the victims suffer, or even still better before there are any potential victims as potential objects of violence. The real challenge, in other words, is the ability to reject any form of participation in a fascist world while that world still enjoys the support of the scientific, religious, and moral authorities. Now that we cannot return to the past and resist the Nazi project, the point is to be able to detect what should be resisted today and resist it. In a sense, every age has its own forms of fascism, and every age's fascists speak in the name of glory, morality, objectivity, truth, and so forth. The point, in simpler words, is to be able to diagnose the little fascist that is inside every one of us. It is helpful to know that little fascist often speaks one's own mother tongue or another highly respected language and acts in a noble, selfless, virtuous, and in fact heroic manner within the ethos in which one happens to be immersed. Without catching that little fascist, one would never be able to see the political equivalents of the Nazi Party out there. If there is one thing we should learn from the twentieth century's forms of fascism, it is that no religion or science could safeguard one from becoming an active fascist. One may regularly assure oneself by thinking something along the lines of, "I care about so many people, animals, places, and memories. I take the side of truth, goodness, and beauty. The people I completely trust have similar views and beliefs." The problem is that all that could be true, and the person nonetheless be an active fascist of their time and place. As a matter of fact, old-fashioned fascists from their most loyal followers would see themselves that way, and they received more assurances than denouncements from the authorities of science and morality around them.

When we are too focused on the obvious representative of falsehood, whether in the past or our contemporary world, we run the risk of creating and empowering another force of falsehood whose true identity remains concealed due to the overwhelming contrast between the opposing camps of the ongoing conflict. Most of us, including some of the most highly educated, tend to think in terms of dichotomies and thus refuse to consider a third possibility. Intellectually (i.e., in principle), human beings are capable of rejecting all the given options and aiming at the realization of what either does not exist yet or is not powerful enough to be visible; nonetheless, the tendency to give in to the simple division of the world between darkness and enlightenment, good and evil, has always been the common tendency, perhaps mainly due to the sense of urgency in every set of circumstances and the habit of intellectual laziness. Century after century the ruling groups have produced new means of barbarism, and this century could be the most barbaric thus far. Fundamentally, the pattern of false dichotomies has not changed over the centuries since the European dark ages. Almost always the falsehood is reproduced unwittingly during the very conflict against falsehood. The enlightenment project's conflict against the forces of anti-enlightenment has been stuck in a similar deadly cycle. It is a cycle of mimesis and false projection.

Assumptions about one's own objective objectivity are inevitably, deeply, and hopelessly ideological. In fact, post-ideological claims about one's own views as supposedly ideology-free judgment could not be more ideological simply because they are symptoms of perfect ideological hegemony, whereby the internalized ideology is completely infused, leaving no trace and thus no reason for the subject's critical faculties of judgment to question their perception of the world. The common understanding of "ideology" is simply the most ideological because it is unaware of its deep partialities. Since ideology is first and foremost a set of truth claims (i.e., a subjective assumption of objectivity), the most ideological positions are necessarily those that profess *unideologicality*. This does not mean that all perspectives are equally false. Rather, it simply means the denial to be immersed in ideology makes the subject more, not less, susceptible to be partial, to perpetuate blind spots in perceptions and interpretations of the social world, than a potential state in which the same subject knows that all perspectives, including her own, are inherently ideological and thus political. The difference is not between taking sides versus not taking sides, but rather taking sides unknowingly versus taking sides consciously. One may or may not take the side of the dominant in any given scenario, one may or may not choose to be a part of particular technology of power, one may be a fascist or an anti-fascist, but assuming neutral objectivity (i.e., unideologicality) makes it more likely for one to unknowingly take the side of the dominant against the silenced, whether or not one is a member of the silenced. This is exactly how ordinary good people end up creating and running machines of mass murder without even being bothered by the occasional sense of guilt, at least while the mass murder takes place. Genocides have always been committed throughout modernity, and ordinary people have always failed to realize their involvement in these genocides. Often the ordinary good people do not recognize the genocides of their age, let alone their own amenability. Currently, if more people realized the direct effects of arms industry and their own democratic role, not to mention the ecological effects of their innocent daily contribution to maintaining the capitalist machine, probably most would alter their political behavior radically. A century from now, people might be amazed by the utter violence, irrationality, and destructiveness in which most of us are taking part simply by fanatically sticking to the supposedly unideological center or a few inches to its left or right.

How could one make a convincing case to a positivist that one's critique of reductionist conceptions of science does not mean the rejection of scientific methods of inquiry in favor of some sort of mysticism or nihilism? One should search for terms other than "science" and "ideology" in such a simplistic, and of course misleading, discourse that is used as if there are ahistorical, metaphysical entities whose existence and eternal endurance is unquestionable. There are plenty of such taken-at-face-value terms in the social sciences and the broader arenas of opinion-making. "Nation" is just one of those terms. A discourse that uses the term "nation" as if it referred to an actual entity out there is already deeply ideological, and a speaker/writer's ignorance of this only makes them more ideological in the sense of false consciousness.

This is precisely why what vulgar empiricists do in the name of research amounts to a mere reaffirmation of the false reality. As Bauman explains, even until World War II, for people in some parts of Poland, national identity or nationality made no sense whatsoever. While the Polish state's bureaucrats were "trained to expect that for every human being there must be a nation to which he or she belonged," "the people they questioned simply could not grasp what a 'nation' was and what 'having a nationality' was like" (2008, 17). In fact this was the case for most populations from the Far East to Latin America until the European colonizers imposed the myth of "nationality." National identity is an elite's invention that is projected on people and later actualized via state institutions. Then, once the identity is created, the nationalist ruling elites narrate a false version of the past according to which "the nation" created the state, whereas the truth is the exact opposite: the state, which is controlled by the elites, systematically constructs "the nation" as some sort of a natural and eternal identity. Immanuel Wallerstein is right to assert that "a systematic look at the history of the modern world will show . . . that in almost every case statehood preceded nationhood, and not the other way around, despite a widespread myth to the contrary" (1991, 81). This matters for exposing the ideological structure of today's "objective" and "neutral" dominant mode of perception, which is a nationalist mode of perception constructed according to and on the basis of the capitalist mode of production. Nationalism, like religion, is an illusion, and like all illusions it is a product of a materialist reality that inevitably perpetuates falsehood. Let us continue this analysis in terms of historical materialism.

Consider Balibar's following passage:

> In appearance, humanity has been unified by the suppression of imperial hierarchies; in fact, however, it is only today that humanity exists as such, though split into tendentially incompatible masses. In the space of the world economy, which has effectively become that of world politics and world ideology, the division between subhumans and super-humans is a structural but violently unstable one. Previously, the notion of humanity was merely an abstraction. But, to the question, "What is man?" which—however aberrant its forms may appear to us—is insistently present in racist thought, there is today no response in which this split is not at work. (1991, 44)

Balibar then adds:

> What are we to conclude from this? The displacements to which I have just alluded are part of what, to borrow a term from Nietzsche, we might call the contemporary transvaluations of racism, which concern both the general economy of humanity's political groupings and its historical imaginary. They form what I have, above, called the singular development of racism which relativizes typologies and reworks accumulated experiences against the grain of what we believe to be the "education of humanity." In this sense, contrary to what is postulated in one of the most constant statements of racist ideology itself, it is not "race" which is a biological or psychological human "memory," but it is racism which represents one of the most insistent forms of the historical memory of modern societies. *It is racism which continues to effect the imaginary "fusion" of past and present in which the collective perception of human history unfolds.* (1991, 44–45, italics added)

I have already moved from the notions of nation and nationalism to race and racism; the same source cited above offers an excellent set of arguments exposing the racist past and present of the notion of "nation." I am in complete agreement with Balibar's statement that "the discourses of race and nation are never very far apart" (1991, 37). In fact, I would add "culture" to race and nation. Culturalism, the perception of human societies in terms of their supposed respective cultural identities, has formed today's most common discourses of nationalism and racism. Culturalism is today's language of idealism. Most children are taught to dismiss the basic, that is material, aspects of human life and instead assume that what makes societies different is the diversity of cultures. Thanks to the culturalist education, the normal view of college students today is that some societies value individual liberties, political democracy, and so on, while others endorse their own cultural values! As absurd as this might sound when problematized, the unspoken assumption is that those other (non-Western) societies must value unfreedom and despotism! They must enjoy destruction instead of prosperity and misery instead of happiness! Then it is only normal for people in Europe and the United States to assume that there is a psychological explanation for every case of mass shooting committed by a White man, whereas if the perpetuator is Brown, psychology is hardly relevant, as if for the Brown human psychology is not applicable, as if the Brown person's behavior is collectively determined, just the way each animal species is collectively recognized according to that species' "nature." Indeed, "culture," precisely like "race," is used to mean "nature" whenever the subject in question is an "Other," whether Chinese, Indian, Arab, African, and so on.

Nation-statism was essentially a European bourgeois invention that in the name of societal difference imposed sameness, and in the name of political plurality imposed oneness. Today's discourse of culturalism, including multiculturalism, is a continuation of the same totalitarian steamrolling of diversity. What skips most educators and opinion makers is that by recognizing cultural diversity, all differences are practically denied simply because "culture" in the first place is a homogenizing and essentializing notion. Of course, these idealist inventions have very real, that is material, roles to play; namely, they are deployed precisely in order to distort the materialist reality, to misplace the attention of those exploited on daily bases, to fictionalize what is otherwise impossible not to grasp. In short, racism, nationalism, and culturalism are mere ideological means for producing and reproducing a false epistemology, thanks to which the more miserable the exploited become, the more fanatically they support their exploiters, the ruling groups in their respective societies and globally.

Race, nation, and culture are mere tools for obscuring the working class's political identity as a class, to replace the political identity they would otherwise form on the bases of their actual experiences under the real condition of their lives with an idealist identity, to replace potential class politics with idealist-identity politics.[8] This is exactly the process of *mobomassification*, or the bourgeoisification of the proletarian, substituting class-mass politics with mob politics, a democratic sphere with a fascistic sphere. Laborers will identify and mobilize not as workers but as patriots. The flag becomes a fetish. The more they suffer, the more fetishistic power the flag will have over them. The more powerless they become to change their life conditions, the more faithfully they obey their actual exploiters and the more mercilessly they brutalize those who are below them in the social hierarchy. It is no wonder that refugees who, even by the standards of a bourgeois society are already extremely disempowered, face increasing discrimination, demonization, and violence at the hands of nationalist mobs. In an idealist pact against the cosmopolitanism of the marginalized, racist, nationalist, and culturalist, bourgeoisification works hand in hand with religious mystification. Men and women who might have no consideration whatsoever for billions of impoverished human beings, including some in their own neighborhoods, mobilize to criminalize a woman who might decide to abort her pregnancy, and without any sense of irony this is done in the name of "the right to life." It is somehow God's will to grant life to the unborn and God's will to deprive most of the already-born of life with dignity. The absurdity is boundless, but seldom have absurdities been stopped by merely exposing them in a piece of writing or a speech. The historical materialist, therefore, understands myths in terms of the existing reality, not reality in terms of myths. For the historical materialist, understanding the reality and changing it are one and the same praxis. Another way to put this is that we cannot imagine a rational alternative world until we change the reality that limits our imagination.

The idealist fallacy I emphasize does not necessarily concern what an author might claim in regard to this or that nation but rather the fact that they attribute anything at all to a "nation." Also, whether or not most people believe in the existence of "nations" does not make nationhood any less idealist and false in terms of the assumed denotation and in terms of the denoted that is falsely assumed to be a superhistorical entity or any entity at all. Idealist ideologies are not just wrong epistemologically, say, in the sense of failure to grasp any historical situation, which is to say all individual and societal circumstances related to humanity, but also false ontologically (i.e., in the sense of attributing predicates to a nonexisting subject). It does not matter if an idealist statement is logical because the idealist is illogically positioned. The very standpoint is a standpoint of inherent falseness. Then the problem is not that the idealist's worldview is ideological (everyone's view is ideological anyway); rather, the problem is that it is a view that does not stand a chance of being not false. By the same token, those who have not negated the idealism they have been born into and been trained to sustain in their interaction with the world around them, speech acts, and uses of the social space are doomed to contribute to their own unfreedom. The falsity of the existing reality is ideologically sustained by our failure to realize the difference between knowledge as a social product and knowledge production as a complex project of power relations; between beliefs and the mechanism of belief manufacturing; between the reality as an actualized falsehood and truth as the not-yet-actualized; or between a reality that is only falsely maintained and a truth whose validity is rationally evident and potentially actualizable.

The historical materialist, on the other hand, is well aware of their own stance as subjectively affirmative of change as emancipation and an objectively negating actor within an oppressive reality but not necessarily part of the oppressive forces. The historical materialist consciously endorses an ideological position to negate the real, *what is*, in the interest of the truth, *what ought be*. That is to say the historical materialist unlike the theological idealist does not deny the existing reality and unlike the positivist idealist does not affirm it metaphysically. Rather, for the historical materialist, the reality is something to be comprehended and negated in a continued intergenerational and cross-generational process of transformation that takes us closer to a moment when freedom and therefore equality are not mere ideals but actual conditions of experience. That is the moment of conciliation between truth and reality, which can only be possible in a world where the real is not actualized on the basis of the negation of the rational. The historical materialist's knowledge (in terms of both historical awareness and revolutionary consciousness for historical transformation) is negative and gained negatively (through negating the dominant order). The idealist's realism will inherently impose submissiveness to the dominant whereas the historical materialist's realism will inevitably entail changing the reality. The idealist's realism leads to the conclusion that it is impossible to change the world. The historical materialist's realism, on the other hand, leads to the exact opposite conclusion: it is impossible to accept the world. This to say that because the existing state of affairs is irrational and, hence, inherently false, the only rational position is negativity.

From the idealist perspective, realism abolishes the horizons of possibility. In contrast, from the historical materialist perspective, some of what has been impossible so far can be realized today. Historically, all the material obstacles that render human emancipation impossible can and must be negated. This is what makes a historical materialist a revolutionary subject. Moving beyond nihilist idealism in all its theological, positivist, bourgeois, and empiricist forms is what makes this subject a postnihilist revolutionary.

Chapter 6

Critical Theory and the Margins

There is an irony that, when exposed, speaks to the utter irrationality within irrationality that characterizes the age of neoliberal capitalism. Namely, whenever the marginalized dare to speak of a world in which inequality is not the norm, they are accused of utopianism. By whom? Often—and here is the irony—by those who do not have an issue with mythical accounts of an afterlife world and other faith-based assumptions that contradict even the most elementary of the laws of physics and biology. However, the irony has been going on unnoticed thanks to the bourgeoisie's totalitarian domination of the means of knowledge production. Given this ideological hegemony, it is imperative for any genuine form of critical thought to seek a different mode of perception and theorization to deliberately and insistently focus on the negation of what is for the sake of what could be realized. That is precisely the forgotten essence of Critical Theory. From its origins in Marx's work to its official launching by Horkheimer, Adorno, and company, Critical Theory was an anti-philosophy philosophy, a negative theory aimed at negating the capitalist and racist order and problematizing the unspoken rules of domination. These stateless outsiders who refused to compromise in return for personal and financial security left us a school of thought that adamantly defies the prevalent order in favor of universal emancipation, which is inherent in the projects of the resistance advanced by the marginalized. In defense of this stance, and negativity as a philosophy of resistance, this chapter offers a new reading of Critical Theory. At the same time, it argues for expanding the potential scope of Critical Theory by enhancing its fidelity to the margins.

The Anti-Enlightenment Nature of Eurocentrism

Insofar as the enlightenment is a project of reclaiming individual autonomy, a project in which the human subject is recognized as a thinking being and a right holder, it has a unique universal significance. Its emancipatory potentialities are especially important for societies that have suffered under various forms of monotheist suppression. The European birthplace of the project does not make it any less universally claimable and defendable, just as the Mesopotamian birthplace of writing, laws, or mathematics does not make writing, laws, or mathematics any less universal or in any sense unique to the Mesopotamians. Contrary to the common culturalist assumptions advanced equally by right-wing Europeans, moral relativists, and religious fundamentalists, none of these projects, from the Ancient Mesopotamian ones to the modern European ones, even at the moment of their emergence let alone their prolong evolution, had been the exclusive accomplishment of an isolated group of people. To the contrary, if they have one thing in common in terms of their origins, it is the metropolitan nature of the social space that allowed for inclusivity in terms of both contributors and contributions. To put this very bluntly, with the historical heterogeneities and complexities implied (rather than omitted), there would not be Aristotle without Athens or Ibn Rushd without Andalusia. Also, there would not be Ibn Rushed without Aristotle or Aquinas without Ibn Rushd (also known by his latinized name, Averroes). There would not be the Renaissance without Aquinas or the enlightenment without the Renaissance. More importantly, Europe would still be in its Dark Ages without the role of the numerous Chinese inventions including agricultural techniques and tools, navigation tools such as compasses, advanced time measuring devices such as mechanical clocks, techniques and instruments of typing and printing, and so forth.

Today, can we even imagine how many more people in Europe and North America would be deprived of essentials including shelter and clothes without the Chinese and other Asian industrial supplies—add to that the Chinese key role in the democratization of computing machines and communication technology. Without Asian industrial mass production, one could easily imagine how devices such as laptops or cellphones would be luxuries like watches were in Europe's mid-nineteenth century, at best. In return, what is exactly the Western ruling groups' contribution to the betterment of the well-being of Asians and Africans? Robbery of raw materials (for the last five hundred years), labor exploitation on unprecedented scales, invention and support of contemporary forms of tribalism including nationalism and fundamentalism, and the invention, use, and dissemination of nuclear weapons are some examples of ongoing imperialist Western practices from which everyone in Africa and Asia has suffered in some way and to some degree. Of course, this does not mean the West's role in modernization should be reduced to these fatal, exploitive, and repressive categories; rather, the point I want to make is that in so far as modernity is an emancipatory project, it cannot be attributed exclusively and racially to Europeans in any reasonable or meaningful way.

The point of this argument is that despite these unmissable civilizational advantages of the Chinese model, Sinocentrism has never become a dominant ideology (even before but especially after) the Maoist communist revolution. If anything, this should be taken as further evidence for the egalitarian potentiality of the Chinese alternative. Furthermore, this prospect of egalitarianism speaks to the more genuine, yes, *democratic* characteristic of the Chinese model, as opposed to European-American so-called world order. The fact that Chinese historians and philosophers are not so obsessed with the production of self-congratulatory media does not make the Chinese contribution to human civilization any less essential. In terms of social psychology, Eurocentrism could be interpreted as a symptom of anthropological narcissism, yet in the age of commercialism, the age of the total dominance of the exhibition value, narcissism may come across as proof for both (metaphysical) soundness and (ontological) preeminence.

One of the most irrational phenomena of this age is the habitual projection of the racist, nationalist, and culturalist typography on historical projects that owe their very potential universalizability to the cosmopolitan openness of their places of emergence. Just as it would be absurd for Mesopotamians to claim cultural ownership of any of the great inventions of the Mesopotamian civilizations, it is absurd when Europeans claim cultural ownership of the enlightenment.

As noted in chapter 4, Baghdad ceased to be a center of civilization when it lost its cosmopolitan diversity, and in fact it even lost its respectability as a city when it claimed a nationalist identity. Similarly, Europe ceased to be the potential capital of the world the moment it racialized and culturalized its boundaries. Today, the refugees who risk their lives crossing deserts, mountains, mine fields, and seas are in fact, for better or worse, the most faithful adherents to the universal and progressive essence of the enlightenment while the European elites who pay oppressive regimes and groups to guard Europe's gates are the ones who are burying the prospects of progress alive. Yet, there is nothing new in this.

Let us keep in mind that the world's leading liberal democracy, the United States, typically spends more on defense than on higher education, and it is by far the most militarized state both geographically and historically.[1] Despite obvious cases of American aggression and endless American threats to other states, somehow the dominant liberal discourse in Western academia portrays the United States as a defender of democracy in the world. If anything, any objective assessment of global politics will conclude that totalitarianism is definitive of liberalism, at least in terms of today's actual state of affairs.

We need to take a step back from the deafening culture industry and at least consider some of the most relevant but indisputable facts. For instance, the rate of imprisonment in any country should be a clear indicator of the exercise of power by state institutions. Aggressions against other countries should be another indicator of anti-democracy, and there is no good reason for not considering a state's foreign relations when we want to gauge the democratic or undemocratic nature of that state. These major indicators matter even more in the case of a state that does not have any excuse for manufacturing weapons of mass destruction or exercising excessive power in international relations.

Let us go over few premises regarding the above criteria. In 2010 more than 1.6 million Americans were in American prisons (US Bureau of Justice Statistics, 2021). The number of American invasions and interventions of other countries places the United States at the very top of the list of aggressive states since the end of the World War II. The American arsenal of weapons of mass destruction is by far the highest in the world. Moreover, it is well known that the American government has supported some of the most violent and racist states in the world, including India, Pakistan, and Turkey, not to mention past regimes such as the Suharto regime in Indonesia and the Pinochet regime in Chile. When these factors are taken into account, it is absurd not to realize that the American world order is totalitarian even by the standard of the traditional definition of totalitarianism, which is "the unlimited exercise of power" (Curtis 1979).

Critical Theory and Emancipation

At least in the United States, but also in most of the West and other regions that are under the American hegemony, Marxism is arguably the only philosophy on which so many people have an opinion without bothering to read even a tiny portion of its vast body of written texts. Most of these "opinions" disturbingly suffer from sameness, compelling even a moderately critical observation to suspect that a regime of unthinking must be at work. The confidence with which first year college students as well as established scholars declare that Marxism/communism is unrealistic/utopian can only be interpreted as a symptom of a totalitarian ideological hegemony. Otherwise, how could so many people have a similar stance about a philosophy that, only counting its primary sources, is composed of tens of thousands of pages. One might be able to form a somewhat educated position about religion without having to read most religious texts, but the same is not true when it comes to a philosophical system for the obvious reason that philosophy is (or should be) a system of reasoning, and it follows that studying its representative texts is essential for taking a position about it.

The suggestion that Marxism is unrealistic or communism is utopian could, perhaps, be defended to a degree or another, but that defense could not be simply assumed if it is not there. Those who defend this fashionable opinion not only fail to offer any sound defense to justify their claim about Marxism being unrealistic or communism utopian, but they also seem to be at home with the most obvious examples of utopianism, which are religions. Somehow, equality is too unrealistic of a goal, but heaven, an afterlife world, and the theologically claimed universal justice are reasonable or at least widely acceptable objects of belief.

Marxism itself is precisely the philosophy that is capable of explaining this kind of irony. Put briefly, Marxism teaches that widely held beliefs and values and commonly adopted modes of perception are for the most part shaped by the relations of domination. That is to say, the dominant modes of belief do not explain but rather sustain social domination. No form of social domination could continue if it does not produce and normalize its own order as the rational, realistic, and moral order. By the same token, what arises as its opposition must be perceived as irrational, unrealistic, and/ or immoral. Truth is entirely sociohistorical and dependent on actual human beings, and none of the postmodernist areas and forms of critique would be imaginable without this main Marxist groundbreaking discovery (that truth is inherently a construction and knowledge could not be anything but a matter of production).

If truth is inherently a product of the dominant, and history is always the history of the dominant, how can emancipation even be articulated? Even if the time and space are somehow torn away from the institutions of the established order, how can the silenced, who are already deprived of the means of knowledge production and much more, produce such a philosopher? Even if that philosopher somehow, through some strange aline-ments of series of mistakes, appears in some forgotten corner, how could they possibly negate the unfreedom that has been structurally totalized even through the institution of language? Precisely because of the hopelessness, the materialist creation of hope becomes a matter of imperativeness for the silenced margins. To Walter Benjamin it is in fact a mission, and he admitted the messianic element, albeit as a historical materialist, as an uncompro-mising Marxist rebel against the existing order and the myths that sustain it. By being faithful to the excluded, by exploiting the state of emergency, the historical agent of the silenced pushes ahead with the struggle against the dominant.

Thus, the enlightenment even before the end of the French and Amer-ican revolutions was claimed by a new class of oppressors. At the same time, however, almost immediately its emancipatory, universalist core became the struggle of the marginalized, silenced, and enslaved. The Haitian Revolution was the first and arguably the truest revolution of the enlightenment. As Fernando Grüner argues, "If this revolution can be said to have 'enlight-ened the Enlightenment' in the Adornian sense, then we can also say that it revolutionized the (French) Revolution." (2020, 193). The freedom of the enslaved was immediately and violently opposed by both republics, the bourgeois heirs of the enlightenment. The Haitians were the universalists, and the French and American ruling groups were the tribalists. Similarly, today the victims of both Islamism and Euro-racism who refuse to give up their entitlement to their humanity, who refuse to become part of either camp of barbarianism or accept the culturalist division of the world, are the true adherences of emancipation.

In the realm of knowledge production, similarly, an anti-metaphysics philosophy in the margins of exiled groups and poor neighborhoods during times stolen from hunger and death was taking shape. Marxism is, in fact, an anti-philosophy philosophy in the sense that it emerges as a negation of the perpetual conditions of unfreedom. The moment history ceases to be the history of domination and the dominant, philosophy, from the Marxist point of view, loses every reason to exist. In other words, the very phil-osophical enterprise is a revolutionary project, an attempt to change the world, a project to rescue the enlightenment from the metaphysical abyss and the abyss of metaphysics. Critical theory, therefore, since its very Marx-ist beginning, has been a theory by the oppressed and for the oppressed. The oppressed as the only true universalist revolutionaries are compelled to either accept their eternal enslavement or own the enlightenment. Critical theory was in this sense a desperate attempt to fight for the emancipatory project. Its founders had to walk hopelessly against the barbarism at its most overwhelming moment. They were well aware of the magnitude of the hopelessness because they knew that the realm of oppression goes far beyond Italian Fascism and German Nazism. To them, the realm of oppression was the enlightenment itself. "Enlightenment is totalitarian," wrote Horkheimer and Adorno in one of their most daring polemics (2002, 4).

Then, they elaborate:

> That fate befell not only his philosophy, as the apotheosis of advancing thought, but enlightenment itself, in the form of the sober matter-of-factness by which it purported to distinguish itself from Hegel and from metaphysics in general. For enlightenment is totalitarian as only a system can be. Its untruth does not lie in the analytical method, the reduction to elements, the decomposition through reflection, as its Romantic enemies had maintained from the first, but in its assumption that the trial is prejudged. When in mathematics the unknown becomes the unknown quantity in an equation, it is made into something long familiar before any value has been assigned. Nature, before and after quantum theory, is what can be registered mathematically; even what cannot be assimilated, the insoluble and irrational, is fenced in by mathematical theorems. (Horkheimer and Adorno 2002, 18)

The crisis, therefore, is that the project of total emancipation itself has become a project of total oppression. The problem is not deception in terms of falsehood but the very modes of inquiry that are inseparable from the technologies of power. While liberalism bases its doctrines on the knowledge of politics, what passed through the liberal measures of autonomous thought undetected is a predetermined politics of knowledge. Since knowledge is a product, the only way in which hegemony could be accomplished is through an ideologically neutralized mode of production, and that is already put in place under capitalism (i.e., under the domination of the capitalist mode of production). By virtue of their standpoint, those who are located outside history and denied the basic conditions for life, whose mere survival becomes a struggle that sucks off their potentialities, are epistemically more capable of detecting the politics according to which knowledge is produced. That is to say, those who are in the position to problematize the politics of knowledge production are those who are pushed outside the totalitarian space and hardly manage to survive precisely because they are so marginalized. It follows that only a few survivors might be able to carry on a spark of the emancipatory project against all odds and by consistently seizing temporal and spatial fragments that fall from the continual states of emergency in which they live. The status of this few can best be described as a mistake within a mistake. They simply exist by mistake, but they existentially seize their state of existence and turn it into a political negation in the interest of the anti-totalitarian struggle. Such a spark is essential for the struggle against totalitarianism if for nothing else because its very momentary existence prevents the hegemonic from accomplishing its totalitarian end. The mistake that escapes the teeth of silencing elimination proves, at least to some other fellow outsiders as well as some insiders who are capable of perceiving/reading it, that there are other possibilities, that the total transparency in which everyone lives in fact amounts to total darkness, that what rules is indeed light but it is the blinding light of totalitarian space, a space in which nothing and nobody can hide, a space where everyone is different but difference is mass produced, and a space in which truth is positivistically quantifiable and pragmatically utilizable. Therefore, the doubly marginalized whose very existence is conditioned by and in the margins of times and spaces are the only hope for the survival of the universalist emancipatory project. Critical Theory was formed by a few such voices of the marginalized and for the marginalized.

In this particular sense, the Frankfurt School's Critical Theory never made it beyond its so-called first generation. To grasp the lost element, we need to go further than the liberal turn at the hand of the School's heirs in both New York and Frankfurt who more or less gentrified both the School as well as the Theory. In my view, one of the reasons that renders Critical Theory worth revisiting is its original negativity, which endured the political and institutional pressures of the American exile, not to mention the Nazi terror. The critical theorists were not prepared to settle for a false light in a world that was drowning in despair.

At the climax of the Nazi reign, Max Horkheimer and Theodor Adorno set out to write an extremely ambitious book addressing the question of humanity's "sinking into a new kind of barbarism," as opposed to "entering a truly human state" (2002, xiv). The task, as they soon realized was more or less impossible if for nothing else because the existing linguistic structures themselves are bound to reproduce hegemony. As Žižek states, "We 'feel free' because we lack the very language to articulate our unfreedom" (2002, 2). Even critique is bound to reaffirm the existing unfreedom unless the totalities of the systems of thought and the dominant institutions that sustain them also become objects of critique within a negative theory of society and knowledge. "In reflecting on its own guilt, therefore, thought finds itself deprived not only of the affirmative reference to science and everyday phenomena but also of the conceptual language of opposition," wrote Horkheimer and Adorno, adding, "no terms are available which do not tend toward complicity with the prevailing intellectual trends, and what threadbare language cannot achieve on its own is precisely made good by the social machinery" (2002, xv). Under total hegemony, we do not have even the linguistic capacity to articulate the ways in which we have been hegemonized. "In the bourgeois mode of production," Horkheimer and Adorno insist, "the denial is so total that it is no longer registered consciously" (2002, 149). This is a reminiscent to the ideology critique that emerges from what has become known as historical materialism. For instance, recall Marx's famous statement in the Preface to *A Contribution to the Critique of Political Economy*, "Just as one does not judge an individual by what he thinks of himself, so one cannot judge such a period of transformation by its consciousness, but, on the contrary, this consciousness must be explained from the contradictions of material life, from the conflict existing between the social forces of production and the relations of production" (2010a, 263). Objectively speaking, the norm for objective judgment itself is immersed in the material modes of production, so the challenge undertaken by Critical Theory is the likelihood of negation, the theoretical capacity to depart from the hegemonic by problematizing the prevalent modes of perception. Therefore, the critical theorists, including Marx and Engels, had no illusions about the deadly nature of the task and the impossibility of victory. Negation, nonetheless, was itself a theoretical goal ever more worthwhile.

What made Horkheimer and Adorno's undertaking especially challenging was the dominant expectation that imposes the use of the established language in terms of clarity, "objectivity," and so on (Horkheimer and Adorno 2002, xvi). The crisis Critical Theory challenges is not the alleged conflict between the enlightenment, as it is represented by positivism, and anti-enlightenment, unreason, faith, superstitions, and so on.[2] Rather, the crisis is precisely the existence of a union between those two worldviews, positivism and theology, (instrumental) reason and faith, bourgeois absolutism and absolutist metaphysics. That union has resulted in various forms of totalitarianism from social space to the discursive realms in the public sphere, and from governmentality to philosophy. Fascism is only a manifestation of this totalitarianism, and as such, genealogically, fascism is hardly distinguishable from the broader ideological elements that are built into the dominant mode of perception.

In such a world, the frame of reference is strictly limited by identitarianism, which is a one-dimensional mode of thinking that is inherently reductionist. Identitarianism aims to ultimately minimize all phenomena, physical entities, conscious agencies, and the world as such into simple dualities, which in turn are reduced to a smaller and smaller number of laws. Essentially, identitarianism is the production of sameness and continual realization of oneness. Such a world is naturally hostile to dialectical thinking. Dialectical propositions, theories, and thought are denied space or treated as heretical polemics at best. Again, notice how Marxism has been endlessly accused of utopianism, yet religious faiths, including beliefs in Disney-like other worlds, are spared from such an accusation. In fact, it is often the believers in heaven and hell and their respectful allies, whether politically conservative or liberal, who habitually and without a sense of irony accuse every communist proposition of being utopian, unrealistic, and so on. This phenomenon is an embodiment of the anti-emancipatory nature of the bourgeoisie's version of the enlightenment.[3] As ironic as the phenomenon may sound once one pays attention to it, it attests to my claim with regard to the totalitarianism that is sustained through a deep alliance between positivism and religiosity, which has rendered identitarianism dominant across the arenas of knowledge production.

Therefore, every conceptual negation, linguistic deconstruction, or dialectical deployment of thought is delegitimized from the outset. Prohibiting negativity only further normalizes the prevailing irrationality in the name of science, and myth in the name of enlightenment. Mythological systems play their ideological trick not by presenting themselves as myths, of course. To the contrary, their language is factual, as opposed to conceptual, affirming, as opposed to negating, and identitarian, as opposed to dialectical. One of the greatest contributions of Critical Theory is its discovery of what can and should be considered the foundation of ideology critique. That is the discovery of the *ideologicality* of all claims of objectivity. In this sense, only what is clearly fictional is nonideological. Here it is worth quoting Horkheimer directly:

> Every human way of acting which hides the true nature of society, built as it is on contrarieties, is ideological, and the claim

that philosophical, moral, and religious acts of faith, scientific theories, legal maxims, and cultural institutions have this function is not an attack on the character of those who originate them but only states the objective role such realities play in society. Views valid in themselves and theoretical and aesthetic works of undeniably high quality can in certain circumstances operate ideologically, while many illusions, on the contrary, are not a form of ideology. (Horkheimer 2002, 7)

In order to mystify the world, mythologies must speak in the language of facts, in order to darken minds, they have to pass through as revelations whose only aim is to enlighten us. In Horkheimer and Adorno's own words, "False clarity is only another name for myth. Myth was always obscure and luminous at once" (2002, xvii). To defy the mythical structures of the enlightenment, negative thought is crucial because "a true praxis capable of overturning the status quo depends on theory's refusal to yield to the oblivion in which society allows thought to ossify" (33).

Horkheimer and Adorno wrote the book in their American exile during what would be some of the darkest years not only personally for them and their relatives and friends but also historically for entire populations. The ultimate horror and suffering inflicted on the most marginalized and the utter irrationality of the capitalist order, of which fascism is only a manifestation, were precisely what made Horkheimer and Adorno so adamant to undertake such an almost impossible project and other projects that sought to diagnose the various historical, sociological, and psychological roots of the new barbarism. Other fellow émigrés, such as Pollock, Löwenthal, Marcuse, Fromm, and Bloch, also aimed at tackling the same question though using different and sometimes overlapping approaches. Unlike most intellectuals and scholars in the United States, they were not prepared to perceive the crisis within the dualist framework of liberalism versus fascism, or in the 1950s, democracy versus totalitarianism. It should go without saying that their rejection of such a clear-cut dichotomy does not mean they were uncertain about what is wrong or they were somehow compromising about certain phases of fascism, as some of Heidegger's liberal disciples had been. Rather, to them, such dichotomies were not clear cut at all. Only falsely can irrationality be represented by one pole of such a dichotomy. The false depiction implies both false solutions to ongoing crises and misleading suggestions about the future. The roots of fascism are deeper, and its horizons are broader, than what philosophers who habitually ahistorize ideologies have been prepared to realize. Its boundaries are blurrier than what identitarian and positivistic thought is capable of conceiving.

Even though Horkheimer and Adorno were living as refugees in the United States, the rising fortress of both capitalism and liberal democracy and the decisive power capable of tilting the balance of forces against Nazism, they announced both capitalism and liberalism guilty of the same irrationality, the same totalitarianism, of which fascism was an example, albeit with immediate and undeniable global effects. In fact, they found the bourgeois enlightenment as such guilty of both irrationality and totalitarianism. Thus, they titled their coauthored masterpiece *Dialectic of Enlightenment*. Of course, it should not escape anyone that "dialectic" already implies that the authors saw in the enlightenment also the viable source of rationality and emancipation. As anti-fascist and anti-capitalist Marxists, they were not anti-enlightenment per se. Like Marx, they were extremely critical of the bourgeois hijacking of the enlightenment. Thus, unlike anti-enlightenment intellectuals, such as romantics and theologians, they were not under the illusion of the plausibility of any redemption outside the enlightenment, outside reason, itself. Their grievance had nothing to do with any potential reluctancy or uncertainty in terms of choosing between reason and superstition. Of course, they were uncompromising about their rejection of all forms of idealism, whether represented by spirituality or nonmaterialist philosophies. They barely saw any need to argue for their rejection of spirituality and every other professed anti-enlightenment force.

The Oppressive Nature of Instrumental Rationality

In terms of practice, instrumental rationality, which is definitive of the bourgeois approach to science, strives to (1) *quantify everything* and (2) totalize power-utilitarianism. By quantifying everything, instrumental rationality eliminates not only aura but also the sphere of conception, especially in terms of the latter's negativity, and in doing so it renders dialectical thinking outdated. The world it depicts in its theory and imposes in its practice is a world free of contradictions with the maximum degree of flatness, a space for absolute efficiency, an object of flawless visibility and total administration. In short, the bourgeois mode of knowledge production both presumes and envisions the world as a single totalitarian space. It is a mode of production that is fundamentally reductionist. Its approach to nature as a realm ruled by a set of absolute laws and principles is not restricted to the natural sciences. Rather, it deploys the exact same reductionist assumptions to the social sciences as well simply because society, like nature, is assumed to be not only instrumentally quantifiable but also managerially controllable. This is precisely why social Darwinism, a major pillar of what would become fascism in the twentieth century, was effortlessly inferred from Darwin's evolution theory. At the end, in the bourgeois universe, knowledge is sought for the sake of controlling nature and engineering the societal development. Therefore, the bourgeois mode of knowledge production is inherently oppressive and totalitarian. By the same token the politics of the bourgeois state cannot be but biopolitics, and, in fact, it is also the perfect locus at which the reductionist fundamentalism of both the natural and social sciences are reunited.

In such a world, power and knowledge finally become one and the same. The space ensures the utilitarian application of power/knowledge without the need or reason for any possible separation between them. In such a world, everything is allowed precisely because difference is made impossible. No difference is possible because all the outcomes are already predetermined. All the conditions are controlled (without having to apply excessive force). There is no need for means of inspection, discipline, and control simply because policing is an indistinguishable feature of the social space itself. In effect, spatiality and history are reduced to eternally and absolutely defined dimensions, of plain surface and a leaner time. Thus, the ideal world of instrumental reason is a geometrical world, a world of plains defined by their geometrical borders. It is a world in which every subject perceives predetermined (directed) exhibition of imagery as events and events as imagery via hyperreal media. It is a space that resembles Plato's allegory of the cave, and the subjects resemble the prisoners in the allegory (Plato, 1992).

Instrumental reason's world is quantified so that knowledge lends itself immediately and pragmatically to power, and power, in turn, is translated into control seamlessly. Therefore, in the bourgeois-positivist ethos, knowledge qua power is the only useful and legitimate (i.e., scientific or objective) form of knowledge. Efficiency, infinite reproducibility, quantitative measurability, and the capitalist totality of value are already built into this form of knowledge before it is allowed to start its societal cycles. In other words, in the very process of knowledge production, within the dominant bourgeois mode of production, both the means of total administration and the end purpose of the totality of capital are already assumed. Thus, when the produced knowledge is released into the social realms, everyone from scholars and intellectuals to bureaucrats and professors, from poets and priests to weapon manufacturers and CEOs, merely consumes it if for nothing else because of their adoption of its frame of reference (i.e., because of having to play within the already determined semiological field). Totalitarianism does not determine what we say but how we speak. It does not eliminate the will to opposition, but it determines limits and forms of opposition. In fact, the presence of dissence in the social space and discursively (i.e., in the public sphere) is essential for an effective hegemony because that is the only way for the totalitarian regime to secure its democratic facade and thus remain legitimate in the eyes of the majority. Totalitarianism makes unfree individuals unable to realize that they are unfree.

From the bourgeois perspective, the perfect mode of knowledge production is the one that produces formula that can be stored and used by so-called artificial intelligence because this would make possible the total utilitarian efficiency without requiring any degree of understanding or even consciousness. Such a formula allows users/consumers to deploy the quantified and codified knowledge without needing to actually have or gain the knowledge, so to speak. At a zero cognitive scale, the total exploitation of the knowledge is guaranteed. That is to say, knowledge is produced to function purely as an instrument. Furthermore, unlike physical instruments, such as a hammer, a shovel, or a needle, it does not necessitate an intelligent interaction from the side of the subject to bring out its instrumentality.

Because management, governmentality, and total administration are already assumed prior to, during, and after the production of knowledge, totalitarianism is simply the normal formation of the bourgeois world. That is to say, in terms of both material and ideological production, totalitarianism is a condition of our experiences. Thus, totalitarianism is definitive of both the produced social space and the nature of subjective cognition. Neither our cognitive systems nor our imagination is capable of prefiguring an alternative, that is, an emancipated world, precisely because of the totalitarian hegemony. Emancipation, therefore, necessitates a dialectical theory that enables us to negate and conceptualize at the same time. With each negation, another space opens up, and from each newly formed space more horizons of possibility emerge, and so on.

In terms of theory, the bourgeois mode of scientific thinking aims to (1) *define everything including what it supposedly admits unknown* and (2) *minimize theories not only in terms of content but also in their numbers.* Within the bourgeois mode of science, the unknown is represented mathematically, and by doing so, the dominant imposes its own metaphysics in the form of epistemological premises, which are entirely fictional, thereby denying the viability of any logic other than its own absolute (il)logic. The prevailed rationality, therefore, is the rationality within an irrational framework. Because its metaphysics enjoys total hegemony, its absolutist logic is constantly at work. Even, and especially, positivist experts do not have the philosophical means to problematize the dominant logic. In fact, the fragmented attempts to criticize the system only end up further normalizing the system's logic as logic per se, and thereby reaffirming the dominant ethos qua not only the universal rationality but also as the definitive determinant of the reality as the only possible world. The bourgeois enlightenment therefore is nothing short of the cosmos insofar as the dominant, the bourgeoisiefied, perceive the cosmos according to such a metaphysical mode of perception.

Oneness, which is the ultimate goal of the bourgeois mode of *scientific conception of science*, is produced through multiple processes of imposing the utilitarian economy of knowledge production. Scientists of the bourgeois enlightenment have not been different than the Medieval philosophers and saints who took the singularity of frame of reference, metaphysics, as an unquestionable matter-of-factness. Even the most genius among them, such as Einstein and Hawking, have made that goal and desire clear in their remarks on the progress of scientific thinking. There is a tendency, as it were, to discover the law of all laws, the ultimate universal equation.[4]

Controlled Environment or Environments of Control

Horkheimer and Adorno write:

> Science stands in the same relationship to nature and human beings in general as insurance theory stands to life and death in particular. Who dies is unimportant; what matters is the ratio of incidences of death to the liabilities of the company. It is the law of large numbers, not the particular case, which recurs in the formula. Nor is the concordance of general and particular concealed any longer within an intellect which always perceives the particular as a case of the general and the general only as the aspect of the particular by which it can be grasped and manipulated. (2002, 66)

Then, they add, "science itself has no awareness of itself; it is merely a tool. Enlightenment, however, is the philosophy which equates truth with the scientific system" (66). This alone suffices to start comprehending why they consider the enlightenment totalitarian (4). The issue here is not the assumed rejection of metaphysics by science; rather, the problem is that the exact opposite is the prevalent case thanks to positivism. In other words, the problem is precisely positivism's reproduction of metaphysics. "Not only metaphysics but the science it criticizes is ideological, in so far as the latter retains a form which hinders it in discovering the real causes of the crisis. To say it is ideological is not to say that its practitioners are not concerned with pure truth" (Horkheimer 2002, 7).

Sociologically, the aggregate of the outcomes guaranteed by scientific methods constitute an environment of control whereby whatever does not confirm the empirically proven yet predetermined outcome/s is treated as an anomaly if not pathology. Ultimately, positivism's scientific controlled environments lead to social and political environments of control. Vulgar empiricism constructs a oneness, a universal unity, from its verified but fragmented truths. The construction of this metaphysics is conducted according to the bourgeois worldview. This is also to say vulgar empiricism through endless ideological state apparatuses aims to create a world that reflects its own metaphysics. In this sense, vulgar empiricism resembles religious fundamentalism. They both abide by a belief system that operates as the a priori truth. The manipulation of conditions is not a quality of the scientific experiment but rather it is the experiment itself. Then, the established truth, the outcome of the experiment, becomes a source of legitimation for manipulating the social reality even more. The society itself becomes a medium for reflecting the truth, an experiment with unlimited possibilities for monopoly until it reaches the point of factual immediacy. Every contradiction with the established truth is taken as a sign of error in the conditions, and therefore more manipulation is called for. Sometimes this translates into genocide as social engineering. Even during the first few decades of the twentieth century, the scientific establishment would not entertain the idea of research to invalidate "race." For race had already been deployed socially and politically in the form of slavery and colonialism. Thus, the space of scientific activity was determined around questions about racial categories. "Race" as a signifier continued to be falsely validated precisely through abandoning any actual examination of the notion itself. In other words, because "race" was already assumed ontologically, research findings were inevitably going to reaffirm it. The dominant mode of knowledge production in every age and society predictably naturalizes and eternalizes its own paradigms even if those paradigms are entirely fictional. Questioning the validity of race during the one hundred years or so prior to 1945 would have sounded like questioning the existence of, say, angels in the Dark Ages.

In a more direct sense, the very occupation of scientists was, and is, situated within a sociopolitically predetermined space. The question of (in) validation of "race" would not even occur to most scientists in Europe and the United States. Thus, all the relevant research could not have but further confirmed "race" regardless of the methods and conclusions of any number of research projects simply because those projects were premised on race. In the same manner, today questioning the conceptual validity of "culture" is not in any way part of the scholarship, and it also follows that whatever the research may be, it will only confirm the primacy of culture. Since the entire frame of reference is based on a false premise, all the "creditable" research will necessarily deepen the falsehood in the name of scientific research. To grasp this point it might be useful to come back to the argument after considering the following proposition: *wars are made, at least in today's world especially since the 1970s, because weapons are manufactured, not vice versa.* Likewise, culture is thought to be so definitive of the human societies because culturalism, the ideology of the dominant groups, is dominant in the world. In fact, in the case of "culture" the confusion is even greater because those who conduct relevant research rarely, if ever, address the what-ness of culture. Instead, they set out to describe subcategories of "culture." For instance, when the research question is something along the lines of "How does Ethiopian culture differ from Egyptian culture in terms of caring for elderly?" or "What are the characteristics of Tibetan culture?" the outcome will, as a matter of course, further confirm the paradigm of culture. The production of knowledge is one and the same as the mystification of the reality. It is the political production of ignorance. It obscures truth by providing false justifications for false truth claims. Therefore, education is literally the problem, not the solution. When students are taught to reproduce cultural talk, they are simultaneously prevented from perceiving even some of the most immediate aspects of the reality. For instance, by looking for answers to cultural questions, they pass over even the most obvious material conditions. This is why the paradigm of culture became dominant exactly during the same decades when the question of class gradually fell out of fashion. Falsehood, or its broader outcome, which is ignorance, is not just a matter of getting things wrong in an innocent contest of intelligences or a harmless game of perceptions. Rather, falsehood, as a product of the dominant mode of knowledge production, directly contributes to unfree-dom, exploitation, and violence. Marx's merciless critique of everything is, therefore, the only rational way of doing philosophy in an unfree world.

The social sciences have further obscured the totalitarian nature of the positivist version of the enlightenment. In their imitation of the pure sciences, they have become more fundamentalist. Moreover, the social sciences are more prone to prejudices because they are held to lower standards of proof in the first place. Add to that the fact that it is almost impossible to disprove whatever becomes a widely held assumption, doctrine, notion, or paradigm in the social sciences. For instance, how could we disprove the notion of "culture" among social scientists? It took us a world war to discredit the notion of "race," which was strongly defined on the basis of life sciences. In principle, it is easy now for a biology major at any American college to falsify the notion of race empirically. However, this time, instead of borrowing the concept from biology, social scientists promoted one of their own inventions, which is "culture," more or less as an effective alternative to "race," allowing for similar discrimination and hierarchicalization of human groups in the name of scientific authority. It is not uncommon, for instance, in anthropology departments to impose not only studying but also conducting so called ethnographic research on graduate students. Technically, the parameters at work in this kind of research methods are the continuation of the openly racist origins of anthropology in the nineteenth century. Even when "culture" was introduced on the basis of what was supposed to be an egalitarian thesis, that culture is not unique to Europeans and that all peoples have culture to falsify the dominant view that perceived most non-Europeans as savages, racism carried on uninterrupted. In fact, the notion of "culture" itself was quickly raced. What contributed to this was the simultaneous rise of nationalism (Balibar 1991b; Lentin 2014) and social Darwinism. The fathers of German nationalism, such as Herder (2002; 2004), Fichte (2008), and, to some degree, Hegel (2001), had already prepared the intellectual climate for the essentialization of culture, which, not surprisingly, was picked up by fascism. Today, neofascists are even keener than others to abide by the culturalist *dogma* (it would be inaccurate to call culturalism a hypothesis). Neofascists, for the most part, have dropped "race" and replaced it with culture, which is something impossible to discredit due to its fictional premises produced by the social sciences.

Thanks to the neoliberal version of diversity, which amounts to exclusion through inclusion, more often than not members of the anthropologized groups are encouraged to carry out such predetermined research, which further normalizes the prevalent Euro-racism. It is extremely common for graduate students who come from non-European backgrounds to carry out research on an aspect of the perceived culture of their own society of origin, and such research necessarily confirms the cultural presumptions by *scientifictionalizing* them, that is, by masking the assumed culturalist fiction with more scientific facades. In fact, often the supposedly researched society is not even considered a society because that would necessitate the recognition of a degree of sociological sophistication and a political space encompassing difference. Instead, what we commonly hear/read about is "community" when it comes to the non-European and non-Europeanized geography.

Today, culturalism is the dominant form of idealism, which in turn is the dominant framework of knowledge production. Notice how many social scientists from top American universities tend to assume the answer to any question that has to do with, say, social forms of violence in Afghanistan, such as those related to gender oppression, or forms of political violence in Afghanistan, such as those related to civil war, lies in the Afghan cultural realm.[5] That is idealism at its purist. A materialist consideration would, to the contrary, start by looking at the life conditions of people to understand everything else, including cultures or prevailing forms of violence. This is not to say that the causal relationship is the reversed formula; rather, the materialist approach simply excludes false premises that are themselves rooted in the dominant ideology, which is itself maintained through social relations of power.[6]

One would think the expert would, if nothing else, take a look at the per-capita average income in Afghanistan before trying to enlighten us about the cultural obscurities that supposedly constitute the Afghan reality. One would think the expert would look at the condition of the most essential needs in a North African society, say, before diving into Islamic theology and so-called culture as if the "Muslim" has a cognitive system uniquely rooted in Islam. Thanks to such experts, the American foreign policy in the region from Afghanistan to North Africa has always been chaotic. Yet, even after the disastrous failure in both the Iraq and Afghanistan wars, somehow social science departments, including political science, do not seem to be prepared to shoulder any of the responsibility or take part of the blame. In a non-idealist world of knowledge production, as a matter of course, an association such as the American Political Science Association (APSA) would perceive any of these disastrous failures of American foreign policy, from Vietnam to Afghanistan, from North Korea to Chile, as a crisis of the prevailing methods, theories, schools, and pedagogies of political science in the United States. The American officials, including those in charge of the armed forces, are so hopelessly immersed in culturalism, they seem to be unable to take into account some elementary facts about a human being anywhere. The American army in Iraq, for instance, was so focused on the so-called Iraqi or Arab culture (often used interchangeably), they so badly neglected the basic human dignity of the people in Iraq, that within three years most of the country became a war zone for them after they had been received with substantial support from parts of the population and without much resistance anywhere in the country. The *Soldier's Handbook to Iraq* includes informative maps and statistics about Iraq and its population, but it is centered around the cultural information. In that context, it includes bizarre pieces of advice for the American soldier deployed to Iraq, such as, "Do not show any type of interest in an Arab woman or female members of an Arab family. Do not photograph them, stare at them or try to speak to them." "**Do Not**," the handbook emphasizes, "stare at an Iraqi woman or maintain eye contact with them" (1st Infantry Division n.d., 3–2, emphasis from original). Then, it warns the American soldier, "do not touch their palm and do not kiss her [sic] hand" (3). In these propositions, notice the utter misogyny, which might pass undetected due to the racist/culturalist normalization advanced discursively and internalized ideologically thanks to alleged multiculturalist education, which is tolerant but only after it inherently essentializes the Other. Again, Zîzêk is among a few European thinkers who noticed that the liberal West tolerates the Other only "insofar as this Other is not really other" (2008b, 41). In the very act of exhibiting cultural respect to this non-other Other, the Other is in fact dehumanized (148).

The tolerated Other, in other words, is an Other who does not exist outside the culturalist mind. The real Other, the person, the human, the right holder, who, qua a human being according to liberalism's fundamental doctrine is entitled to universal rights, is in fact denied ontological recognition, let alone political respect. In the name of cultural education, the culturalized is completely denied any sense of personhood while the culturalizer both implicitly and explicitly claims ownership of universal values of human equality and liberty. This speaks to liberalism's illiberal and Eurocentric core because through its very exclusive and idealist claim of universal liberty it undermines both universalism and freedom. Like Islam or Christianity, in practice, liberalism is exclusionary not despite but because of its claim of universalism. Chinua Achebe puts it very well when he states, "To suggest that the universal civilization is in place already is to be willfully blind to our present reality and, even worse, to trivialize the goal and hinder the materialization of a genuine universality in the future" (2000, 91). It is not that Achebe would oppose "a universal civilization," but the basic fact that we cannot afford to deny is that such civilization "is nowhere yet in sight" (104). This is precisely the point Mahatma Gandhi tried to make when an English journalist in London asked what he thought of "Western civilization" and he replied, "I think it would be a good idea" (qtd. in Higgs and Smith 2007, 58).

Such idealist forms of universalism are inherently contradictory because they are based on moralist (factually false) premises that universalize discrimination. Therefore, liberalism's enterprises for liberation, like Islamic and Christian political missions for enlightenment, cannot be but imperialist. Since the Other's status is perceived as something to be politically liberated, spiritually enlightened, or conditionally tolerated, the subject who does the Othering is certainly tribalist, illiberal, and anti-universalist while the Othered may or may not be tribalist, illiberal, and anti-universalist, depending on each particular movement and circumstance. There are certainly many Afghan and Iraqi jihadi movements who, by virtue of being Islamist, hold imperial and anti-universalist worldviews, but bear in mind there are also many Afghan and Iraqi anti-Islamist movements composed of women and men who are engaged in a daily existential struggle in defense of universalism and liberty and against the Islamist project of universal discrimination. Ironically, while universal discrimination is characteristic of only the far right in the Third World, including places where the social fabric and societal progress have suffered extreme disruption due to poverty and wars, in the West the commonly held views by the center, the right, and even many on the left is universal discrimination in the form of culturalism. If absolute relativism is taught in Islamic schools in Afghanistan, Pakistan, Iraq, Iran, and Somalia, in the liberal democracies it is taught across the board, in public, private, secular, and religious schools. Thus, when it comes to the essentialization of culture and culturalization of human societies, Khamenei and Judith Butler hold similar views. Indeed, both of them perceive the extreme far right as the legitimate representative of a Muslim or an Arab society.[7]

As someone who lived in Iraq for three decades and is fluent in the common languages in the country, I am certain one would be considered mentally challenged if one expressed "excellence" as the *Soldier's Handbook to Iraq* advises, "with open palms toward the person" or "OK" by "touching the outer edge of one's eyes with the fingertips"(3) although the latter gesture might be interpreted, as anywhere else, to indicate that one is both-ered by a strange body in one's eye! Luckily for Iraqis, the *Handbook* also includes reasonable pieces of advice such as, "DO NOT: Patronize or talk down to an Iraqi, even if he does not speak English well" (3–8)—as if in some "cultures" it is alright to patronize and talk down to people! Overall, the cultural education reads more like information for learning about the nature of a particular species. For instance, there are certain ways to handle deferent animals. Whether one wants to domesticate an animal or hunt it, it is useful to know the collective nature, body language, and so on, of that animal in its natural environment. That is precisely how the anthropolo-gized, culturalized, and essentialized Other is assumed to be.

Therefore, the knowledge production, including research methods, pedagogy, and premises, merely confirm the racist prejudices, some of which are three hundred years old, while the terminology could be traced back to the nineteenth century or the post–World War II era when "race" for the most part was replaced with culture and ethnicity depending on the discursive register, context, discipline, social settings, and so on (Essed 1991; Wright 1998; Lentin and Titley 2011). Culturalist social scientists today continue to reproduce the reality racist scientists helped produce and repro-duce for more than two centuries. In controlled environments, the scientific system discovers its truths, and in environments of control it produces a reality that reflects those truths. The social sciences have further reduced the process whereby the induction of truth from reality and the reproduction of engineered reality take place simultaneously.

After the French Revolution, it became clear that religion did not stand a chance of winning the war against the enlightenment. The more decisive conflict, however, was taking place within the enlightenment camp in terms of both philosophy and politics. The enlightenment rejected mythology but did not move quite beyond it thanks to the bourgeoisie's triumph in Europe. In many ways, the enlightenment was bound to reproduce mythology unless the emancipatory project was taken into its ultimate conclusion by abolish-ing all the institutions of oppressive power including class and patriarchy. Horkheimer and Adorno write:

> In short, enlightenment turned against the bourgeoisie as soon
> as that class, as a system of rule, was forced to suppress those
> it ruled. By virtue of its principle, enlightenment does not stop
> short at the minimum of belief without which the bourgeois
> world could not exist. It does not render to power the reliable

services which had always been performed for it by the old ideologies. Its antiauthoritarian tendency, which communicates, if
only subterraneously, with the utopia contained in the concept
of reason, finally made it as inimical to the established bourgeoisie as to the aristocracy, with which, indeed, it lost no time
in forming alliances. Ultimately, the antiauthoritarian principle
necessarily becomes its own antithesis, the agency opposed to
reason: its abolition of all absolute ties allows power to decree
and manipulate any ties which suit its purposes. (2002, 73)

With the rise of the bourgeoisie to power, the enlightenment was
utilized as an anti-emancipatory enterprise. As Horkheimer writes, "Bourgeois thought begins as a struggle against the authority of tradition and
replaces it with reason as the legitimate source of right and truth. It ends
with the deification of naked authority as such (a conception no less empty
of determinate content than the concept of reason), since justice, happiness, and freedom for mankind have been eliminated as historically possible
solutions" (Horkheimer 2002, 72). From the bourgeois point of view, the
democratization of politics had to be restricted in ways that would prevent
the otherwise inevitable and obvious egalitarian outcomes across societies.
While it has become the norm to accuse "the masses" for the rise of reactionary and oppressive movements, it was the bourgeois elites who stood
diametrically against the enlightenment's project of universal emancipation,
and in fact mapped such political and human geographies that are structured
around unprecedented and unimaginable inequalities. The masses did not
invent nationalism. Bourgeois European philosophers, especially the German
romantics such as Fichte and Herder, did. It was European elites, not masses,
who enslave nearly half of the African population. The division of Africa into
colonies to be robbed and exploited was similarly a bourgeois imperialist
plan. Finally, normalizing a world of inherently oppressive entities, nation-
states, was a bourgeois project par excellence. In every stage of turning the
enlightenment into barbarism, including the fascist enterprises, the masses
became the object of intensive bourgeois ideological campaigns to mobilize
them and recruit them in wars. Philosophers, scientists, poets, musicians,
and religious authorities made those ideological campaigns possible. The
same thing is true for every nation state that was created in the former
colonies. Namely, national elites conducted ideological campaigns to create
and institutionalize social inequality in the name of national sovereignty. The
masses who were supposedly sovereign now immediately became the objects

of new campaigns by the national bourgeoisie to mobilize and brutalize them, replicating the colonial and fascist experiments endlessly.

The Haitian Revolution was in fact decisive for determining the fate of the enlightenment project as what it claimed to be in its clearest moment of philosophical and historical expression, as a universalist project of freedom, the triumph of the human subject over all the institutions that enslaved her, whether mentally, socially, or politically. The suppression of the Haitian Revolution at the hand of the official heirs of the enlightenment was the first fallback of the enlightenment into its opposite, the abyss of irrational rationality, universal discrimination, and absolutist relativism, which would reach its maturity in fascism by the end of the second decade of the twentieth century. Yet not all hope was lost. In Europe itself, the newly risen dominant class faced two decisive moments, either of which could have saved the world, including Europe, from the long fascist chapter. The 1848 revolutions across the continent of Europe and, albeit more desperately, the 1871 Commune Revolution in Paris were the most recognizable moments of rescuing the enlightenment project in the century. The subjugation of the continent of Africa during the last two decades of the nineteenth century and the first half of the twentieth should be seen as the ultimate murder of the enlightenment at the hands of the European ruling groups. The enlightenment became a totalitarian project of unprecedented barbarism. By the end of the 1930s, with or without religion, fascism had succeeded in turning modernity into an anti-enlightenment project and the scientific system of experimentation into an anti-modernist scheme for engineering barbarism and manufacturing genocide. Fascism continues under new names and flags, and the enlightenment is yet to be saved from the abyss its racist claimers and fanatic enemies have actualized. The confident representatives of instrumental reason who speak authoritatively in the name of science have more intellectual kinship with the theologically licensed enemies of science than what either side seems to realize.

The bourgeoisie's diminution of reason to instrumental rationality had provided the most essential climate for fascism. That is to say, regardless of the various moral perspectives of the bourgeois groups, including the bourgeois philosophers and politicians, the capitalist mode of production as a matter of inevitability must reduce reason to instrumental rationality alone just as it reduces the laborer to her labor. The more extreme the reductionism, the better, in terms of the ultimate goal of the creation and accumulation of surplus value (i.e., capital). Also, keep in mind that under capitalism, by definition, capital is the ultimate source of power. Capital can be converted into every other source of power including social privileges and political influences, but the reverse is not always true, which reaffirms the proposition that capital is power in its most concentrated and universal form under capitalism. Therefore, instrumental rationality both as form and essence can best be described as technique. Technique has functionality but not consciousness. Installed within a technological framework, it could function independent of not only human purposes but humans as such. Technique, in other words, is rationality reduced into pure instrumentality for the purpose of maximizing the efficiency of production. Thus, within a utilitarian world framed by instrumental rationality, technology, as a system of techniques designed and operated for reaching specific outcomes, is totalitarian independent of the morality and intention of its inventers and beneficiaries. Since the ultimate goal against which efficiency of any technique and technology is measured is the purest form, or the utility, of power, fascism is the inevitable outcome of the bourgeoisie's instrumental rationality.

A technologically organized institution, such as the state, is far more totalitarian than its non-technological equivalents. For technology, within the framework of capitalism, is essentially the utilitarian formula of power. It is a formula that maximizes the efficient use of power and minimizes everything else that goes into the production. The panopticon is the classical example. In the Panopticon the maximum number of inmates can be policed (i.e., made feel that they are watched constantly) using the minimum number of inspectors, which could be one or even zero simply because the inmates are completely deprived of the ability to verify the presence or absence of people in the inspection tower. The panopticon, therefore, is the embodiment of a utilitarian technology of power that is invented by instrumental rationality. What is produced by that technology is a social space that is, along with its users, fully subjected to the gaze of power (Foucault 1980, 151; 1995, 202–10; 2008, 67; Ahmed 2019d, see chapter 3).

Knowledge aimed at materializing technique essentially serves the utility of power. The unlimited exercise of power is inherent in the technologies of power, so the transition to fascism is not a qualitative transformation. The particularity of fascism in its various ideological and organizational forms has to do with the angle from which unlimited power is exercised. For instance, given the extreme exclusionary tendency of fascist movements, the internal Othered other could be subjugated by the police apparatuses more openly, collectively, and rigorously than the members of, say, the racial or religious majority. A concentration camp with gas chambers is an enterprise of social engineering, and most of those who take part in running it are merely "doing their jobs." Ultimately, no single person could be held responsible for the enterprise in its totality simply because the operation of isolation and elimination of the condemned is conducted by the mechanical function of the system. Obviously, we do not want to exempt anyone who works in such a place from full responsibility for the particular role they play whether or not they comprehend the larger picture and their role within the system's mechanism.

The problem arises when we move on to the stage of determining actual individual liability. For instance, are we ready to blame the Nazis who were not aware of the overall operation of the Nazi establishment? In a Nazi concentration camp, take for instance anyone from the guards to the workers who had not known that where they worked was or would ever be called a "concentration camp." How can we determine the ways in which this guard or worker is more criminal, less innocent, more immoral, or less moral than those who work in other prison systems? It seems a person's possession of a comprehensive picture (of what takes place as a whole and the way in which their work is utilized within the immediate technique and the broader technology that causes suffering for other human beings) would necessarily make a difference in determining the degree of their liability. Of course, then there are other details regarding the person's willingness, ability, and efforts to obtain the necessary knowledge. Put briefly, it is only reasonable to affirm that we are responsible for our deeds, including the mechanical contexts and instrumental utilities of those deeds. In other words, the common excuse of "I was just doing my job" or "I was merely executing orders" cannot exempt a human being from liability. That is to say, it is everyone's ethical responsibility to learn about the fuller picture in which their jobs, deeds, votes, and so forth are situated and utilized.

The problem is that in a world so deeply shaped by the division of labor to the narrowest possible micro levels and managed by gigantic systems of administration, technologies of power, and mechanisms of exchange, it is hard to see how anyone would reasonably be able to obtain a picture accurate and comprehensive enough to enable her to realize the consequences of her work and thus determine the relevant political and moral implications. A mine worker could very well be involved in part of the long process that ends with the production of a deadly weapon that, in turn, will be used for systematic elimination of a certain population on the other side of the world. If we make the picture actually comprehensive and somewhat accurate, we realize the same thing could be said about a mathematics teacher, a cook, a bus driver, and so on, simply because the dictating framework of our lives and knowledge has instrumentalized us in such a totalitarian way that renders reasonable liability, freedom of choice, and autonomous thinking virtually impossible. As we compete for ripping away whatever possible from the value created by our labor or other nameless and faceless people's labor, we actively participate in operating the global machine that imposes utter passivity on each one of us. This is the world of instrumental reason and the unlimited power of capital. It is the universal framework that instrumentalizes and contextualizes everything from science to poetry, from intellectual curiosity to spiritual mysticism, from social institutions to aesthetics.

The ability to problematize, conceptualize, and articulate the scale of the totalitarianism and depict the depth of our unfreedom is the essential condition for stepping toward the horizon of universal emancipation. The totalitarian hegemony invests in the actualized alienation and hopelessness in the form of the happiness industry, which simply perpetuates the cycle of unhappiness and consumption. In the meantime, as we "merely do our jobs" under different local and regional names and with various ideological contents, fascism continues to rise.

Epilogue

Fascism with a Thousand Faces

One hundred years ago, in the aftermath of the World War I, fascism began to emerge in Europe. Simultaneously, and at the other end of the spectrum, there was a popular cosmopolitan will to bring about an egalitarian world free of imperialism, colonialism, and class-based social exploitation. Most societies that had just left behind the rule of emperors were at a crossroad between regression into a tribal space now defined as nationalism or progression toward the birth of a cosmopolitan world in which all identities could be equally housed without discrimination. The conflict between the cosmopolitans and the chauvinists still continues and takes new forms. Now we are standing at a crossroad strikingly similar to what happened one hundred years ago, but it seems there are fewer believers in cosmopolitan egalitarianism. Unless this changes, the rise of fascism could expand over generations and inflict irreparable damage on life on the planet as such.

Today, resisting the rise of fascism is not merely a political question, in the narrow sense of the word. Rather, it has serious implications for those who are part of the regime of knowledge production. We are living a decisive historical moment at which the world is standing on its head, and it will inevitably fall either to the left or the right. While we have many indicators suggesting that it is falling to the right, as always educators and other opinion makers can and do play crucial historical roles in terms of what tomorrow's reality would look like. Granted there is a rise of exclusionary movements across different parts of the world including large and powerful nation-states such as India and the United States, but what we do not hear about is the voices of the world's marginalized (simply because they are marginalized). Most textbooks and news agencies, historians and journalists, political scientists and politicians echo the dominant voices and worldviews thereby further drowning the voices of the marginalized. Thanks to the nationalist ethos and intelligentsia, it has become a habit in the public sphere, including the academy, to use a country's name in reference to (a) the government in power, (b) the state, and (c) the population, all at the same time as if they, a, b, and c, were one entity. "Russia," for instance, is typically used to refer to the ruling regime, the nation-state that is the Russian Federation, Russian elites, and/or the population that live in the vast territory called Russia (including the vast majority who are silenced and oppressed by the Putin regime and its and social and political allies). The same goes for China, India, Iran, Nigeria, Brazil, and so forth. The ease with which the many references of each such nouns are interchanged is indicative of the irrationality of the mode of perception that is prevalent thanks to the elites who run the ideological apparatuses of nation-states.

"The reality" is the elites' discursive depiction of the world, and that system of representation structurally perpetuates falsehood, partiality, and irrationality. Therefore, the natural starting point of critical theory advanced on behalf of the marginalized is the point of total negation. The given is incomplete, irrational, and distorted, so negating it is imperative. The normal frame of reference is ideologically tilted, so the very linguistic patterns, even on levels that are below sentence structure, must be problematized. It is not that there is no truth, as some nihilists like to claim, but the truth is a matter of production and presentation followed by endless cycles of reproduction and representation. Critical theory's intervention should negate representations and question their respective frames of signification where the ideological distortions are obliquely built into the operational rationality. Ultimately, through total negation, the critical theorist's systematic analysis should be able to reach a point at which the regime's sensory perception become a subject of problematization. This is the only possibility we have for de-normalizing the dominant mode of perception prior to the historical point at which the mode of production at large, in both material and ideological realms, will have altered. At the same time, the negative intervention to problematize the dominant modes of perception become an effective factor in the historical transformation from the current mode of production to a nonexploitive one. This is also the emancipatory capacity of critical reason. More to the point, through unmasking the normalized, voicing the silenced, de-naturalizing the naturalized, critical reason is able to fracture the iron system of instrumental rationality, and from the faults the irrational increasingly flows out exposing the mythical nature of the prevalent order. The reality and truth will then start to enter a new relationship. This amounts to re-educating the educated via helping them to unlearn norms that are falsely rationalized and structures that are socially naturalized. Such a re-education, in turn, is an imperative in the process of social emancipation.

Without such a principle of negativity, whether theories or pedagogies call themselves critical or not, whether institutions and constitutions are considered democratic or not, the produced knowledge is necessarily part of the dominant groups' totalitarian regime of truth, and, as such, they actively partake in perpetuating oppressive social relations structured on the basis of privilege and marginalization. Then, when the bourgeoisie demolishes the wealth on which the petty bourgeoisie has situated itself, capitalism gives way to an abrupt rise of fascism. Needless to say, the academy's continued refusal to deploy the term fascism to denote the rising exclusionary movements will not prevent those movements' increasing violence and destruction from taking place. In fact, forms of denialism, apology, and bad-faith optimism will only contribute to the lack of immunity against fascism and thus the weakening of anti-fascist democratic action.

Whatever the shortcoming of the American liberal democracy may be, its decline will have catastrophic effects on democracy everywhere. The fall of the state into the hands of exclusionary and illiberal forces that are openly and militantly antagonistic to the very idea of democratic participation, representation, institutions, and practices is something that will harm everyone and every prospect of egalitarianism and peace even on local levels. Such a fallback will bring about too much violence before the society could have a chance to create new emancipatory ways out of extremism.

In their *Prophets of Deceit* (first published in 1949), Löwenthal and Guterman argue that the American fascist agitator does not follow a specific ideology but instead focuses on stirring feelings of persecution among the members of the ingroup (2021; also see chapter 2 of this book). That means when fascism takes over, it will not necessarily be identified as such. It follows that fascism can always be denied even after it takes over. While keeping in mind that the Nazis had already borrowed a great deal from the ruling elites in the United States in terms of the latter's treatment of native Americans and African Americans, it is crucial to emphasize that American fascism even in the 1930s and 1940s had an extremely different form than Italian and German fascism. In the 1940s, Löwenthal and Guterman noted the adapted formula and adaptable nature of American fascism. In that regard, the following passages are worth reproducing here:

These preliberalistic and revolutionary elements of the fascist appeal in Europe served to mask the actual meaning of the movement. In practice Nazi totalitarianism was no more feudal than it was socialist. Its break with contemporary society took place only on the cultural and ideological level; the old liberalistic values were ruthlessly pushed aside for the needs of an industrial war machine. Old forms of economic and social coercion were perpetuated and strengthened. The American agitator, however, has no preliberalistic tradition on which to fall back; he does not find it expedient to pose as a socialist, and he dares not explicitly repudiate established morality and democratic values. He only indirectly and implicitly assumes the mantle of charismatic leadership. He works, by necessity rather than choice, within the framework of liberalism.

Study of our themes shows that this limitation does not prevent him from conveying the principal social tenets of totalitarianism to his audience. The themes point to the disintegration of existing institutions, the perversion and destruction of democracy, the rejection of Western values, the exaltation of the leader, the reduction of the people to regimented robots, and the solution of social problems by terroristic violence. The American agitator shows that manipulation of people with a view to obtaining their conscious or unconscious adherence to his movement need not take the detour of preliberalism or perverted socialism; that the psychological attitudes and social concerns that flow from the crisis of liberal society provide a sufficiently fertile soil for the growth of anti-democratic tendencies. It is as though the American agitator had evolved a method of directly converting the poisons generated by contemporary society into the quack remedies of totalitarianism; he does not need to resort to pseudofeudal or pseudosocialist labels. His themes could be transplanted to another country, much more easily than corresponding Nazi slogans could be transplanted to the United States. The mythical notion of the pure-blooded Nordic Aryan German superman would have to undergo many profound changes before becoming an effective appeal in this country, but the agitator's Simple Americans could be used in other countries as Simple Germans, or Simple French, or Simple Britishers, and so on. One is tempted to say that the American agitation is a

standardized and simplified version of the original Nazi or fascist appeals. Because the American agitator dispenses with such
secondary labels, his methods of appeal are also more universal
in scope, and are not bound to any specific national tradition
or political situation. Despite his professions of Americanism,
not a single one of his appeals refers to concerns of situations
specific to the United States. The feelings that he stirs are in no
sense limited to this country, for the social abscesses on which
his invectives thrive can be found in any modern industrialized
society. (2021, 153–54)

The American version of fascism is more flexible in terms of its capacity for allowing discursive reappropriation and ideological remodeling than
(both old and new) European versions. Obviously, American fascists have
always needed to establish a discourse not so tidily linked to claims about
ancient history or blood and soil, which at least partly explains the overall
minimalist specifications of American fascism. A distinguishing aspect of the
American formula is the strong presence of libertarian themes including the
hostility toward so-called big government. It might come across is paradoxical that many libertarians are attracted to Trumpism, but if we investigate
the history of their type of hostility toward the state, their present illiberal,
and overall fascist, tendencies become less puzzling. The American libertarians were antagonistic toward the Union's abolitionist intervention. Put
plainly, many anti-abolitionists argued that the state has no right intervening
in or limiting (White) Americans' right to property, and of course enslaved
individuals were considered mere property by the anti-abolitionists and the
confederates (for more on this see Losurdo 2015).

Trump was (and might come back as) an optical illusion. In fact, if
anything, in terms of personal inclinations toward war policies, he was less
aggressive than most of his predecessors, including Obama. The danger is
in what he represents and the forces that might be empowered through his
presidency. What Trump represents is the real fascist danger. He represented
and continues to represent a rising *mobomass* movement that is arguably
the most fascistic compared to any sizable part of the constituencies of
any former American president at least since Nixon. Like the vulgar facade
of everything in Trump's world, his personal shallowness is a mere front,
behind which what takes place is anything but a joke. Behind Trump there
are numerous White supremacy demagogues like Steve Bannon, right-wing
militias like the Proud Boys, bourgeois tycoons like Sheldon Adelson, and

mobomassdividuals prepared to go violent like Patrick Wood Crusius. The Biden victory in the 2020 elections will, arguably, end up meaning little more than the last chapter before the fascist takeover. Since Ronald Reagan and George H. W. Bush, the Republican Party has consistently moved toward the right. The far right in the government and the streets made it clear that they are prepared to unleash total terror even against their own allies who do not support a terroristic takeover. Let us also remember that in 2020 Trump votes increased by more than eleven million compared to the votes he got in 2016 (CNN 2021). About half of American voters are Trump *followers*.[1] These include militant fascist groups. While it of course matters that those in the other half of the American population are not Trump followers, we need to bear in mind that the actual impact of extremism tends to exceed the voting ballots and democratic institutions. Not to mention the fact that it takes a couple hundred well-organized fanatics to take over a town of ten thousand peaceful residents.

The implications of these basic considerations should cause serious concerns with regard to the imminent rise of fascism in the United States. A common objection is that most of those Trump voters/supporters are not fascists but just frustrated working class members who themselves are disadvantaged and feel betrayed by the political elite in Washington, DC. What such objectors do not realize is that the above description applies to most of the supporters of any rising fascist movement. To use the concept that I developed in chapter 3 of this book, the social backbone of a fascist movement are the *mobomasses*, people who are *mobomassified* by right-wing demagogues and agitators to defend, whether knowingly or unknowingly, the interests of the bourgeoisie. This is true in the cases of Bolsonaro's, Modi's, Khamenei's, and Erdogan's supporters as well. In fact, this was the case even for Hitler's followers in the 1930s.

On August 4, 2019, hundreds of Latin American immigrant workers were arrested in their workplaces in Mississippi just one day after the El Paso mass shooting that targeted Latin Americans as a political act of White supremacy. What is no less alarming is the fact that the mass arrest of the Mississippi immigrant workers, even in such a context, did not result in nationwide anti-government protests of a significant size. Let us recall that what has become known as the Night of Broken Glass, the first nationwide violent on attack on Jews, didn't make enough Germans upset enough to stop Hitler. We should have the courage to realize that the fascist chapter has already started. The Biden victory does not translate even to a temporary halt on the rise of fascism simply because the fascist fronts will use the time to reorganize, recruit, and prepare for the next, and maybe ultimate, takeover. It should be certain by now that the liberal elites who systematically acted as if Trump was the only problem share a great deal of the responsibility for the rise of fascism.

During the 2016–2020 Trump administration, mass arrests of immigrant workers, detention and separation of Latin American children in military camps, and the use of the military against peaceful demonstrations, not to mention open dissemination of racist beliefs, were tested frequently in the United States, repeatedly proving that there is neither civil society willingness nor institutional mechanism to legally prevent such practices. Therefore, the ultimate loss of the freedoms that are taken for granted under the American democracy could be just a matter of time.

What happened between November 3, 2016, and January 6, 2021, and given Trump's behavior throughout the term of his presidency and the fact that he received over seventy-four million votes in the 2020 presidential elections, suggests the following:

1. Sexual assaults are no longer scandalous enough to have serious consequences and future presidents could be given a degree of implicit impunity against persecution for issues related to sexual assault against women.

2. Science and the scientific authorities, including those appointed by the state officials, are subjected to the leader's judgment.[2]

3. The deployment of highly misleading fabricated information and news is justified for the purpose of maintaining or seizing power.

4. Loyalty to the leader has priority over respect for laws, public institutions, democratic practices including elections, and all the social contracts on which the state was founded including the constitution.

5. Everyone, including the vice president, may be subjected to mob violence if they do not continually prove their unconditional allegiance to the leader regardless of everything else including laws, democratic practices, and protocols.

6. The use of armed forces against movements of dissent is deemed acceptable.

7. Depriving refugees from their fundamental human rights is deemed acceptable.

8. The members of the president's family may be given decisive roles in both national administration and foreign policy.

9. The leader may deploy whatever means at his disposal, including mob violence, to bring down any state institution, including the highest legislative body in the country.[3]

These are things that had already been widely accepted under Trump's rule from 2016 to 2020. Those who measure fascism on the basis of a rigid set of criteria deduced from the interwar Italian and German fascism should also notice that none of the above would make the movements Trump represents any less anti-democratic or illiberal than what they might call fascist. Moreover, regardless of the viability of measurements, scales, and meters we may or may not use to determine what constitutes fascism, the destruction of the American liberal democracy under the rule of the next Republican president is not only within the realm of possibilities but also a grave threat worth serious consideration.

Trump's wide popularity indicates a degree of nihilism that is arguably unprecedented in the history of the United States. Taking this, along with the increasing economic and ecological crises, into account, one can anticipate the continuation of the rise of fascism in the United States. Naturally, this kind of argument will face denialism by those who are in the position of privilege and lack the ability to be shocked by fascist phenomena. Let us not forget, while many of us, including the author of this book, anticipated events in the vicinity of what took place on January 6, 2021, that is, the attack on Capitol Hill by Trump supporters (Ahmed 2020),[4] when the event did take place, reporters of the main news outlets repeatedly expressed their shock and admitted that they had never anticipated such a thing to take place in Washington, DC. What did prevent so many journalists from perceiving what was about to happen? At least due to the nature of their profession, they are better informed about political events than most of us, yet it seemed most of them did not see it coming at all. The answer to this puzzle in one word is *denialism*.

Leaving the denialist positions aside, there are two main directions among those who were not (and are not) so optimistic about the situation. First, there are those who anticipated the rise of the unparallel threat to liberal democracy but did not label the rising exclusionary movement "fascist." In other words, they raised the concern without seeing a need to call the phenomenon "fascist," and of course different observers have had different reasons for their respective approaches including the use and unuse of the term "fascism."

Leaving the denialist positions aside, there have been important works that warned the public and experts about the rise of the far right. Timothy W. Luke's work quite accurately anticipated the move toward the far right in the Republican Party especially since the 1980s. In fact, Luke's warning came as early as 1989 in his *Screens of Power* (2021). Luke also offered a rich analysis of the populist mood that led to the Trump moment, as the embodiment of a form of ideological extremism by the far right that successfully exploited the widespread sense of frustration and marginalization among the White working class in the southern and mid-southwest states that suffered from decades of deindustrialization (2022). There are also those who anticipated the crisis of the upsurge of the far right and argued that what we were witnessing was the rise of fascism. Especially in 2016 and the following three years, a relatively large number of articles and books, both journalistic and academic, maintained this position (e.g., Burley 2017; Stanley 2018). Their arguments are mainly formed around similarities between the new right in the United States on one side and the interwar period fascism in Europe, especially Italian Fascism and German Nazism, on the other side. Of course, many of these authors did not miss the chance to compare Trump with Mussolini and Hitler.

While I think the crisis cannot simply be analogized to the interwar fascism, I argue that it is nonetheless a fascist phenomenon. What distinguishes my theoretical position is my approach to the concept of fascism. There are fascist ideologies, as opposed to a single one. What makes these ideologies fascist is their *form*. There is a long history of searching for the definitive characteristics of fascism as an ideology. However, we are arguably further than ever from reaching a semi-consent in this regard. What distinguishes these definitions is not necessarily degrees of accuracy in terms of the characteristics they attribute to fascism. In most cases, the scholars have studied and indeed observed the features they adopt as definitive of fascism.

However, as *conceptualizing* "fascism" captures an ideology form (as in chapter 3), we will have more productive debate and more effective tools of analysis. If fascism is a form, then what I need to grasp is the form, the traits of that particular class of ideologies, which is a more effective method of diagnosis of fascism. Using "fascism" as a concept has the merit of both accuracy and flexibility while maintaining a definition that is neither too broad nor too narrow. This is compatible with the Frankfurt School's interdisciplinary methods of inquiry, as opposed to reductionist accounts that inevitably result in endless historical and historiographical disputes centered around what should and should not be considered decisive for the definitional construction and instrumental applications of the term "fascism."

Universal Discrimination and the Democratic Camouflaging of Culturalism

The ideology that initiated the anti-leftist campaigns of 2020–2021 in the United States and France has been developing democratic discursive strategies for the last seventy-five years, since the fall of old fascism in Europe. For instance, the race talk is no longer part of the official and academic discourse; instead, the culture talk is prevalent, which is by far more effective for the racist mobomassification of people and the normalization of exclusionary fanaticism among ordinary people.

Despite its democratic-sounding claims of plurality, the culturalist mentality is racist through and through. There is a long history of anthropologizing the non-White Other, and in accomplishing that racist purpose, the paradigm of "culture" has been decisive especially since the demise of internationalism in the 1980s. The collapse of communism as an international/ist movement meant the immediate rise of neofascist ideologies. Thanks to the paradigm of culture, it has become possible for fascist worldviews to find a home in liberal discourses. The mystifying and pseudoscientific notion of "culture" makes essentializing all non-Europeans possible without having to use the outdated term of "race" *and* at the same time allowing the speaker/writer to sound like someone who believes in diversity. Today's fascists and liberals alike take it for granted that the world is composed of different cultures, and those cultures are at the essence of "identities."

The unspoken, and sometimes spoken, assumption is that Europeans, Euro-Americans, and Euro-Australians represent a civilization whereas others in the world embody "cultures." *The* civilization, by definition, entails infinite potentialities and universal freedoms whereas culture is definite anthropologically, local geographically, closed up communally, and a finished product historically. The essentializing premises of culturalism are not among the subjects of the dispute between liberals (including many self-proclaimed leftists) and extremists on the right. Rather, the main subjects of the dispute have to do with the degree to which the West should be open toward other "cultures." While this difference is not insignificant in terms of state policies, the essentialist mentality of the-West-and-the-Rest is deeply racist and tribalist. The implicit premises of culturalism alone are enough to render adherents of culturalism fanatic sectarians—contrary to their image of themselves as faithful embodiments of a democratic, pluralist, and tolerant canon.

Culturalism is the direct offspring of the mentality that justified committing true barbarianism on every continent in the name of a war of the "civilized" against "barbarians." Some of today's spokespersons of the enlightenment's "liberalism" and *the civilization* are not liberal enough to even tolerate the term "colonialism," which is precisely why postcolonial studies has become the new racist campaign's latest obsession in both France and the United States. While the new object of this old phobia is postcolonial studies, the real targets are neither postcolonialisms nor studies. The real target is the same old one: universal equality and leftists who still dare to struggle for it.

Let us take an example of the discourse that embodies the old universal discrimination presented in a language of what should be termed "democratic camouflaging" of cultural racism or culturalism. Ian Buruma (2021), a professor at Bard College and the former editor of the *New York Review of Books* wrote a commentary supposedly defending classics and the enlightenment liberalism against scholars who, God forbid, dare to question some of the premises in those fields and criticize the prevalent homogeneity in the relevant scholarship.

The accused in this case is Dan-el Padilla Peralta, an educator, historian, and scholar of classics, featured in the *New York Times Magazine* (Poser 2021). To start, nowhere does Dan-el Padilla Peralta call for abandoning classics or European philosophy, contrary to the false claims Buruma uses to make a case of red herring. Buruma expresses grievances that the term "white" is used in the article, but he has no problem using the term "black" for the purpose of racializing Dan-el Padilla Peralta. To show how Buruma's self-deceiving mentality actually commits White-racism at the very moment it denies it, we need to examine the implicit premises in his language. For instance, he writes, "The two Western democracies established from revolutions based on liberty and reason were France and the United States. People of both countries like to claim the universality of their values." A few paragraphs later, he writes, "Blacks, Asian-Americans, Latinos and others would like to assert their own cultures, their own values, their own representations, their own 'souls.' " Putting these two statements together, it becomes evident that it is Buruma who thinks in terms of race, perceives the world in terms of race, and classifies societies in terms of race because his unspoken premise is that the people of the United States are White. The rest are American by some sort of indirect association. For if he actually thought Blacks and others as part of the subject, "the people" of the United States, he would not pen both of those statements simply because on the basic logical level both assertions could not be true at the same time.

Buruma's class of "the people" whose project is based on the universal values of "liberty and reason" designate all Whites including those who slaughtered the native peoples, the Confederates, the members of the Ku Klux Klan, and the Trump supporters, but not any Blacks. Even the Blacks who led the Civil Rights movement, not to mention those who fought for the Union in the nineteenth century, are excluded. Buruma could not have been more mistaken in his judgment. Had he reversed the subjects or predicates, he would have been less wrong. Historically and presently, African Americans have been leading the most democratic and emancipatory movements in the United States. All one needs to consider in order to reach this conclusion is the anti-slavery uprisings in the 1700s and 1800s, the Civil Rights movement in the 1950s and 1960s, and the ongoing Black Lives Matter movement.

The fundamental intellectual problem with denialism is the double deception, inwardly and socially. That is to say, denialists do not know that they do not know. They deny their denial of truth so meticulosity that they might genuinely be clueless about what they deeply believe. What they deeply believe, however, will inevitably be embedded in their discourse. Such a contradiction in utterances is not necessarily a sign of hypocrisy if we take hypocrisy to be conscious or premeditated behavior. Rather, it is simply the way things appear to the kind of mentality that is formed within and around privilege if that mentality is not challenged according to an emancipatory epistemology.

Buruma advises anti-racist critics not to racialize the enlightenment unaware of the fact that what he does is exactly that. He claims universality using a language that is itself racializing and exclusionary. Repeating the same logical fallacy of contradiction, in his very defense of the enlightenment against racialization he actually does nothing but racialization of the enlightenment. Instead of including the local, say the French, in the universal (the enlightenment), he reduces the universal to the local. Instead of rejecting tribalism universally, he universalizes his own tribalism. Having internalized the ideological distortions that are built into neoliberalism, he mistakes a globalized form of tribalism for the globally human. Also, like most other denialists, he denies racism but recognizes race, instead of rejecting race and recognizing racism.

Buruma is upset that the neutralized/racist monopoly on universality is challenged by "a black critic of classics education." Being so certain and confident, not only does he unknowingly commit the fallacy of logical contradiction, but he also projects his own epistemological crisis on the critics of racism. In the court of the dominant, the victim is found guilty twice: for existing and for speaking up. Victims of social inequality are habitually blamed for daring to speak about victimhood. The real falsehood, we are told, is the result of a false perception of the victims, who falsely claim victimhood.

To meet the liberal criterion of openness and thus show that he is capable of seeing both sides of the issue, Buruma admits that there have been "blindspots" and "blemish[es]," yet, as usual, we are supposed to believe that the abused is the actual abuser simply because they dare to speak of abuse. The underprivileged as bodies and voices are normally exiled from public space because the cancellation of their existence is the norm. On the other hand, if the privileged are held accountable for their acts on any level, we are told that freedom of speech and inquiry is under attack due to "cancel culture." Ironically, it has become typical for those who are intolerant of the voices of the silenced to preach about "freedom of speech." Within the same absurdity, the ideological heirs of anti-abolitionists, American libertarians, present themselves as the true believers of freedom. To the anti-abolitionists in the nineteenth century, freedom included the freedom to purchase and sell human beings without the intervention of the state, and when the state tried to put an end to slavery, they adamantly opposed the state.

During the COVID-19 pandemic, to the libertarians, freedom entailed spreading the virus as they wished without the intervention of the state. Somehow, their freedom seems to always entail death for others. That in itself should tell us how fanatically they try to further unfreedom, violence, and death for the majority of human beings outside their clans. Similarly, the "liberty" that has been translated into so many wars and genocides, embargos and famines, planetary destruction and ecological catastrophes, is anything but universal liberty. Rather, it is the liberty of a small number of people to inflict suffering on living beings and destruction of the conditions of life. It is no wonder that libertarians and neofascists, assuming that they are distinguishable, support the same racist and fanatic kind of political leadership.

A typical characteristic of denialism is the habit of suppression, which in turn is based on the assumption that if we do not talk about the problem, the problem does not exist. To denialists, those who talk about racism are guilty of racialization, just as feminist women are often blamed for the degeneration of the institution of family or accused of discrimination against men. We are supposed to believe the way things are should not be disturbed or the natural balance of existence as such will be destroyed. Those who are at the bottom of the hierarchy should learn how to be positive. They should be taught that their misery is some sort of good luck. They should be taught that happiness is a state of mind. How else could so much misery and oppression be sustained socially?

At the heart of historical marginalization is silencing the oppressed. The guardians of social privilege who fanatically identify with power and all that represents power cannot stand the voice of the silenced. The moment the silenced speak up, the entire social reality is disrupted. The elites who benefit from social hierarchy and are paranoid about losing their privileges react to serious critique in ways that are semi-instinctive. Theory, philosophy, and politics are all driven by those naturalized interests, not vice versa. In fact, the "natural" modes of knowledge production and perception in a hierarchical society simply reproduce hierarchy. That is precisely why without a philosophy of negation committed to solidarity with the silenced and their struggle for equality, education will only deepen unfreedom. In hierarchical societies, which are almost all societies under the prevalent patriarchy and capitalism, education is part of the problem, not the solution, unless it is founded on the pedagogy of unlearning. The social world we are born into is founded on inequality, so the value systems and modes of perception that we learn as we grow up serve the regime of unfreedom, and education is more like a process of cementing intellectual bureaucracy for the purpose of sustaining the existing inequalities.

According to the racist worldview, "Whiteness" and "Blackness" can only be references to skin color. In anti-racist discourses, on the other hand, these terms should be used as references to social conditions *plus* politics. One could be born into the social conditions of "Whiteness" but choose a politics that is anti-racist, re-educate oneself by unlearning racist prejudices, and even join the politics of "Blackness" as a struggle for universal liberation. In this sense, all revolutionary subjects are Black.

When "Blackness" became an indicator of progressive political awareness, it became even more liberating, both qualitatively and quantitatively, precisely because it inspired a new political space that was progressive, emancipatory, and inclusive.[5] That is to say, the racial categories were politicized, allowing for the transformation of identities on the basis of a free and freeing politics. In the case of South Africa, this progressive transformation of the frame of reference led to the birth of a struggle for not only the social emancipation of Blacks but also the epistemological emancipation of those who might not be identified as Black in the racial system of classification. In other words, the racist social regime of Whiteness versus Blackness was confronted with a revolutionary movement inclusive of all those who rejected the racist order. Blackness is the title of emancipatory politics for not only those born into racially disadvantaged social conditions but also those born into epistemologically disadvantaged social conditions. The struggle for Black freedom opened a horizon for being not only free as Black but also Black as free. A robust form of cosmopolitanism aimed at the realization of personal, social, and political freedoms necessitates a Black proletarian politics.

Politically, the social condition into which one is born matters only insofar as what one would make out of it. The first anti-racist rule should be evident: there is nothing inherently valuable or devaluing in any particular social construct such as "race." Of course, we are born into societies where those identities are predetermined in terms of social advantages or disadvantages, but the point of emancipation is precisely to reject (not deny) such a reality, to unlearn its knowledge, to negate its episteme, to bring down its oppressive institutions and constitutions, and simply to take the side of the oppressed whoever they may be in any given society at any given time. These rejections and negations are what constitute one's emancipatory politics. In principle, *politically* every person can aspire to become Black. If one is not born into Black social conditions, one could and should unlearn until one's social conditions are radically undone. That is a process of self-emancipation, which is a precondition for emancipatory social movements capable of changing the world. Those who are born into social privileges are sometimes even more unfree not despite but because of those privileges. At least intellectually, everything else being equal, the underprivileged are better situated to comprehend what freedom entails. Therefore, the struggle for universal liberty is located in the margins of the margins and led by the most marginalized.

Buruma takes it upon himself to defend some of the enlighten-ment *philosophes* in an imaginary trial in which his (long dead) clients are, allegedly, defamed. He sets out to prosecute all those who fail to under-stand (what to him is) the universality of the French and American projects and the inherent neutrality of Whiteness. He actually writes, "Voltaire may have disparaged Africans, but he was an avid reader of the 13th-century Persian poet Saadi." As if Diderot's Encyclopedia has not been published yet, Buruma preaches to the reader about his version of the enlightenment values. Even more shamelessly he minimizes the significance of racism in the works of European philosophers to "blindspots" inside quotation marks and followed by a disclaiming "but" sentence.[6] It is true they had some inappropriate views about Africans, and that is due to the era they lived in, but Voltaire knew of an Iranian poet, as Buruma enlightens us. The implied point is that the European philosophers were not universally dis-criminatory. It seems Buruma suggests that the Eurocentric (racist) views on Africans were somehow justified because, in Buruma's thought, Africans did not have great poets. Recall Fanon's line: "I made myself the poet of the world. The White man had found a poetry in which there was nothing poetic" (1986, 98).

One might get the impression that Buruma is trying to make a tran-sition to the entertainment industry, but what is truly disturbing is the fact that Buruma makes these explicit and implicit claims without a sense of irony. According to Buruma: "The founders of both countries were very much children of the enlightenment. And leaders of both countries, from Napoleon to George W. Bush, believed that their nations had a mission to spread universal liberty to less-enlightened peoples." He adds: "The bad con-sequence of claims to universality are equally clear. People do not like more powerful nations imposing their beliefs or values on them, especially if this is done by force. Napoleon had no right to subjugate other nations by extolling the superior virtues of liberty, fraternity and equality. American efforts to invade countries in the name of democracy have been equally misguided. The notion of universality imposed by force is never a good idea" (2021). Does Buruma think that Ronald Reagan and George W. Bush thought people like being bombed? Perhaps the missionaries of the enlightenment did not know that people are not particularly crazy about being burned alive. Perhaps, the "mission to spread universal liberty to less-enlightened peoples" was misunderstood by the "less-enlightened peoples" who did not sit in Buruma's classes to be prepared for the somewhat painful operation of enlightening. The statement "American efforts to invade countries in the name of democracy have been equally misguided" (Buruma 2021) amounts to saying that there had been some mistakes in the methods the United States has used to liberate Koreans, Vietnamese, and Iraqis, not to mention Cubans, Guatemalans, and Chileans. Due to the "misguided" efforts, instead of delivering the enlightenment philosophers' books, bombs were utilized to introduce liberty to the "less-enlightened peoples."

If we go by Buruma's banal assertions while considering his proclamation that the "American efforts" to carry on the mission of liberty were "misguided," the events of the last four decades seem even more absurd. When the United States actively supported jihadis in the 1980s, perhaps the intention was purely Voltairean! In the 2001 invasion of Afghanistan to remove those same jihadis, that is, the former allies, perhaps, the enterprise's aim was, still, spreading "universal liberty." In 2020, however, the American government made a deal with the Taliban, perhaps to hand over the enlightenment project once more to the jihadis. The experiment in Iraq was more or less similar. First Saddam Hussein was supported. Then, to remove Saddam Hussein the entire population of Iraq was starved for more than a decade. Eventually, the country was invaded to remove Saddam Hussein. Today, thanks to the neoliberal missionaries of universal liberty, entire generations are impoverished, and Islamist militias rule the ruined country, where nobody is safe.

Being faithful to the principle of universal discrimination, Buruma sees the same problem of "identity politics" in the United States where "more and more people feel that a set of values—a civilization, if you like—is being imposed on them, a civilization loosely based on the Enlightenment, on liberalism, on the classics, and, above all, on 'whiteness' " (2021). Notice Buruma puts "whiteness" in quotations because he allegedly rejects racialization.

Somehow Buruma manages to commit red-herring, covert racism and projection, all at the same time. First, those who protest against racial inequality "feel that . . ." and so on. In addition to grouping entire populations of faceless, nameless, and voiceless human beings together and making a claim about how this imaginary collective *feels*, it is worth noticing Baruma's word choice to refer to what motivates *their* politics. In and according to the dominant modes of knowledge production, just as femininity has typically been associated with emotions, which in turn is posed as the antipode of rationality, the racialized Other is typically depicted as collectives whose main motivations are rooted in raw feelings, which have already been posted as the opposite of objectivity or reason.

Buruma, who allegedly rejects racism—after all, everyone rejects racism even though somehow racism is alive and well—protests against the use of the term "whiteness" to racialize what is (to him) truly nothing but universality, or "a civilization, if you like." Thanks to the confidence that comes with privilege, which is at the same time an obstacle for personal enlightenment, Buruma puts a finger on *his* problem when he announces that "the main problem is the confusion of race, ethnicity and culture." Thus, even if cultural racism did not exist, Buruma would invent it.

Clearly, Buruma does not realize that the language of racism has already been updated since the 1950s and 1960s when "racial identity" became "ethnicity" and "race" became "culture" (2021), allowing educators and scholars like himself to preserve and disseminate the old ideology using more democratic-sounding terminology. However, even by the standards of democratic camouflage, Buruma quickly re-exposes his problematic worldview using the expression "high cultures." The main point of the politically correct language of culturalism is the alleged rejection of hierarchy inherent in the old language of race, but Buruma unknowingly ruins the culturalist persona immediately exposing his old self when he uses the obvious substitute for "superior races." Culture talk in the first place was invented to mask the deep belief in racial hierarchy, superior versus inferior, high versus low, but Buruma's democratic camouflaging is just as embarrassing as his (mis)representation of the universality of the enlightenment.

Let us pause again on the claim Buruma makes so confidently about non-White Americans while he allegedly rejects racialization: "Blacks, Asian-Americans, Latinos and others would like to assert their own cultures, their own values, their own representations, their own 'souls.'"

I suggest the following revision of Buruma's statement to make it less false, less racist, and more fitting to the enlightenment Buruma's liberalism scandalously fails to defend: "Blacks, Asian-Americans, Latinos and others would like to *be included as equal members of the republic and not be discriminated against in the name of* their own cultures, their own values, their own representations, their own 'souls.'" The Burumas who run the dominant regime of knowledge production simply project their problematic views of humanity on humanity in the name of universality. In their very arguments for the "universality" of the enlightenment, they manage to racialize the enlightenment. In essence, what the Burumas of the world are claiming is that all the non-White peoples have cultures, in the anthropological sense of the term, but the (White) European has produced the "high culture," in the philosophical and sociological sense, a universal project for all humanity, a civilization.

In their alleged attempt to refute relativism or absolutism, they reproduce the worst form of relativism and absolutism, which is absolute relativism. By attributing universality to themselves in a culturalist/racist manner, they prove to be the true global tribalists. Never mind the enlightenment philosophy, all that is needed to expose this kind of imperialist affection for the mythology of the dark ages is some basic Aristotelian logic.

In the culturalist mindset, "Whiteness" is not a social condition; rather, it is the state of being pure, the neutral state of being a human, the founder of the civilization, and the missionary of liberty. This universal confusion and habitual categorical distortion cannot be excused in terms of blind spots. It is dark-agism. It is the curse of certainty that comes with the unlimited sense of entitlement and undeterred embracement of the social conditions of privilege. It is a mode of perception that mythologizes the world in the name of objective knowledge (of course claimed by the in-group self). Christian and Islamic theology claim enlightenment too. They too speak in the name of the universal truth. They too in the name of universality and truth mythologize the world. However, unlike religion, the enlightenment can and should be defended philosophically especially against the chauvinists who try to turn it into another form of universal tribalism.

The civilization is threatened by Eurocentrists, from culturalist liberals to White supremacists, and by other absolute relativists such as religious fundamentalists who, similarly, divide the world according to an in-group versus out-group dichotomy. The logical contradictions committed by these ideologies of universal discrimination are similar. The difference is their respective discursive strategies. The strain that developed democratic camouflaging of culturalism is arguably the most fatal one for the universalist horizons of the enlightenment project given this strain's ability to operate on behalf of democracy's immune system (i.e., with unlimited authority). Today, culturalists not only have access to the most powerful platforms of opinion making but also enjoy a kind of authority that is by far more totalitarian globally than any other authority in history. If somehow a voice of critique against this total hegemony makes it to an influential platform, that voice is immediately Othered, criminalized, or racialized to ensure that the unlimited hegemony is maintained.

It is interesting that fanatic missionaries of liberalism typically do not include Marx in the list of the great philosophers of "universality." Marx was, in fact, a *universalist*, and what scares the missionaries of liberalism about universalism or cosmopolitanism is the adherence to true equality, an equality that exceeds the constructed walls among nations, republics, and classes. From Marx to Benjamin, egalitarian universalists, those who struggled to save the enlightenment project from falling into the abyss, were denied a place in Europe and its universities. There is a pattern that cuts through philosophy and politics, from pedagogy and education to nationalism and patriotism. *Those who want to make it great again, in practice, try to make it barbarian again.* Those who criminalize critique are the enlightenment's worst possible representatives.

One can only feel sorry for the state of the enlightenment project when educators like Buruma are its defenders. Surely, such advocates of the enlightenment are its true destroyers. Just to be clear, one should defend the enlightenment especially against chauvinist and racist attempts to use it as a tool for universal discrimination. Just as we should remain conscious of its catastrophic side represented by fascism, colonialism, and imperialism, the enlightenment must be defended against chauvinism. Also, let us not be deceived by racist distortions and culturalist tribalism advocated through discursive strategies of Euro-chauvinism, what is worth defending in the enlightenment has always been a universalist project of humanity as such. There would have been no enlightenment without discoveries and inventions that are universally human, including those that had emerged in China, India, Central Asia, Mesopotamia, and Africa. Just as writing, for instance, is inseparable from the human civilization despite the fact that it was first discovered in Mesopotamia and Egypt, the enlightenment cannot be claimed based on a chauvinistic frame of reference that is itself a product of an anti-enlightenment movement, best represented by cultural racism. In reality, the enlightenment today is defended by those in the margins of the margins, the women and men who resist capitalism, imperialism, and internal colonialism at the same time. The communists in the Indian subcontinent, Rojava-Bakur revolutionaries, Zapatistas, Black Lives Matter activists, and their allied anti-fascists are the true defenders of what is worth defending in the enlightenment. Revolution represents a leap in the human emancipation insofar as the revolutionaries realize the inherent universality of reason and the inevitable rationality of emancipation.

"Islamo-Leftism": Another Oxymoron Invented by the Right

Islamo-leftism is one of the latest rhetorical inventions of the right-wing propagandists in France and the United States. This term is just another device to obscure reality by classifying the perceived enemies of White nationalism under one term. Equating political Islam and leftism can only be a sign of (1) genuine political and historical ignorance or (2) racism.

To unpack this, let us analyze the terminology and look at a few historical facts. Let us also be charitable in our interpretation and assume that those who adhere to the term "Islamo-leftism" do not mean to implicate "Islam" as such simply because that would be absurd given that "Islam" refers to a religion with thousands of variations and hundreds of millions of believers, just like Christianity.

Needless to say, even in that case, religiosity, whether Islamic or Christian, falls under conservatism, not leftism. Even "liberation theology" inevitably falls short of maintaining a leftist position unless it becomes "liberation from theology." Marx's assertion that "even a critical theologian remains a theologian" may sound like stating the obvious (1994, 57), but it is precisely the statement that makes the problem obvious. If this reasoning is not convincing enough, the Iranian regime is a living example of "liberation theology." In its first year of rule, the regime massacred thousands of leftist academics, communists, Kurds, Bahais, and Balochis as a part of its long list of its religious campaigns, which have never stopped since then (see Amnesty International 2017).

What about Christian "liberation theology" or "Black theology"? To answer this and grab the issue from its roots, we may ask a different kind of question: Would there be any need to speak of "liberation theologies" had these theologies themselves not been at the heart of colonial campaigns of genocide and enslavement? It is as if worshiping the same God as that of the colonizers has spared Native Americans or Africans from the fate of genocide and impoverishment. Submitting to the imperial religion in fact crowned the process of subjugation whether in the case of Islamic or Christian imperialism. Spirituality is a nice term for turning one's attention away from what *matters* and to focus on a presumed realm of absolute truth and metaphysical justice, thereby surrendering the body to endless chains, the iron sounds of which is music to sadomasochism. Theology has always claimed liberation. How else could it make people call murder sacrifice, genocide holy war, and submission virtue? How else could total domination be internalized on the account of it being total freedom?

Thus, if those who use the term are not so ridiculously oblivious to implicate "Islam" as such, by the "Islam" part of the term "Islamo-leftism" they must mean what is known as political Islam, jihadism, Islamic fundamentalism, or (hereafter) "Islamism." However, even with this charitable interpretation of the term "Islamo-leftism," that is assuming that it is meant to associate Islamism and leftism, the far-right intelligentsia's adoption of the term is indicative of their ignorance and disturbing racist mindset. Islamism is an ultra-right ideology through and through—socially, politically, historically, and geopolitically. If "right-leftism" made any sense, then "Islamo-leftism" would make sense too. Yet, perhaps there is such a thing as "right-leftism" as a form of self-contradicting-ideocracy, but in that case, such an orientation belongs to the same camp of White racism despite the appearances, which means the right intelligentsia in the West should consider so-called Islamo-leftists as their fellow ideological travelers because of their shared racist modes of perception.

To show the pseudo-rationality of the term, it is sufficient to simply recall two basic facts with regard to the relationship between Islamism and leftism. First, Islamism is inherently, universally, and fanatically anti-leftist. A mere elementary level of historical awareness of social movements in the last one hundred years or so is enough for anyone to comprehend that leftists have been Islamism's most uncompromising traditional enemy. Whether we look at the contemporary history of Indonesia, Pakistan, Afghanistan, Iran, Iraq, Turkey, and wherever else Islamists in one way or another triumphed or we compare the two sides' respective discourses, the diametrical opposition between Islamism and leftism could not be more evident. Communists have been at the frontline against Islamist movements. In fact, only after the brutal eradication of communism as a popular social movement did Islamism gain a global sphere of influence. It barely needs to be mentioned that the bloody eradication of communists was committed by a wide anti-leftist coalition that included local nationalists, Western colonial powers, and Islamists, which brings us to the second point.

The second basic fact that the right in the West needs to be reminded of is that Western governments and politicians, including some of the right's own celebrated heroes, share a major part of the blame for the rise of Islamism. All one needs to do is to check the American Congress's resolutions in the 1980s to find out that jihadis from various backgrounds were openly and proudly supported with positive propaganda, logistics, funds, and weapons in their fight against the communists in Afghanistan, not to mention the wide scale of American and British discreet support for anti-communist Islamist and nationalist military juntas throughout the second half of the twentieth century.

Can the discursive act of grouping leftists with Islamists be a sign of anything other than obliviousness? Given the fact that the term "Islamo-leftism" is mostly used in the European and American contexts, perhaps by

"Islamo-leftists," rightists mean to refer to Western intellectuals who support Islamism as some sort of anti-imperialism. Indeed, that is an existing phenomenon with which the left is cursed and, thus, deserves to be addressed from a leftist angle. A well-known example of a post-Marxist intellectual who is counted on the left and, at the same time, is sympathetic to Islamism is Judith Butler. While I personally like to consider intellectuals like Jodi Dean, Alain Badiou, Slavoj Žižek, and Franco Berardi as the representatives of the left in the West because they unapologetically stayed faithful to universalism, we have to admit that post-Marxist culturalist "leftists" are not marginal in Western universities.

Given the post-Marxist liberal leftists' flirtations with Islamism, one might think rightists are justified on some level to use the term "Islamo-leftism," but in this case, they would still be guilty of racism simply because they (1) cannot differentiate between "Islamist" and "Muslim," and (2) take the Muslim identity as a racial identity.

This mentality is incapable of imagining a non-White society that is not homogeneous. It is a mentality that defines all non-Whites anthropologically through the paradigm of culture and mythology. Unsurprisingly, such a mentality cannot imagine that the politics of right and left also exist in a so-called Muslim society because it perceives all the members of such a society through the supposed cultural/religious identity. Therefore, according to the White-culturalist mentality, even if some sort of leftism exists in such a society, it can only be Islamic leftism. Universalism is reserved for the White European. The non-White's world is assumed to be inherently local, tribal, sectarian, and culturally predetermined. Even in the proclaimed multiculturalist age, to this mentality the White stands above and beyond the anthropological notion of culture, playing the role of the all-loving lord while the non-Whites are expected to be grateful for this infinite semi-divine kindness.

By the same token, while feminism in the West has to be described by its epistemologies, theories, doctrines, and waves, if "feminism" could exist in the Middle East and North Africa, it cannot be but Islamic. This mentality, whether it claims anti-Eurocentrism or not, whether it is sympathetic to the perceived Other or not, whether it is for or against multiculturalism, whether its rhetoric comes across as cultural humility or supremacist mythology, is racist for the simple reason that it perceives the world through the lenses of "race" and "culture," both of which are Eurocentric, mythic inventions devised to create a metaphysical distance between White and non-White. It is a racist mentality because it presumes that only Whites could have developed a complex politics of left and right, secular and liberal, progressive and conservative, and so on. Regardless of good and bad intentions, the premises that stem from culturalism indicate the dominance of a racist episteme.

Given that Western post-Marxist leftists and the anti-Marxist right share this culturalist mentality, they should not be so hard on each other. After all, ideologically they are more similar than they think they are, and their differences are merely evaluative. Granted one side may see the non-White as an object of pity deserving kindness or an aesthetic element of diversification of the natural colors of the world while the opposite side may see the non-White as an object of scorn and permanent threat or a continental if not planetary agent of contamination, epistemically both parties are plunged in racism. Self-proclaimed leftists who abide by the culturalist ethos commit racism as a matter of course. Therefore, no matter how many "ethnic dishes" they like or how "culturally diverse" their social relations might be, they effectively partake in the reproduction of a retroactive world. Critical thought is not a matter of intentions or moral sentiments; rather, it is first and foremost the struggle of breaking free from the dominant modes of perception and thereby operating against the ethos where the premises and paradigms of domination are normalized.

However we look at "Islamo-leftism," it is nothing but an intellectual scandal. I have taken the "Islam/o" part of the term "Islamo-leftism" to mean political Islam or Islamism. Nonetheless, regardless of the intentions of the term's adherents, the choice of the word is not free of immediate ideological implications, so we should not completely ignore the inherent ambiguity. Essentializing those who are perceived as Muslim by totalizing a perceived homogeneous religious identity on them is itself an act of "de-specification," to borrow Domenico Losurdo's concept (2015, 55). De-specification is an act of Othering a group of people through the use of discursive devices that essentially dehumanize them. For instance, repeated attribution of certain collective behavior to the targeted population is done in order to de-specify them. De-specification is at the core of a process of justifying forms of treatment that are otherwise unjustifiable, at least in terms of human-to-human treatment. Once the Other's image is established as fundamentally different than us, the stage is ready for their full dehumanization. We should also keep in mind that "us" remains to be the signifier that normatively designates the species of humans in the most neutral sense, in the sense of the universality of reason, morality, and the beautiful. Therefore, the out-group's dissimilarity with the in-group amounts to falling off the class of humanity insofar as the full membership in the species is measured by the degree of resemblance with the civilized.

The act of de-specification is often committed in preparation for justifying the use of violence against the Other. This is a typical fascist procedure. Old-fashioned fascists liken the Other with insects, animals, viruses, and so on to create a popular climate of opinion in which ordinary people of the in-group would demand a heavier hand on the excluded, marginalized, Other. The antagonized masses may very well even take matters into their own hands via the mobilization of armed militia who would organize insurrections and assassinations. At a certain stage, the accumulated hatred against the de-specified Other could easily be utilized by fascist agitators to instigate mobs to commit spontaneous acts of lynching, pogrom, stoning, and so on. However, it is crucial to keep in mind that de-specification can only be launched by elites who control the means of opinion making.

The rightist intellectuals and governments are not going after Islamism. How many Western academics have boycotted Turkish universities in protest of the vast Islamification campaign of Turkish universities? In terms of international politics, how many Western governments have cut ties with Erdogan's regime, given that it is the most powerful pole of Islamism in today's world? In fact, NATO's second largest standing army, under Erdogan's leadership, is directly involved in supporting jihadist groups from Libya to Syria, not to mention its violent campaigns against Kurds.

To expose the propagandist tactic devised in the term "Islamo-leftism" as part of a much broader campaign we need to go further back into the history of fascism. Historians of fascism are familiar with terminologies such as "Jewish Bolshevism," "cosmopolitan Jews," and similar right-wing linguistic devices that were at the heart of the antisemitic campaigns throughout the first half of the twentieth century. Associating Jewry and leftist international conspiracies and revolutions by the reactionary writers and politicians has a long history (see for instance Hobsbawm 1995, 119–20; Traverso 2016, chapters 1, 2, and 8). It is well known that the Nazis regularly depicted communism as an international Jewish conspiracy. For example, in 1935, in the Nazi Party's congress, Joseph Goebbels proudly delivered a speech advancing such an antisemitic and anti-communist conspiracy theory, and he was thrilled to see that Hitler was "genuinely enthused" (1935).[7]

Of course, fascists did not create antisemitic conspiracy theories from scratch; rather, as in many other issues related to policies of genocide, they borrowed a page from the more experienced colonial powers. As Losurdo writes, "The initial head of the crusade against the Judeo-Bolshevik conspiracy was Henry Ford, the American automobile magnate" (2015, 178). At the beginning of the first decade of the rise of fascism in Europe, the 1920s, Ford's publishing company published an antisemitic booklet titled, *The International Jew*, in four volumes. *The Ford International Weekly*, on the first page of its May 22, 1920 issue, published an article under the headline of "The International Jew: The World's Problem."[8]

Looking back, we could see how plain the rationale of the hate campaign was. Namely, it associated the ideological enemy, Marxism, with the race enemy, in this case Jews, to turn individual human beings of flesh and blood into legitimate targets of discrimination and violence. Of course, there are many differences between the nuances of anti-Semitism and those of other forms of racist campaigns, but the overlap is the association of the Othered with "leftism" to impose homogeneity more forcefully in the production of both social space and knowledge.

The image of the in-group is packaged and sold as the rational, free, democratic, tolerant, and even universal whereas the excluded is presented as a threat to all that constitutes "our way of life," which is simply the culturalist alternative expression for racial purity, with the exact same phobias and anxieties common among old fashion fascist groups who use terminologies of biological racism.

The irony is that racists, sectarians, extremists, and nationalists attribute what is characteristic of themselves to leftists, many of whom, or at least the Marxists among them, are deemed a threat on the existing relations of domination precisely for their doctrines of cosmopolitan equality. At the end of the day, despite their fantastic images of themselves and psychological means of projection, denial, and defense, the right in the West, including White supremacists, are extremely similar to Islamists in terms of their hierarchical views of the world and xenophobia. They are similar not only in their anti-leftist violent tendencies but also in the propaganda tactics they deploy against leftists.

Pairing communism with fascism, especially since 1951 when Hannah Arendt published *The Origins of Totalitarianism* (1979), is a well-known trick to undermine the legitimacy of communism through its alleged shared features with fascism (Hobsbawm 1995, 393).[9]

Communism was fascism's number one enemy across Europe from Italy, Spain, and Germany to Yugoslavia, Romania, and Ukraine. As soon as fascism lost the war and its political power, it also lost its attraction to many in the academy and intelligentsia. Furthermore, it became a useful term for criminalizing communism. However, simply associating fascism with its arch enemy, communism, would have been laughable. Therefore, a third concept was needed to be deployed as mediator, and "totalitarianism" was quickly turned into that gluing agent. Thus, somehow, communism along with fascism became the *other* of capitalist liberalism in the post–World War II ethos.

There is an existing example of this criminalization-via-pairing tactic at work, and it is more directly similar to the French invention of "Islamo-left-ism." The example to which I want to draw attention is the Erdogan regime's habitual pairing of the leftist, pro-democracy, pro-Kurdish-rights, feminist liberation movement represented by several political parties in Turkey and Syria, such as Peoples' Democratic Party (HDP) and Democratic Union Party (PYD), with ISIS. In addition to the obvious and complete ideological opposition between this leftist movement on one side and Islamists from the Muslim Brotherhood to ISIS on the other side, there is a bloody ongoing existential conflict between the two camps. Moreover, it is Erdogan's regime that has been actively supporting Islamists across the Middle East and North Africa. In fact, today Erdogan's regime is by far more influential than the Iranian regime in terms of Islamist mobilization, populism, and reactionary radicalization. "Islamo-leftism" is thus just the latest propagandist tool that is put forward by those whose mindset, worldviews, and policies are exemplary of exclusionism and extremism.

To Asian and African leftists—whether Javanese or Bengali, Punjabi or Pushto, Kazakh or Persian, Baluchi or Kurdish, Turkish or Arab, Darfuri or Nubi, Nigerian or Amazigh—who are part of everyday struggles, from the Indian subcontinent and Central Asia to the Eastern shores of the Mediterranean, from Mesopotamia to Central and West Africa, the term "Islamo-leftism" would sound laughable.

Notes

Introduction

1. This is evidently clear from exit polls (e.g., see CNN 2021).

2. I have advanced in "Negativity as the Compass of Revolution" (2022a). It is also explained in more detail in my book, *Revolutionary Hope after Nihilism* (2022b).

3. This text intentionally combines the gender pronouns to maintain neutrality. Often both feminine and masculine pronouns are used together as the singular "they." Sometimes, "he" is used when the subject is typically a man, such as "the father figure" even though the expression is not used in the literal sense. In some other cases, "she" is used as a neutral third person pronoun, for instance to refer to a subject, the Othered, and so on.

4. For example, see Timothy Luke (2022) for Trump's strategy of treating "myths as facts, facts as fictions" (13).

Chapter 1

1. In the 1980s, the Islamists were funded, armed, and politically supported by the US and its allies to fight the Afghan government and the Soviet army in Afghanistan. Back then, the Islamists were called "freedom fighters" by American officials, while Islamists called—and continue to call—themselves *mujahideen*, or religious warriors. In fact, Senate Concurrent Resolution number 74 in 1984 bluntly states, "The freedom fighters of Afghanistan have withstood the might of the Soviet Army for over four years and gained the admiration of free men and women the world over with their courageous sacrifice, bravery, and determination," adding that "it would be indefensible to provide the freedom fighters with only enough aid to fight and die, but not enough to advance their cause of freedom" (US Congress Committee on Foreign Affairs 1985, 352).

2. Recall that when Napoleon banned slavery in 1815, thirteen years after restoring it, slave trade continued to thrive in the United States for another forty-five years.

3. One would think, if nowhere else, under liberalism, abortion and same-sex marriage would be undisputed rights, as opposed to some sort of half justifiable political demands that would require a referendum. Not to mention, any genuine liberal order would not make a woman's right to abortion something determined by male voters. Similarly, a genuine liberal rationality would not politicize same-sex marriage. If it becomes the subject of a political referendum, then one would think marriage as such should be the question because there is nothing democratic in allowing the majority to decide about the personal lives of the minority.

4. This is the subject of the last chapter of my book *Totalitarian Space and the Destruction of Aura* (2019d) and my upcoming book, *Postnihilism: The Dialectics of Hope and Despair*.

5. In Thesis XII of "On the Concept of History," Benjamin writes, "The subject of historical knowledge is the struggling, oppressed class itself" (2006c, 394). This same line is quoted on his grave in Portbou, Catalonia (Rollason 2002, 3). In Thesis IX, he offers his famous description of the angel of history (2006c, 392).

6. This is an expression used more than once by Benjamin (e.g., see 2006a, 441).

7. The extraordinary parallelism between these two characters is the subject of one of the chapters of my upcoming book, *Postnihilism: The Dialectics of Hope and Despair*.

8. This is a reference to Benjamin's statement "Only for the sake of the hopeless ones have we been given hope" (2004, 356).

9. For more on this, see the fourth and fifth chapters of my book *Totalitarian Space and the Destruction of Aura* (2019d).

10. This is explained in detail in chapter 3 of my book on totalitarian space (2019d) and an article titled "Panopticism and Totalitarian Space" in *Theory in Action* (2018).

11. For a well-grounded account of the correlation between virtual reality and the phenomenon of mass shooting, see Berardi's *Heroes: Mass Murder and Suicide* (2015).

Chapter 2

1. For instance, Mussolini's designated philosopher of fascism, Giovanni Gentile, states, "The first point, therefore, that must be established in a definition of Fascism, is the totalitarian character of its doctrine, which concerns itself not only with political order and direction of the nation, but with its will, thought and sentiment" (2002, 21).

2. For instance, among recent books written on fascism is Jason Stanley's *How Fascism Works* (2018), which warns the American public about resemblance between Trumpism and twentieth-century Fascism and Nazism.

3. For instance, among Iranian nationalists, old race talk, especially Aryanism and anti-Arab racism, are not uncommon (for more on this see Ahmed 2017; Zia-Ebrahimi 2011). Pan-Arab nationalists, especially when addressing their own constituents, do not make much effort to hide their intolerance for perceived Jews. Islamists might differ on endless issues from the secular nationalists, but they have anti-Semitism in common (Ahmed 2017; also see Ter-Matevosyan 2015; Hanioglu 2014).

4. I propose the term as a critical alternative to the term "massification," which has anti-democratic connotations. The base term "mobomass" is meant to simultaneously allude to mob-mobilization, the bourgeoisie/bourgeiosiefied, and "mass/ification" to suggest that it is a reference to neither "the mass" nor a mob per se but to individuals who are ideologically bourgeoisiefied and depoliticized precisely in order to be instrumentalized for anti-egalitarian political agenda. More on this in the next chapter.

5. For more on this, see Ahmed 2022b.

Chapter 3

1. For more on the differences and similarities between Arendt's account of "the mass" and "the mob," see chap. 10 of Arendt's *The Origins* (1979).

2. See for instance Leo Löwenthal's notes on this (1989, 49–50).

3. Leo Löwenthal and Norbert Guterman observed that the Fascists in Italy and the Nazis in Germany exploited the working class's distrust of the liberal governments in both countries, respectively, for their own mobilization purposes and the eventual fascist takeover of all the state institutions (2021, 94–95).

4. Adorno states:

Even the fascist leader's startling symptoms of inferiority, his resemblance to ham actors and asocial psychopaths, is thus anticipated in Freud's theory. For the sake of those parts of the follower's narcissistic libido which have not been thrown into the leader image but remain attached to the follower's own ego, the superman must still resemble the follower and appear as his "enlargement." Accordingly, one of the basic devices of personalized fascist propaganda is the concept of the "great little man," a person who suggests both omnipotence and the idea that he is just one of the folks, a plain, red-blooded American, untainted by material or spiritual wealth. Psychological ambivalence helps to work a social miracle. (Adorno 2001, 142)

5. Löwenthal and Guterman write:

The self-portrait of the agitator is thus a culmination of all his other themes, which prepare the audience for the spectacle of the great little man acting as leader. Taking advantage of all the weaknesses of the present social order, the agitator intensifies his listeners' sense of bewilderment and helplessness, terrifies them with the specter of innumerable dangerous enemies and reduces their already crumbling individualities to bundles of reactive responses. He drives them into a moral void in which their inner voice of conscience is replaced by an externalized conscience: the agitator himself. He becomes the indispensable guide in a confused world, the center around which the faithful can gather and find safety. He comforts the sufferers of malaise, takes the responsibility of history and becomes the exterior replacement of their disintegrated individuality. They live through him. (2021, 202–3)

6. I have called this "the negativity thesis." For more detailed accounts of it, see Ahmed 2022a; 2022b, chap. 6.

7. There is no clearer example of this than *Faith's Checkbook* (2020), a book authored by Charles Spurgeon, an English pastor. The book was first published in 1888, but it is still in print. The new editions have been made more and more "appealing," for instance some of them are designed as actual bank checkbooks.

8. Benjamin notes: "According to its economic nature, bourgeois society cannot help insulating everything technological as much as possible from the so-called spiritual [Geistigen], and it cannot help resolutely excluding technology's right of determination in the social order. Any future war will also be a slave revolt on the part of technology" (2005, 312).

9. "*The logical outcome of fascism is an aestheticizing of political life.* The violation of the masses, whom fascism, with its *Führer* cult, forces to their knees, has its counterpart in the violation of an apparatus which is pressed into serving the production of ritual values" (Benjamin 2006b, 269. Italics from original).

Chapter 4

1. To clarify this point, the chapter builds on some of my previous works (e.g., see Ahmed 2015; 2019b; 2021a; 2021b).

2. This should not be taken as a generalization of all anthropological accounts of "culture." The following passage by Susan Wright is worth reproducing here:

Although anthropologists have developed new ways of thinking about "culture," these "old ideas of culture" have percolated out from academic discourse and, as will be shown below, are still in widespread use in public parlance. The main features of this, still-current "old idea of culture" are:

bounded, small scale entity

defined characteristics (checklist)

unchanging, in balanced equilibrium or self-reproducing

underlying system of shared meanings: "authentic culture"

identical, homogenous individuals. (1998, 8)

3. See Lentin and Titley (2011) for more on multiculturalism as "racism in a neoliberal age."

4. Also see Žižek 2008, 41, 148.

5. Žižek (2008b, 76–77) offers a similar analysis of the 2005 riots in the French suburbs.

6. See Bonnett (2005) for a helpful discussion of the evolution of "the West" as a "ubiquitous [supremacist] category in the articulation of the modern world" (2005, 15).

7. On a number of occasions in Canada and the United States, complete strangers have asked me what religion I practice, not because there is anything about me that could remotely suggest I follow any religion, but I assume merely because of my Middle Eastern appearance. In one of these cases in Montreal in 2007, a White Canadian woman had already deduced I was Muslim, perhaps because of both my appearance and my two Iranian companions who had already identified themselves as Muslims. When I replied, "I have no religion," she enthusiastically responded, "Don't be ashamed of your religion!" before proudly divulging her own (non-Muslim) religious affiliation. Her response speaks to the very heart of the matter: the Other can only have a cultural, not personal, identity. Therefore, if I say I am not Muslim, that must only be because I am ashamed to admit my beliefs to a "non-Muslim."

8. Not surprisingly, conservative and liberal versions of culturalization often coexist in practice, with "multicultural" reforms—such as the superficial acknowledgment of Aboriginal populations in Canada's citizenship guide (Jafri, 2012) or Australia's National Curriculum (McAllan, 2011)—serving to offset the continuation or introduction of overtly racist policies.

9. Over the last couple of years (2020–2022), I discussed two versions of what became this section with Judith Friedlander, the author of *Being Indian in Hueyapan*. Of course, my goal was to use her anthropological research to further reinforce my anti-culturalist position, yet precisely because of this, I needed to be careful not to impose my interpretation on the book. Friedlander kindly read and edited the section closely.

Chapter 5

1. Ernst Toller is an example, among many others, of this idealist figure. Toller is a relatively underappreciated revolutionary writer, activist, and poet who

belonged to the same generation as the Frankfurters. Like Benjamin, he killed himself in 1939. Horkheimer and Toller knew each other, and at some point Toller was mistaken for Horkheimer. Like many other German exiles, he ended up in the United States, deeply alienated by the pragmatic, consumerist, and commodifying aspects of American life.

2. For empiricists, Horkheimer states, "There are nothing but facts, and the entire conceptual apparatus of science serves to determine and predict them. When the relation of consciousness to the objective world does come under consideration, it is in turn treated as a collection of facts, such as habits conditioned physiologically or in a similar way. Any other mode of consideration is meaningless" (2002, 154).

3. Nagarjuna's writings are considered fundamental for Madhyamika. Accordingly, most of the interpretations of the two truths in Madhyamika refer to Nagarjuna.

4. To be more accurate, Jesus goes on committing the same fallacy, so even if one goes by the biblical text, as any student of logic should be able to conclude, the Jewish interlocker/s make/s a valid and sound argument demanding reasonable proof.

5. Notice, in Arabic, the word for light in the strict physical sense is *dhaw'*, a variation of which is also shared by some other related languages such as Maltese, *dawl*. However, the Arabic word for fire, *nar*, is phonetically closer to *noor* than *dhaw'*.

6. Thus, in Islamic history, the pre-Islam age is called the Age of Ignorance. Even today, Islamic theologians are referred to as "scientists," *ulamaa* in Arabic, indicating their religiously licensed knowledge authority.

7. Positivism—fortunately for it—does not need to be atheistic since objectified thought cannot even pose the question of the existence of God. The positivist sensor turns a blind eye to official worship, as a special, knowledge-free zone of social activity, just as willingly as to art—but never to denial, even when it has a claim to be knowledge. For the scientific temper, any deviation of thought from the business of manipulating the actual, any stepping outside the jurisdiction of existence, is no less senseless and self-destructive than it would be for the magician to step outside the magic circle drawn for his incantation; and in both cases violation of the taboo carries a heavy price for the offender (Horkheimer and Adorno 2002, 19).

8. Hannah Arendt makes the connection between the rise of "tribal nationalism," including fascism, and "declassed" masses (1979, 232, 261, 315–17; also see chapter 3 of this book).

Chapter 6

1. The American federal spending on "national defense" for the 2021 fiscal year was 754.8 billion USD or 11 percent of the total federal spending, whereas the total federal spending for education, training, employment, and social services was 296.6 billion USD or 4 percent of the federal spending (Data Lab; MTS). In the 2022 budget, that so-called defense budget has been increased to 777.7 billion

USD (US Office of Management and Budget, 2021a). For a detailed statistical comparison between military budgets of the United States and China, see GFP, 2021. In terms of the American federal government's IT (information technology) budget distribution, below is a brief overview of some information from the 2021 fiscal year. The Department of Defense alone, which does not include Veterans Affairs or Homeland Security, was allotted an IT budget of 38,815 million USD, while the Department of Education was allotted 887 million USD (US Office of Management and Budget, 2021b). The ratio for education to defense is about 1 to 43.76. The Department of Veterans Affairs alone was allotted 7,761 million USD from the federal government IT budget, which amounts to more than 8.7 times what the Department of Education received. Similarly, the Department of Homeland Security was allotted an IT budget of 7,298 million USD, which amounts to over eight times more than the Department of Education's federal IT budget.

2. Indeed, Horkheimer makes this point very clear. For instance, he writes, "In maintaining this doctrine of the necessary limitation of knowledge to appearances or rather in degrading the known world to a mere outward show, positivism makes peace, in principle, with every kind of superstition. It takes the seriousness out of theory since the latter must prove itself in practice. If non-positivist metaphysics must exaggerate its own knowledge (since by its nature it must claim autonomy for itself), positivism, on the contrary, reduces all possible knowledge to a collection of external data" (2002, 38).

3. As I will explain, that is also the main thesis of Horkheimer and Adorno's *Dialectic of Enlightenment.*

4. Hawking writes:

Unfortunately, however, these two theories are known to be inconsistent with each other—they cannot both be correct. One of the major endeavors in physics today, and the major theme of this book, is the search for a new theory that will incorporate them both—a quantum theory of gravity. We do not yet have such a theory, and we may still be a long way from having one, but we do already know many of the properties that it must have. And we shall see, in later chapters, that we already know a fair amount about the predictions a quantum theory of gravity must make. (2011, 12)

5. Average annual income per capita during the American administration of Afghanistan never reached 1,000 USD. While the annual income per capita in Afghanistan was 561.86 USD in 2016 (IMF 2019), the average American lower- to middle-income consumer spent 69–82 USD (averaging 76.23 USD) per day from July 2016 to July 2017 (Gallup 2017). This means that over eight days a typical American consumer would have spent more than the equivalent of the annual income of an average Afghan citizen. If we look at holiday shopping, consumers in the United

Kingdom spent an average of 732 GBP (about 1,082 USD) in 2015 (Rubicon Project 2016), about 2.35 times the annual income of an average citizen of the Democratic Republic of the Congo, which was 460 USD in 2015 (World Bank 2018).

6. Also, keep in mind that in 2002–2003, the United States had only seven thousand troops in Afghanistan, while, in the same year, more than 35,000 civilian police were actively deployed to New York City (Barfield 2010, 313). This alone should tell us, everything else being equal, Afghans are certainly not more violent than New Yorkers. By the same token, New Yorkers, of all racial and cultural backgrounds, are not more violent than any other population when people are not deprived from the most basic life necessities.

6. Horkheimer provides a very useful materialist account for culture explaining that at some point a certain practice would have been beneficiary, for instance, to establish some sort of social order, but at another point in history the same practice becomes reactionary and oppressive (2002, 52–53; 60–64).

7. In 2006, Butler said, "Understanding Hamas, Hezbollah as social movements that are progressive, that are on the Left, that are part of a global Left, is extremely important" (quoted in Zalloua 2017, 62). This is especially insulting to the Palestinian left who have been marginalized by the global right Butler assumes to be critiquing.

Epilogue

1. In the context of the 1968 elections, Marcuse made the point that Richard Nixon had followers, as opposed to the other two who had *voters* (Marcuse 2021, 35), and I think that distinction makes even more sense in the case of the 2020 presential elections.

2. Note that the anti-science tendencies have been growing for decades in the United States, and it got especially worse during the last two decades, but with Trump the denialism and nihilism reached an absurd level whereby science is simply mocked and demonized and scientists are humiliated publicly in the White House. Recall the visible intimidation of Anthony Fauci, the director of the National Institute of Allergy and Infectious Diseases (NIAID), during several White House press conferences in 2020. Soon, Fauci became a target of attacks by right-wing radio agitators.

3. Next time, it is very likely the right-wing president, whether Trump or someone else, might not need a coup attempt, such as the one that took place on January 6, 2021 (Breuninger 2021), to put an end to the fragile liberal system in the United States.

4. About eight months before the January 6, 2021, attack on the Capitol Hill, I wrote, "In December 2020 and January 2021, if things get out of control, it will be Trump's supporters who will use those same machine guns to take over what is left of the state" (Ahmed 2020).

5. The Black Consciousness movement in South Africa aimed to actualize something similar in terms of revolutionizing Blackness. For instance, the prominent revolutionary figure in the Black Consciousness movement, Steve Biko, states, "Being black is not a matter of pigmentation—being black is a reflection of a mental attitude." Then he adds, "Merely by describing yourself as black you have started on a road toward emancipation, you have committed yourself to fight all forces that seek to use your blackness as a stamp that marks you out as a subservient being" (1987, 49).

6. This is one of the common strategies in racist discourse (for more on this see Bonilla-Silva 2010; Van Dijk 2011).

7. By the way, the depiction of communism as a Jewish international conspiracy is typical of many Islamist ideologues (for instance, see Azzam 1980). In fact, Iraqi communists were accused by Islamists (and nationalists) of being part of such an international conspiracy (for instance, see Janahi 2010).

8. Well after World War II, anti-Semitic and anti-communist rhetoric continued. For instance, Frank Britton, an American nationalist, published a book insisting on the anti-Semitic and anti-communist conspiracy theory (2012). *Journal of Historical Review*, which was published between 1980 and 2012, is an example of a platform that perpetuated that rhetoric. More broadly, leftist exile intellectuals who escaped Nazi Germany to the US were systematically subjected to hate speech. For instance, the members of the Frankfurt School were typically accused of aiming to corrupt the American society through utilizing their project of cultural Marxism. *American Free Press* is an ongoing platform that is still obsessed with "cultural Bolshevism," "red plagues," and so on.

9. For more on this, see the first chapter of my book *Totalitarian Space and the Destruction of Aura* (2019d).

References

1st Infantry Division. (n.d.). *Soldier's Handbook to Iraq*. Available online: https://fas.org/irp/world/iraq/1IDguide.pdf.

Achebe, Chinua. 2000. *Home and Exile*. Oxford: Oxford University Press.

———. 2009. *Things Fall Apart*. London: Penguin.

Adorno, Theodor W. 1973 *Negative Dialectics*. London: Routledge and Keegan Paul.

———. 2000a. *Problems of Moral Philosophy*. Edited by Thomas Scröder. Translated by Rodney Livingstone. London: Polity Press.

———. 2000b. "On Popular Music." *Soundscapes: Journal on Media Culture* 2: 3–13. http://www.icce.rug.nl/~soundscapes/DATABASES/SWA/On_popular_music_1.shtml.

———. 2001a. "Freudian Theory and the Pattern of Fascist Propaganda." In *The Culture Industry: Selected Essays on Mass Culture*, edited by J. M. Bernstein, 132–57. London: Routledge.

———. 2001b. "Culture Industry Reconsidered." In *The Culture Industry: Selected Essays on Mass Culture*, edited by J. M. Bernstein, 98–106. London: Routledge.

———. 2001c. "The Schema of Mass Culture." In *The Culture Industry: Selected Essays on Mass Culture*, edited by J. M. Bernstein, 61–97. London: Routledge.

———. 2001d. "Transparencies of Film." In *The Culture Industry: Selected Essays on Mass Culture*, edited by J. M. Bernstein, 178–86. London: Routledge.

———. 2004. "Antisemitism and Fascist Propaganda." In *Stars Down to Earth and Other Essays on the Irrational in Culture*, edited by Stephen Crook, 218–32. London: Routledge.

———. 2006. *The Culture Industry: Selected Essays on Mass Culture*. Edited by Jay Bernstein. London: Routledge.

———, Walter Benjamin, Ernst Bloch, Bertolt Brecht, and Georg Lukacs. 2007. *Aesthetics and Politics*. Translated and edited by Rodney Taylor. London: Verso.

Ahmed, Saladdin. 2015. "Culture as 'Ways of Life' or a Mask of Racism? Culturalisation and the Decline of Universalist Views." *Critical Race and Whiteness Studies* e-journal 11, no. 1: 1–17.

———. 2018. "Panopticism and Totalitarian Space." *Theory in Action* 11, no. 1 (January): 1–16. doi: 10.3798/tia.1937-0237.1801.

———. 2019a. "The 21st-Century Crossroad of Islamism and Enlightenment." *TelosScope*, last modified December 10, 2019. https://www.telospress.com/the-21st-century-crossroad-of-islamism-and-enlightenment-part-1-the-historical-crossroad-of-an-ideological-crisis/.

———. 2019b. "The Left's Culturalism and Rojava." *Contours Journal* 9: 1–20. http://www.sfu.ca/content/dam/sfu/humanities-institute/Images/contours/issue 9/9.11.pdf.

———. 2019c. "One Hundred Years After World War I, Are We Heading Back to the Abyss." *OpenDemocracy*, June 30, 2019. https://www.opendemocracy.net/en/transformation/one-hundred-years-after-world-war-i-are-we-heading-back-abyss/.

———. 2019d. *Totalitarian Space and the Destruction of Aura*. Albany, NY: State University of New York Press.

———. 2020. "When We Lose the Ability to be Shocked, Fascism has Already Arrived." *Institute for Social Ecology*. http://social-ecology.org/wp/2020/05/when-we-lose-the-ability-to-be-shocked-fascism-has-already-arrived/.

———. 2021a. "Why 'Islamo-leftism' is Just another Conspiracy Theory." *International Journal of Socialist Renewal LINKS*, March 5, 2021. http://links.org.au/islamo-leftism-conspiracy-theory.

———. 2021b. "Universal Discrimination and the Democratic Camouflaging of Culturalism." *International Journal of Socialist Renewal LINKS*, March 27, 2021. http://links.org.au/universal-discrimination-democratic-camouflaging-culturalism.

———. 2022a. "Negativity as the Compass of Revolution: A Marxist Rejection of the No-Alternative Ethos." *Science & Society* 86, no. 3 (July): 409–38.

———. 2022b. *Revolutionary Hope After Nihilism: Marginalized Voices and Dissent*. New York: Bloomsbury Academic.

Allardyce, Gilbert. 1979. "What Fascism Is Not: Thoughts on the Deflation of a Concept." *The American Historical Review* 84, no. 2: 367–88. https://doi.org/10.2307/1855138.

Amnesty International. 2017. *Blood-Soaked Secrets*. London: Amnesty International Ltd. https://www.amnesty.org/download/Documents/MDE1394212018ENGLISH.PDF. Also in Persian: https://www.amnesty.org/download/Documents/MDE-1394212018PERSIAN.PDF.

Arendt, Hannah, ed. 1969. "Introduction: Walter Benjamin: 1892–1940." In *Illuminations: Essays and Reflections*, Walter Benjamin, translated by Harry Zohn, 1–55. New York: Schocken Books.

———. 1979. *The Origins of Totalitarianism*. New ed. San Diego, CA: Harcourt Brace.

———. 1994. *Essays in Understanding*, edited by J. Kohn. New York: Harcourt Brace.

———. 1998. *The Human Condition*. Chicago: University of Chicago Press.

Aronowitz, Stanley. 2002. "Introduction." In Max Horkheimer. *Critical Theory: Selected Essays*. Trans. Matthew J. O'Connell and others, xi–xxi. New York: Continuum.

Azzam, Abdullah Yusuf. 1980. *Al-Saratan Alahmar* [The red cancer]. Amman: Maktabat al-Aqsa, 1980.

Balibar, Ètienne. 1991a. "Is There a "Neo-Racism"? In *Race, Nation, Class: Ambiguous Identities*, edited by Etienne Balibar and Immanuel Wallerstein, 17–28. London: Verso.

———. 1991b. "Racism and Nationalism." In *Race, Nation, Class: Ambiguous Identities*, edited by Etienne Balibar and Immanuel Wallerstein, 37–67. London: Verso.

Barfield, Thomas. 2010. *Afghanistan: A Cultural and Political History*. Princeton, NJ: Princeton University Press.

Baudrillard, Jean. 2002. *The Perfect Crime*. Translated by Chris Turner. Reprint ed. London: Verso.

Bengio, Ofra. 2016. "Game Changer: Kurdish Women in Peace and War." *Middle East Journal* 70, no. 1 (Winter): 30–46.

Benjamin, Walter. 1999. *The Arcades Project*. Edited by Rolf Tiedemann. Translated by Eiland and Kevin McLaughlin. Cambridge, MA: Harvard University Press.

———. 2004. "Goethe's Elective Affinities." In *Selected Writings, Volume 1, 1913–1926*, edited by M. Bullock and M. W. Jennings, translated by S. Corngold, 297–360. Cambridge, MA: Harvard University Press.

———. 2005. "Theories in German Fascism." In *Walter Benjamin: Selected Writings, Volume 2, Part 1, 1927–1930*, edited by Michael W. Jennings, Howard Eiland, and Gary Smith, translated by Rodney Livingstone, 312–321. Cambridge, MA: Harvard University Press.

———. 2006a. *Walter Benjamin: Selected Writings, Volume 4, 1938–1940*. Edited by Howard Eiland and Michael W. Jennings. Translated by Edmund Jephcott et al. Cambridge, MA: Harvard University Press.

———. 2006b. "The Work of Art in the Age of Its Technological Reproducibility: Second Version." In *Walter Benjamin: Selected Writings, Volume 3, 1935–1938*, edited by Howard Eiland and Michael W. Jennings, translated by Edmund Jephcott and Harry Zohn, 101–33. Cambridge, MA: Harvard University Press.

———. 2006c. "On the Concept of History." In *Walter Benjamin: Selected Writings, Volume 4, 1938–1940*, edited by Howard Eiland and Michael W. Jennings, translated by Harry Zohn, 389–400. Cambridge, MA: Harvard University Press.

Berardi, Franco Bifo. 2015. *Heroes: Mass Murder and Suicide*. London: Verso.

Bernstein, J. M. 2001. Introduction to *The Culture Industry: Selected Essays on Mass Culture*, by Theodor Adorno, 1–28. London: Routledge.

Biko, Steve. 1987. *I Write What I Like: Steve Biko; A Selection of His Writings*. Edited by Aelred Stubbs C. R. Johannesburg: Heinemann.

Bloch, Ernst. 2018. *On Karl Marx*. Translated by John Maxwell. London: Verso.

Bobo, Lawrence D., and Ryan A. Smith. 1998. "From Jim Crow Racism to Laissez-Faire Racism: The Transformation of Racial Attitudes." In *Beyond Pluralism: The Conception of Groups and Group Identities in America*, edited by W. F. Katkin, N. Landsman, and A. Tyree, 182–220. Urbana: University of Illinois Press.

Bonilla-Silva, Eduardo. 2010. *Racism without Racists: Color-Blind Racism and the Persistence of Racial Inequality in America*. 3rd ed. Lanham, MD: Rowman and Littlefield.

Bonnett, Alastair. 2005. "From the Crises of Whiteness to Western Supremacism." *Critical Race and Whiteness Studies* 1: 8–20. https://www.acrawsa.org.au/files/ejournalfiles/96AlastairBonnett.pdf.

Breuninger, Kevin. 2021. "Top U.S. Gen. Mark Milley Feared Trump Would Attempt a Coup After His Loss to Biden, New Book Says." *CNBC*, July 15, 2021. https://www.cnbc.com/2021/07/15/mark-milley-feared-coup-after-trump-lost-to-biden-book.html.

Britton, Frank L. 2012. *Behind Communism*. London: Ostara Publications.

Burley, Shane. 2017. *Fascism Today: What It Is and How to End It*. Chicago, CA: AK Press.

Buruma, Ian. 2021. "Racism & Enlightenment." Persuasion, February 22, 2021. https://www.persuasion.community/p/ian-buruma-racism-and-enlightenment.

Césaire, Aimé. 2001. *Discourse on Colonialism*. Translated by Joan Pinkham. New York: Monthly Review Press.

CNN. 2021. "Exit Polls." *CNN*. https://www.cnn.com/election/2020/exit-polls/president/national-results/5.

Cox, Robert W. 1981. "Social Forces, States and World Orders: Beyond International Relations Theory." *Millennium* 10, no. 2: 126–55.

Curtis, Michael. 1979. *Totalitarianism*. New Brunswick, NJ: Transaction Books.

Data Lab. 2021. "Federal Spending by Category and Agency." Fiscal Service, US Department of Treasury. https://datalab.usaspending.gov/americas-finance-guide/spending/categories/.

Del Boca, Angelo, and Mario Giovana. 1970. *Fascism Today: A World Survey*. Translated by R. H. Boothroyd. London: Heinemann.

Deleuze, Gilles, and Felix Guattari. 1987. *A Thousand Plateaus: Capitalism and Schizophrenia*. Translated by Brian Massumi. Minneapolis: University of Minnesota Press.

Derrida, Jacques. 2002. "The Animal that Therefore I Am (More to Follow), translated by David Wills." *Critical Inquiry* 28, no. 2: 369–418.

Eagleton, Terry. 1976. "What Is Fascism?" *New Blackfriars* 57, no. 670: 100–6. http://www.jstor.org/stable/43246521.

Eco, Umberto. 1995. "Ur-Fascism (Book Review)." *New York Review of Books* 42, no. 11 (June 22): 12. https://search.proquest.com/docview/1311529717?accountid=14637.

Eriksen, Thomas Hylland, and Finn Sivert Nielsen. 2001. *A History of Anthropology*. London: Pluto Press.

Essed, Philomena. 1991. *Understanding Everyday Racism: An Interdisciplinary Theory*. Newbury Park, CA: SAGE.

Fanon, Frantz. 1986. *Black Skin, White Masks*. Translated by Charles Lam Markmann. London: Pluto.

———. 1994. *Toward the African Revolution: Political Essays*. Translated by Haakon Chevalier. New York: Grove Press.

Fichte, Johann Gottlieb. 2008. *Fichte: Addresses to the German Nation*. Edited by Gregory Moore. Cambridge: Cambridge University Press.

Flax, Jane. 1987. "Postmodernism and Gender Relations in Feminist Theory." *Signs* 12, no. 4: 621–43. http://www.jstor.org/stable/3174206.

Ford International Weekly. 1920. "The International Jew: The World's Problem." May 22, 1920. https://upload.wikimedia.org/wikipedia/commons/3/34/19200522_Dearborn_Independent-Intl_Jew.jpg.

Foucault, Michel. 2008. *Birth of Biopolitics: Lectures at the Collège de France, 1978–1979*. Edited by Michel Senellart. Translated by Graham Burchell. Basingstoke, UK: Palgrave Macmillan.

———. 1980. "The Eye of Power." Interview by Jean-Pierre Barou and Michelle Perrot. In *Power/Knowledge: Selected Interviews & Other Writings, 1972–1977*, edited and translated by Colin Gordon, 146–65. New York: Pantheon Books.

———. 1984a. "Nietzsche, Genealogy, History." In *Foucault Reader*, edited by Paul Rabinow, 76–100. New York: Pantheon Books.

———. 1984b. "The Body of the Condemned." In *Foucault Reader*, edited by Paul Rabinow, 170–178. New York: Pantheon Books.

———. 1995. *Discipline and Punish: The Birth of Prison*. Translated by Alan Sheridan. New York: Vintage Books.

———. 1998. "Nietzsche, Freud, Marx." In *Aesthetics, Method, and Epistemology: Essential Works of Foucault 1954–1984, Vol. 2*, edited by James D. Faubion, translated by Robert Hurley et al., 261–69.

———. 2000. "Truth and Juridical Forms." In *Power*, edited by James D. Faubion, translated by Robert Hurley et al., 31–45. New York: New Press.

Friedlander, Judith. 2006. *Being Indian in Hueyapan*. Basingstoke, UK: Palgrave Macmillan.

Fromm, Erich. 1965. *Escape from Freedom*. New York: Avon Books.

Gallup. 2017. U.S. Lower- and Middle-Income Consumer Spending from July 2016 to July 2017, by Month (in U.S. Dollars). Statista. https://www.statista.com/statistics/205250/us-self-reported-lower-income-consumer-spending-by-month/.

Gentile, Emilio. 2003. *The Struggle for Modernity: Nationalism, Futurism, and Fascism*. Westport, CT: Praeger.

Gentile, Geovanni. 2002. *Origins and Doctrine of Fascism: With Selections from Other Works*. Translated by A. James Gregor. New Brunswick, NJ: Transaction Publishers.

Gessen, Masha. 2014. *Words Will Break Cement: The Passion of Pussy Riot.* New York: Penguin.

GFP. 2021. "Comparison of United States and China Military Strengths (2021)." *Global Fire Power Utility.* https://www.globalfirepower.com/countries-comparison-detail.php?country1=united-states-of-america&country2=china.

Goebbels, Joseph. 1935. "Communism with the Masks Off." Calvin University's German Propaganda Archive. https://research.calvin.edu/german-propaganda-archive/goeb58.htm.

Gramsci, Antonio. 1957. *The Modern Prince: And Other Writings.* London: Lawrence and Wishart.

———. 1978. "Elemental Forces." In *Selections from Political Writings (1921–1926)*, edited and translated by Quintin Hoare. http://marxism.halkcephesi.net/Antonio%20Gramsci/1921/04/elemental_forces.htm.

Gregor, A. James. 1974. "Fascism and Modernization: Some Addenda." *World Politics* 26, no. 3: 370–84. https://doi.org/10.2307/2009935.

———. 2006. *The Search for Neofascism: The Use and Abuse of Social Sciences.* Cambridge: Cambridge University Press.

Griffin, Roger. 1991. *The Nature of Fascism.* London: Routledge.

———. 2008. *Our Fascist Century: Essays by Roger Griffin*, edited by Matthew Feldman et al. New York: Palgrave Macmillan.

———. 2012. "Studying Fascism in a Postfascist Age. From New Consensus to New Wave?" *Fascism* 1, no. 1: 1–17. doi: https://doi.org/10.1163/221162512X623601.

———. 2018. *Fascism: An Introduction to Comparative Fascist Studies.* Cambridge: Polity Press.

Grüner, Fernando. 2020. *The Haitian Revolution: Capitalism, Slavery, and Counter-Modernity.* Translated by Ramsey McGlazer. London: Polity Press.

"Guerrilla Girls of the PKK—Turkey." YouTube, posted by journeymanpictures. 24 October 2007, http://www.youtube.com/watch?v=pRsw5s28jxY.

Gurnah, Abdulrazak. 2020. *Afterlives.* London: Bloomsbury.

Habermas, Jürgen. 2015. *The Structural Transformation of the Public Sphere: An Inquiry into a Category of Bourgeois Society.* Translated by Thomas Burger. Cambridge, MA: MIT Press.

Hanioglu, M. Sükrü. 2014. "Turkism and the Young Turks, 1889–1908." In *Turkey Beyond Nationalism: Towards Post-Nationalist Identities*, edited by Hans-Lukas Kieser, 3–19. London: I. B. Tauris.

Harding, Sandra G. 1986. *The Science Question in Feminism.* Ithaca, NY: Cornell University Press.

Hawking, Stephen. 2011. *A Brief History of Time.* London: Random House.

Hegel, Georg W. F. 2001. *The Philosophy of History.* Translated by J. Sibree. Kitchener. Ontario, Canada: Batoche Books.

Herder, Johann Gottfried von. 2002. "Treatise on the Origin of Language (1772)." In *Philosophical Writings*, edited and translated by Michael N. Forster, 65–166. Cambridge: Cambridge University Press.

———. 2004. "Governments as Inherited Regimes" In *Another Philosophy of History and Selected Political Writings*, translated by Ioannis D. Evrigenis and Daniel Pellerin, 121–29. Indianapolis, IN: Hackett.

Higgs, Philip, and Jane Smith. 2007. *Rethinking Our World*. Cape Town, South Africa: Juta.

Hobsbawm, Eric. 1995. *The Age of Extremes: The Short Twentieth Century 1914–1991*. New York: Vintage Books.

Horkheimer, Max. 2002. *Critical Theory: Selected Essays*. Translated by Matthew J. O'Connell and others. New York: Continuum.

———. 2005. "The Jews and Europe." In *The Frankfurt School on Religion: Key Writings by the Major Thinkers*, edited by Eduardo Mendieta, 225–42. London: Routledge.

———, and Theodor Adorno. 2002. *Dialectic of Enlightenment: Philosophical Fragments*. Edited by Gunzelin Schimid Noerr. Translated by Edmund Jephcott. Stanford, CA: Stanford University Press.

Hosseini, Anahita. 2016. "The Spirit of the Spiritless Situation: The Significance of Rojava as an Alternative Model of Political Development in the Context of the Middle East." *Critique* 44, no. 3: 253–65. https://doi.org/10.1080/0 3017605.2016.1199631.

Huntington, Samuel. 2010. *The Clash of Civilizations? The Debate*. 2nd ed. New York: Foreign Affairs.

IMF. 2019. "The 20 Countries with the Lowest Gross Domestic Product (GDP) Per Capita in 2016 (in U.S. Dollars)." Statista. https://www.statista.com/ statistics/256547/the-20-countries-with-the-lowest-gdp-per-capita/.

Jafri, Beenash. 2012. "National Identity, Transnational Whiteness and the Canadian Citizenship Guide." *Critical Race and Whiteness Studies* 8, no. 1: 1–15. https:// www.acrawsa.org.au/files/ejournalfiles/179CRWS201281Jafri.pdf.

Janahi, Mahmud Hassan. 2010. *"Alsila bayn Alarab wa Alshuiaiya—Haqaiq wa Arqam"* [The connection between Jews and Communism: Facts and numbers]. *Maqalati: Hassan Mahmud Janahi*, August 19, 2010. http://maqalati.com/56.htm.

Jefferson, Thomas. 1999. *Notes on the State of Virginia*. London: Penguin Books.

Kallis, Aristotle A. 2003. "'Fascism,' 'Para-Fascism' and 'Fascistization': On the Similarities of Three Conceptual Categories." *European History Quarterly* 33, no. 2 (April): 219–49. https://doi.org/10.1177/02656914030332004.

Klein, Hilary. 2019. "A Spark of Hope: The Ongoing Lessons of the Zapatista Revolution 25 Years On." *NACLA* (January 18). https://nacla.org/news/2019/01/18/ spark-hope-ongoing-lessons-zapatista-revolution-25-years.

Knapp, Michael, Anja Flach, and Ercan Ayboga. 2016. *Revolution in Rojava: Democratic Autonomy and Women's Liberation in Syrian Kurdistan*. Translated by Janet Biehl. London: Pluto Press.

Köves, Margit. 1997. "Lukács and Fascism." *Social Scientist* 25, no. 7/8: 27–38. https://doi.org/10.2307/3517602.

———. 2004. "Fascism in the Age of Global Capitalism." *Social Scientist* 32, no. 9/10: 36–71. https://doi.org/10.2307/3518207.

Kroeber, Alfred. L., and Kluckhohn, Clyde. 1952. *Culture: A Critical Review of Concepts and Definitions*. Cambridge, MA: Peabody Museum of American Archaeology and Ethnology.

Landa, Ishay. 2018. *Fascism and the Masses: The Revolt Against the Last Humans, 1848–1945*. London: Routledge.

Lefebvre, Henri. 1991. *The Production of Space*. Translated by Donald Nicholson-Smith. Malden, MA: Blackwell Publishing.

Lentin, Alana. 2005. "Replacing 'Race,' Historicizing 'Culture' in Multiculturalism." *Patterns of Prejudice* 39, no. 4: 379–96.

———. 2014. "Post-Race, Post Politics: The Paradoxical Rise of Culture after Multiculturalism." *Ethnic and Racial Studies* 37, no. 8: 1268–85. https://doi.org/10.1080/01419870.2012.664278.

———, and Gavan Titley. 2011. *The Crises of Multiculturalism: Racism in a Neoliberal Age*. London: Zed Books.

Losurdo, Domenico. 2015. *War and Revolution: Rethinking the Twentieth Century*. London: Verso.

Löwenthal, Leo. 1989. *Critical Theory and Frankfurt Theorists: Lectures-Correspondence-Conversations*. New Brunswick, NJ: Transaction Publishers.

———, and Norbert Guterman. 2021. *Prophets of Deceit*. London: Verso.

Luke, Timothy W. 2021. *Screens of Power: Ideology, Domination, and Resistance in Informational Society*. Candor, NY: Telos Press.

———. 2022. *The Travails of Trumpification*. Candor, NY: Telos Press.

Luxemburg, Rosa. 2004. *The Rosa Luxemburg Reader*. Edited by P. Hudis and K. B. Anderson. New York: Monthly Review Press.

Marcuse, Herbert. 2021. "Forward to the Second Edition." In *Prophets of Deceit*, Leo Löwenthal and Norbert Guterman, xlii–xliv. London: Verso.

Marx, Karl. 1967. *Writings of the Young Marx on Philosophy and Society*. Translated and edited by L. D. Easton and K. H. Guddat. Garden City, NY: Doubleday.

———. 1990. *Capital: A Critique of Political Economy*. Vol. 1. Reprint ed. Translated by Ben Fowkes. London: Penguin Books.

———. 1994. *Karl Marx: Selected Writings*. Edited by Lawrence H. Simon. Indianapolis, IN: Hackett.

———. 2012. *Economic and Philosophic Manuscripts of 1844*. Translated by Martin Milligan. Mineola, NY: Dover.

———, and Frederick Engels. 2010a. "A Contribution to the Critique of Political Economy: Part One." In *Marx and Engels, Collected Works, Col. 29: Marx 1857–1861*, 257–420. London: Lawrence and Wishart.

———. 2010b. *Economic and Philosophic Manuscripts 1844*. In *Marx and Engels, Collected Works, vol. 3*, translated by Clemens Dutt, 229–346. London: Lawrence and Wishart.

McAllan, Fiona. 2011. "Getting 'Post-Racial' in the 'Australian' State: What Remains Overlooked in the Premise 'Getting Beyond Racism'?" *Critical Race and White-*

ness Studies 7, no. 1: 1–21. https://www.academia.edu/3040568/_Getting_post_racial_in_the_Australian_State_Cultural_specificity_and_getting_beyond_racism_.

Mentinis, Mihalis. 2006. *Zapatistas: The Chiapas Revolt and What It Means For Radical Politics*. London: Pluto Press.

Morris, Amanda. 2014. "Twenty-First-Century Debt Collectors: Idle No More Combats a Five-Hundred-Year-Old Debt." *Women's Studies Quarterly* 42, no. 1/2: 242–58. http://www.jstor.org/stable/24364928.

MTS. 2021. "Monthly Treasury Statement (MTS)." Fiscal Data, US Department of Treasury.

Nagarjuna. 1970. *Mulamadhyamakakarika*. Translated by Kenneth K. Inada. Tokyo: Hokuseido.

Nicolescu, Ionut. 2018. "Cases of Equality: Idle No More and the Protests at Standing Rock." *Canadian Journal of Urban Research* 27, no. 2: 1–13. https://www.jstor.org/stable/26542032.

Nietzsche, Friedrich. 1982. *The Portable Nietzsche*. Edited by Walter Kaufmann. New York: Penguin Books.

Nolte, Ernst. 1965. *Three Faces of Fascism: Action Française, Italian Fascism, National Socialism*. Translated by Leila Vennewitz. New York: New American Library.

———. 1979. "What Fascism Is Not: Thoughts on the Deflation of a Concept: Comment Author." *American Historical Review* 84, no. 2 (April): 389–94.

Pasolini, Pier Paolo. 1987. *Lutheran Letters*. Translated by Stuart Hood. New York: Carcanet Press.

Paxton, Robert. 1998. "The Five Stages of Fascism." *Journal of Modern History* 70, no. 1: 1–23. https://doi.org/10.1086/235001.

———. 2005. *The Anatomy of Fascism*. New York: Vintage Books.

Pew Research Center. 2012. "The Global Religious Landscape." Pew Research Religion and Public Life Project, December 18, 2012. http://www.pewforum.org/2012/12/18/global-religious-landscape-exec/.

Plato. 1961. *The Collected Dialogues of Plato, Including the Letters*. Edited by Edith Hamilton and Huntington Cairns. New York: Pantheon Books.

———. 1992. *Plato Republic*. Translated by G. M. A. Grube. Indianapolis, IN: Hackett.

Polanyi, Karl. 2001. *The Great Transformation: The Political and Economic Origins of Our Time*. Boston: Beacon Press.

Poser, Rachel. 2021. "He Wants to Save Classics from Whiteness: Can the Field Survive?" *New York Times Magazine*, February 2, 2021. https://www.nytimes.com/2021/02/02/magazine/classics-greece-rome-whiteness.html.

Razack, Sherene H. 2001. *Looking White People in the Eye: Gender, Race, and Culture in Courtrooms and Classrooms*. Toronto, Canada: University of Toronto Press.

Reich, Wilhelm. 1970. *The Mass Psychology of Fascism*. Edited by Mary Higgins and Chester M. Raphael. New York: Farrar, Straus, and Giroux.

Rodat, Simona. 2017. "Cultural Racism: A Conceptual Framework." *Revista de Stiinte Politice* 54: 129–40.

Rodney, Walter. 1972. *How Europe Underdeveloped Africa. Dar es Salaam: Tanzania Publishing House.*

———. 2018. *How Europe Underdeveloped Africa.* London: Verso.

Rollason, Christopher. 2002. "Border Crossing, Resting Place: Portbou and Walter Benjamin." *Lingua Franca* 5, no. 8 (August 25): 4–9. http://www.yatrarollason.info/files/BenjaminPortbouWBRSversion.pdf.

Roy, Arundhati. 2011. *Walking with the Comrades.* New York: Penguin Books.

Rubicon Project. 2016. "Average Spending on Holiday Shopping in the United Kingdom (UK) in 2015 and 2016 (in GBP Per Capita)." Statista. https://www.statista.com/statistics/633617/christmas-shopping-average-spending-capita-uk/.

Said, Edward. 1998. "The Myth of the "Clash of Civilizations." Lecture at University of Massachusetts. https://www.youtube.com/watch?v=aPS-pONiEG8.

———. 2000. *Reflections on Exile and Other Essays.* Cambridge, MA: Harvard University Press.

———. 2003. *Orientalism.* New York: Vintage Books.

Santideva. 1995. *The Bodhicaryavatara.* New York: Oxford University Press.

Smith, John E. 1994. *Quasi-Religions: Humanism, Marxism, and Nationalism.* New York: St. Martin's Press.

Spurgeon, C. H. 2020. *Faith's Checkbook.* Abbotsford, WI: Aneko Press.

Stanley, Jason. 2018. *How Fascism Works: The Politics of Us and Them.* New York: Random House.

Sternhell, Zeev. 1994. *The Birth of Fascist Ideology: From Cultural Rebellion to Political Revolution.* Translated by David Maisel. Princeton, NJ: Princeton University Press.

Tax, Meredith. 2016. *A Road Unforeseen: Women Fight the Islamic State.* New York: Bellevue Literary Press.

Ter-Matevosyan, Vahram. 2015. "Turkish Experience with Totalitarianism and Fascism: Tracing the Intellectual Origins." *Iran and the Caucasus* 19 (4): 387–410. doi: https://doi.org/10.1163/1573384X-20150408.

Tolokonnikova, Nadezhda, and Slavoj Žižek. 2014. *Comradely Greetings: The Prison Letters of Nadya and Slavoj.* Translated by Ian Dreiblatt. London: Verso

Traverso, Enzo. 2016a. *Fire and Blood: The European Civil War, 1914–1945.* Translated by David Fernbach. London: Verso. Apple Books.

———. 2016b. *Left-Wing Melancholia: Marxism, History, and Memory.* New York: Columbia University Press.

———. 2019. *The New Faces of Fascism: Populism and the Far Right.* Translated by David Broder. London: Verso.

Turner, Henry Ashby. 1972. "Fascism and Modernization." *World Politics* 24, no. 4: 547–64. https://doi.org/10.2307/2010456.

Tylor, Edward Burnett. 2010. *Primitive Culture: Researches into the Development of Mythology, Philosophy, Religion, Language, Art, and Custom.* Vol. 2. Cambridge: Cambridge University Press.

US Bureau of Justice Statistics. 2021. "Number of Prisoners under Jurisdiction of Federal or State Correctional Authorities from 2005 to 2020, by Gender." Chart. Statista. December 14, 2021. https://www-statista-com.libproxy.union.edu/statistics/252828/number-of-prisoners-in-the-us-by-gender/.

US Congress Committee on Foreign Affairs. 1985. *Survey of Activities: 98th Congress*. Washington, DC: US Government Printing Office. https://play.google.com/store/books/details?id=OiEVqkWbwmA.

US Office of Management and Budget. 2021a. *Budget of the U.S. Government: Fiscal Year 2022*. Washington, DC: The White House. https://www.govinfo.gov/content/pkg/BUDGET-2022-BUD/pdf/BUDGET-2022-BUD.pdf.

US Office of Management and Budget. 2021b. "Federal Government Information Technology (IT) Budget in the United States from FY 2015 to FY 2022, by Department (in Million U.S. Dollars)." Chart. June 8, 2021. Statista. https://www-statista-com.libproxy.union.edu/statistics/605501/united-states-federal-it-budget/.

Van Dijk, Teun A. 2011. "Discourse Analysis of Racism." In *Rethinking Race and Ethnicity in Research Methods*, edited by John H. Stanfield, II, 43–66. Walnut Creek, CA: Left Coast Press.

Wallerstein, Immanuel. 2006. *World Systems Analysis: An Introduction*. Durham, NC: Duke University Press.

Wodak, Ruth, and Martin Reisigl. 2015. "Discourse and Racism." In *The Handbook of Discourse Analysis*, vol. 1, edited by Deborah Tannen, Heidi E. Hamilton, and Deborah Schiffrin, 576–96. West Sussex, UK: Willey Blackwell.

World Bank. 2018. "GNI Per Capita, Atlas Method (Current US$)." World Bank. https://data.worldbank.org/indicator/NY.GNP.PCAP.CD?locations=CD.

Wright, Susan. 1998. "The Politicization of 'Culture.'" *Anthropology Today* 14, no. 1: 7–15.

Zalloua, Zahi. 2017. *Continental Philosophy and the Palestinian Question: Beyond the Jew and the Greek*. London: Bloomsbury.

Zia-Ebrahimi, Reza. 2011. "Self-Orientalization and Dislocation: The Uses and Abuses of the "Aryan" Discourse in Iran." *Iranian Studies* 44, no. 4: 445–72. Accessed April 16, 2021. http://www.jstor.org/stable/23033306.

Žižek, Slavoj. 2002. *Welcome to the Desert of the Real! Five Essays on September 11 and Related Dates*. London: Verso.

———. 2008a. *In Defence of Lost Causes*. London: Verso Books.

———. 2008b. *Violence: Six Sideways Reflections*. New York: Picador.

———. 2012. "Christianity Against the Sacred." In *God in Pain: Inversions of Apocalypse*, by Slavoj Žižek and Boris Gunjevis, 43–72. New York: Seven Stories Press.

———, and Boris Gunjevis. 2012. *God in Pain*. New York: Seven Stories Press.

Index

abortion, 17, 20, 210n3

absolutism, 63, 130, 141, 142, 199; cultural, 6

Achebe, Chinua, 3, 172–73

Adelson, Sheldon, 185

Adorno, Theodor: on anti-Semitism, 82; on barbarism, 160–61, 163; and Benjamin, 21, 22; on bourgeois individualism, 99–100; vs. Brecht, 23, 90; on capitalism, 41, 67; critical theories of, 7, 10, 13, 153; on the culture industry, 6, 56, 77–80, 83–84, 97–99; *Dialectic of Enlightenment*, 164; on emancipation, 92; on enlightenment, 130, 158, 159, 174–75; on fascism, 211n4 (Chapter 3); Löwenthal's lecture on, 68; on marginalization, 50; on the masses, 69, 71, 72, 73–74; Marxism of, 4; on materialism, 123, 126; *Negative Dialectics*, 2; negative epistemology of, 3, 137, 138; on positivism, 126; on science, 167–68

Afghanistan, 18, 171, 173, 197, 202, 209n1 (Chapter 1), 215–16n5

Africa, 175, 176

al-Khwarizmi, Muhammad ibn Musa, 116–17

Allardyce, Gilbert, 42, 43

American Political Science Association (APSA), 171

anarchism, 92

anthropology, 104, 105, 135, 170, 212–13n2

anti-abolitionism, 185

antiauthoritarianism, 18, 175; *see also* authoritarianism

anti-capitalism, 164; *see also* capitalism

anti-colonialism, 24; *see also* colonialism

anti-communism, 64, 69, 217n8; *see also* communism

anti-democracy, 156; *see also* democracy

anti-enlightenment, 130, 161, 164; *see also* enlightenment

Antifa, 11

anti-fascism, 27, 40, 49, 57, 64, 101–2, 164, 200; *see also* fascism

anti-imperialism, 203; *see also* imperialism

anti-Marxism, 41, 42, 76, 78; *see also* Marxism

anti-materialism, 133; *see also* materialism

anti-modernism, 64; *see also* modernism

anti-panopticism, 16; *see also* panopticism

anti-racism, 27, 61–62, 194; *see also* racism

anti-Semitism, 50–51, 80, 81, 205–6, 211n3 (Chapter 2), 217n8

231

www.ingramcontent.com/pod-product-compliance
Lightning Source LLC
Chambersburg PA
CBHW020345270326
41926CB00007B/320